What people

America and Other Fictions

In this book you'll rediscover America, the enchanted and cursed. For an age haunted with reactionary nostalgia, Ed Simon haunts readers with an American greatness that is both lovely and perverse, through masterfully told tales that look their subjects' original sins straight in the eye. His America is more than a country, more than an idea or a history or a code of laws; it's a system of worship, hitherto little-known as such to its own devotees.

Nathan Schneider, author of *God in Proof: The Story of a Search from the Ancients to the Internet*

Ed Simon's powerful, searching essays are conversant with a startling range of subject matter: Augustine and Whitman, Bob Dylan and Thomas Paine, Catholicism and Cathars, Cotton Mather and Martin Luther. Simon's mind goes, quite simply, everywhere. His goal as an essayist is a kind of secular reenchantment of the old, dead creeds—to acknowledge, and cherish, truths that go deeper than mere belief. Most remarkable of all is how often he succeeds.

Tom Bissell, author of *The Disaster Artist and Apostle*

From dusty reliquaries to Walt Whitman's odes, from Tomas Paine to Thomas Moore and all across the persistently stubborn landscape of the American religious imagination, Ed Simon's essays help readers to understand how we got to this complicated moment in American religious history. Deft, thoughtful, and creatively told, this book reaches across the divides between left and right, popular and academic, into something greater and more significant: the American imagination.

Kaya Oakes, author of *Slanted and Enchanted: The Evolution of Indie Culture* and *Radical Reinvention: An Unlikely Return to the Catholic Church*

America and other Fictions

On Radical Faith and Post-Religion

To Nathan,

Thank you for all of your support!

— *[signature]*

America and other Fictions

On Radical Faith and Post-Religion

Ed Simon

Winchester, UK
Washington, USA

First published by Zero Books, 2018
Zero Books is an imprint of John Hunt Publishing Ltd., No. 3 East St., Alresford,
Hampshire SO24 9EE, UK
office1@jhpbooks.net
www.johnhuntpublishing.com
www.zero-books.net

For distributor details and how to order please visit the 'Ordering' section on our website.

Text copyright: Ed Simon 2017

ISBN: 978 1 78535 845 6
978 1 78535 846 3 (ebook)
Library of Congress Control Number: 2017953611

A CIP catalogue record for this book is available from the British Library.

Design: Stuart Davies

Printed and bound by CPI Group (UK) Ltd, Croydon, CR0 4YY, UK

We operate a distinctive and ethical publishing philosophy in
all areas of our business, from our global network of authors to
production and worldwide distribution.

Contents

Other Titles by the Author

The Anthology of Babel, Punctum Books, 2018

What kind of world does one see when one experiences it from the point of view of two and not one? What is the world like when it is experienced, developed and lived from the point of view of difference and not identity? That is what I believe love to be.
Alan Badiou, *In Praise of Love*

For Meg

Preface

Several of these pieces appeared before in various forms or permutations, and those places of first publication deserve my thanks and gratitude, especially the editors whom I worked with and who helped me refine both my ideas and my prose. Versions of "An Augustinian Left," "The Death of God, Again," "Apocalypse is the Mother of Beauty," "The Crucified God," "Utmost Malice of their Stars," and "Debts Owed to Death" all appeared in *The Marginalia Review of Books,* a channel of *The Los Angeles Review of Books,* where I contribute as a senior editor. Thanks should be offered to Simon Rabinovitch, Samuel Loncar, Brad Holden, and Dana-Tanner Kennedy for their assistance in editing those pieces, and for giving me the opportunity to regularly write at *Marginalia.*

"Scriptures for a Dead God," "The Page to Damascus," "Speaking in Tongues of Fire," and "Remember that the Devil is Quite a Gentleman" all first appeared in *Killing the Buddha;* thanks are due to editor Brook Wilensky-Lanford. "The American Apocalyptic Sublime and the Twilight of Empire" and "The Remembrance of Amalek" first appeared in *The Revealer,* and I am grateful to Kali Handelman for her editorial work on them. "For Sister Frances Carr" first appeared in *Religion Dispatches;* thanks to both Lisa Webster and Evan Derkacz. All three of these sites are instrumental to what I've called the New Religion Journalism, and I am thankful to be involved with those excellent publications.

Russell Bennetts at *Berfrois* has consistently been a supporter, and versions of several of these essays were first published at that site. These include "Daddy, What Did You Do in the Culture Wars?," "New Jerusalem in the Alleghenies; or, the Madman of Bedford County," "Chair'd in the Adament of Time: On 'America' and Other Fictions," "I Dreamed I saw Bob Dylan," and "American Jezebels: Let Us Now Praise Anne Hutchinson and Mary Dyer." A shorter version of "Wheresover They Come They Be at Home" first appeared in *Jacobin*; thanks to Bhaskar Sunkara. "The Sacred and the Profane in Pittsburgh" was first published in *Belt Magazine*; thanks to Martha Bayne.

Many of these pieces were written while I was finishing my PhD at Lehigh University; thanks should be offered to my colleagues who made composition of these essays possible through both institutional support and conversation. Finally I must thank my family for their patience and encouragement, in particular my wife, Meg, to whom this book is dedicated.

Introduction: The Good Fight of Wisdom

Thomas Paine was busy in the afterlife. Paine had been dead for 43 years by 1852, but according to a spiritualist by the name of Charles Hammond, the American revolutionary and radical pamphleteer was once again preparing for war. Hammond, a medium who had contacted Paine through that strange and popular antebellum ritual of the séance, claimed that the slight Englishman with his thin shoulders and his short stature, known for rambling through the crooked streets of Greenwich Village with ink-stained fingers and smudged clothes, was now bedecked in both martial helmet and crown, with spear in hand so as to "fight the good fight of wisdom." Paine's was a uniform that, as scholar Bret E. Carroll explains, symbolized the pamphleteer's "spiritual authority and leadership over those below him." For the separation between that undiscovered country where Paine (and Washington, and Jefferson, and Franklin) now lived was gossamer thin, and the unseen connections between those celestial realms and the reality of everyday life were legion. With the passing of that revolutionary generation, Hammond believed that the heavens had acquired a just, righteous, egalitarian, radical group of men that fought against authoritarianism on Earth with both pugilism and honor. Paine, who had prophetically called for a war of liberation against Britain while alive, assured Hammond, from his perch in the great beyond, that a war for emancipation against slavery was now approaching. That great struggle of universal redemption initiated by the Revolutionary War would continue, as that departed generation organized their troops in heaven. Much as William Blake's Miltonic liberator Lucifer once had, these men were preparing to topple that hideous inequity which they had either been too hypocritical, or expedient, or immoral to dismantle when they were actually alive. Paine was not the only departed American revolutionary

3

assuring a living spiritualist that a war for emancipation was coming. In the same year that Hammond chatted with Paine, a Rochester New York medium named Isaac Post discoursed with no less an eminence then George Washington, who promised the spiritualist that he regretted his role in a "government [that] was formed with such an element" as slavery, an institution "so filled with wretchedness, misery, cruelty, debauchery and every wickedness." The General, prefiguring Abraham Lincoln's famous "House Divided Speech" which was first delivered in Springfield some six years later, said "I see that it is utterly impossible for Slavery and Liberty, for a great length of time to continue together."

As abolitionists prepared for the possibility of war in the world of the living, spirit armies were being organized concurrently in heaven by men like Paine and Washington. Though Paine's was a reputation for notorious atheism during his own lifetime, his presumed surprise at finding his consciousness survive death seemed to be fleeting. There was no time for ruminating on such a little inaccuracy as having doubted the immortality of the soul. For as there was oppression to fight on Earth, so there were hierarchies to topple in the spirit realm as well. Conjuring Christ in his harrowing of hell, or of Dulle Griet, a Flemish woman who invaded perdition according to a feminist Flemish folktale, Paine had written in 1791's *The Rights of Man* that "Tyranny, like hell, is not easily conquered." Some of the pious ministers of the American backcountry, especially by that period of religious revival known as the Second Great Awakening, assumed that hell was precisely where a rationalist, materialist, Epicurean, and republican like Paine was ultimately destined. Hammond thought Paine was in heaven, but according to the medium the state of affairs was such that regardless of what supernatural realm the writer now found himself in, the act of conquering was once again precisely his righteous cause. Seven years after Washington spoke to Post, and that holy prophet of righteousness John Brown raided Harper's Ferry, eight years after Hammond spoke to Paine, and the Civil War would finally, inevitably begin. Those complicated, contradictory men hadn't been lying after all, perhaps they had been organizing phalanxes, and regiments, and militias in heaven, preparing for that assault on America's most wicked iniquity which they had done so little to eliminate when they were actually alive. Because upon some field of celestial battle, these flawed, often mistaken, often intolerant men could perhaps ultimately redeem themselves, for they were assembling, training, and arming themselves, so that living men could fight through them and thus eliminate bondage from this American land forever. One hell of an image.

Do I think that this really happened? That's the wrong question, predicated upon an epistemological and metaphysical category mistake that assumes certain literal things about how "truth," "reality," and "fiction" operate. In a literal, correspondence-theory-of-truth model, I think that the reality of such an epic conflagration happening in some heaven situated in a direction towards which no human can point is largely semantically meaningless. But despite its not being *real,* it is very much *true,* as any foundational myth must be. More so, it conveys a fundamental accuracy about not just what the story represents, but more specifically about the nature of myths in general. Everything in the affairs of humans – "secular" or not – is bolstered by an unseen phalanx of mythic soldiers, of theological regiments. I am agnostic as to whether Post was actually conversing with General Washington (probably not), indifferent as to whether Hammond had literally made contact with Paine (unlikely). What the story demonstrates, by way of allegory, is how the totality of our institutional edifice, that is our politics, ideology, economics and so on – is at its core fundamentally theological, and is completely religious. Whether or not you literally believe in a God, or a supernatural order, is irrelevant to the fact that by definition you must be a participant in some religious system.

Not all theologies are equal, and not all theologies are good, but there is nothing that is not in some way a theology.

All systems of humans which are constructed and make reference to abstract principle are haunted by the theological; they must in some way be handmaid to a variety of fideism. To reduce theology to mere matter of belief in a supernatural order is to define religion inaccurately, to reduce it to faith is to perseverate too much on the power of creeds, confessions, and denominations, a particular fallacy which we can trace to the earliest days of the Reformation, and which has resulted in obscuring how much of the transcendent theological permeates every single aspect of human culture. Those who marched in battle at Antietam, Gettysburg, and Appomattox during our last civil war might not have been literally animated by the possessing spirits of long-dead revolutionary war ghosts, but they might as well have been. What either side, blue or grey, Union or Confederate, represented was their own particular religious vision, albeit contradictory religious visions. And that war, like any and all wars, was a crusade insomuch as "secularism" as conventionally understood is an impossibility. Furthermore, secularism is a theological construct in its own right (even if it is also an ideal worth striving for and defending). That both sides in our first civil war were to varying degrees fighting on behalf of a secularized religious doctrine is not to claim that they are morally equivalent – far from it. Just as there are angelic interpretations, there are diabolical ones, and if theology bolstered both the angelic train of abolitionist and democratic political thought, then the Confederate justifications for inequity and bondage surely had the whiff of sulfur about them. As the British philosopher John Gray has pointedly made clear, "Modern politics is a chapter in the history of religion." I'll go a step further – everything is a chapter in the history of religion. Religion, like language, is inescapable. Whatever our individual religion, or our feigning of having none at all (its own type of religion of course), theology is the medium in which we communicate. To ask if religion is "good" or not is a simplistic question, a bluntly stupid question. It would be equivalent to asking if language is "good" or not. After all, couldn't the hypothetical anti-language equivalent of the "New" Atheist piously declare that without means of communication, organized warfare would be impossible? Yet obviously language is what we have, facilitating both good and evil, and so it is the same with religion, for just like those soldiers in the Civil War, we are animated and possessed by theologies, faiths, and religions, ones that we are sometimes scarcely aware of. As the prophet Robert Zimmerman once said, "You're gonna have to serve somebody."

The observation that a hidden theological undergirds culture is certainly not in and of itself a new observation, even if I want to push it to the extreme. And though a type of materialist metaphysics grounds much radical discourse, particularly of the Marxian variety, I am also certainly not the first leftist to make such a claim. In contemporary philosophy, probably one of the most famous passages to describe this perspective can be found in the radical Marxist and unrepentant kabbalist Walter Benjamin's 1940 essay "Theses on the Philosophy of History." Benjamin supplied a parable similar to the one that I began this introduction with, and for much the same purpose. He recounted the tale of an eighteenth-century mechanical Turk, a chess-playing automaton who toured the mighty capitals of Europe, beating prodigious players of the game. Observers were amazed that such a contraption of gears and levers could muster the analytical acumen to not just play the game, but indeed to be a veritable chess prodigy. How did such a seemingly artificially intelligent robot, in an era before the Industrial Revolution no less, manage to excel at the most subtle and sophisticated of games? From whence did this Enlightenment era Deep Blue find its programmer?

The answer was that the entire thing was an elaborate ruse, the mechanical Turk was no actual automaton, but merely a clever puppet which concealed a dwarf who happened to be a chess prodigy, and who played and won those games on the Turk's behalf. For Benjamin, the story provided the metaphorical scaffolding for what he understood as one of the central interpretive lessons of history. He writes regarding the Turk that one:

> can envision a corresponding object in philosophy. The puppet called 'historical materialism' is always supposed to win. It can do this with no further ado against any opponent, so long as it employs the services of theology, which as everyone knows is small and ugly and must be kept out of sight.

And so it is with our antebellum spiritualists: they have the Ouija boards, and rapping desks, and automatic writing, and the Fox sister cracking their joints to the rhythm of the dark cosmic mysteries. As the Turk is Benjamin's refugee of esoterica from that past Cabinet of Curiosities, so let Charles Hammond and Isaac Post's missives from the moldering and dead Founding Fathers be mine. For my parable expresses much the same sentiment as that of Herr Benjamin's. Just as it is easy to interpret the events not just of the Civil War, but indeed of any period of American, or human history, by recourse to base and superstructure, or ideology, or economics, or if you're of a certain noxious political bent, "biology," in reality the motivating agent must always be theology. The explanation called "historical materialism" is supposed to be sufficient. But it is only sufficient when we remember that it employs the services of theology, which we know is subtle, and mysterious, and hidden, and not always identifiable, just like an ectoplasmic specter conjured by some magician in a heavy and dark antebellum parlor.

That is the central unifying insight of all of the essays gathered in *America and Other Fictions: Radical Faith and Post Religion.* Whether in a theoretical piece which reads technological transhumanism as its own heretical faith, or a literary biographical treatment of Walt Whitman or Anne Hutchinson, or a historical account of the colonial King Philip's War, the thread which connects all of these pieces is the intuitive understanding that this is religion, nor are we out of it (to paraphrase Mephistopheles). But of course identifying everything as being at its core theological, and reading all of culture as the contrast of competing and sympathetic theologies, only gets one so far. Each historical juncture relates to the idea of theology in different ways, and the totalizing understanding of faith which we associate with medieval Catholicism is obviously a different religion than the totalizing understanding which we associate with contemporary neo-liberalism. In the beginning may have been the Word, and all language may be mediated through a sacred mechanism, but not just the language, the *idea of language itself* perennially alters. Now is an era of literalism, girded by the twin forces of fundamentalism and positivism. Literalism is in opposition to a potentially more expansive understanding of allegorical language, one which existed in the pre-modern world and which is now largely confined to poetics and literature (which explains, in part, my concern with those disciplines).

Scriptural rhetoric from the Bronze Age will be interpreted differently in separate eras, where the admixture of how differing theologies relate to one another may shift. Theological language and how it operates, how it is used, will change from historical period to historical period. And there are certainly ruptures or crises of faith in which the operation of language and its correspondence to experience may undergo traumatic change. Consider monotheism's emergence during the Axial Age, or classical paganism's crisis during the Augustan Age, the Protestant Reformation, or the Enlightenment with its subsequent Death of God. All are examples of certain hinge moments when the interrelationships within theologies radically changed, where the floor dropped out. And yet from those crises came solutions that were incredible in their creative ferment, from the biblical prophets in the Axial Age, the radical writings of the second generation of the Reformation, and the dark prophecies of the Death of God theologians. We face a similar crisis of faith today, and the question is what resurrections we will see as old gods die and must be born again, as our old faiths are eclipsed? What we must demand is a new resurgence of a new theological language, singing new hymns in a new tongue. In short, radicalism (including of the political variety) must rely on what Jürgen Habermas calls the "semantic potential" of theological language, or rather we have got to be taken to church.

If my first motivating instinct is that everything is fundamentally theological, my second instinct is that awareness of that condition must alter how we speak, and that biblical and theological language can be repurposed independently of the sermons of the dying conventional churches in favor of a new gospel, a new prophecy, a new hymn, a new scripture, a new faith. In the service of the radical redistribution of wealth, the equality of the sexes, and races, and genders, in the elimination of imperialism and oppressive economic, social, and political arrangements. And most of all, potentially in the transformation of the individual. What is required is a re-enchantment of our language, a new sacred rhetoric. To interpret this as requiring that "traditional" religion co-opt radical discourses is a category mistake; we must not be concerned with the questions of "traditional" religion. We don't need to answer the "New" Atheists' demeaning, simplistic, reductionist questions; we can reject the questions themselves as meaningless and embrace a faith which lies beyond either mere theism or mere atheism. Theological concepts and scriptural language are our great inheritance, and it is our responsibility to use them and not leave them for the literalists (whether fundamentalists or positivist materialists). As I will explore in a later essay in this collection, there is great mystery, power, and transcendence in the deconstructionist theology of the so-called "Death of God" theologians, but it should be remembered that God dies during every historical crisis of faith. What "semantic potential" is there in the coming resurrection of theological language, in the endowment of those old words with new significance and new meanings, all ablaze in glorious light?

Again, don't confuse me here – I am not advocating for the literal truth of Christianity or any other faith, and certainly not for biblical inerrancy. The literal questions of theology do not interest me; the incarnation, hypostatic union, Trinitarian Christology are signifiers without signifieds. Complex rhetorical systems that do not correspond to an empirical reality in the manner that scientific language does, which is precisely their strength and importance. With such a perspective, the irrelevancy of the inquiry of "How can different religions both be 'correct?'" becomes immediately obvious. We must not be concerned with how, or which, religions are "correct" or "real," only which theologies are true, beautiful, just. And behind every idea, every ideology, and every system there is a theology, as surely as each Union soldier in that great Civil War was "possessed" by one of those enlisted in Paine and Washington's heavenly legions. Capitalism is a totalizing theology and religion, as surely as Marxism, or socialism is. Neo-liberalism is a religion, Trumpism and fascism are different religions. That everything can be understood as a religion is not to equivocate or apologize for this multiplicity of faiths; it's to pledge one's self to the elimination of diabolical religions, such as Trumpism or fascism. In an April 2015 review in *The Revealer* of Nigel Smith's excellent anthology *A Collection of Ranter Writings: Spiritual Freedom and Sexual Liberty in the English Civil War*, I wrote that "the only means of resistance is at its heart religious, but the paradox is that the only systems ever worth resisting are, in themselves, also religious." I continued by explaining that "the mark of God and the mark of Cain are everywhere, even if they're secretly hidden behind a faux-secularism.... For oppressive systems of government, the market, and organized religion aren't.... Profane," rather they are their own type of "sacred system, albeit one that is corrupt and that must be abolished – Mammon is a god after all." I prescribe the "manipulation of religious language, texts, images, and ideas" as the "greatest means of resistance to Moloch's armies, against the 'dark satanic mills' of today's modern day all-encompassing pagan religion, capitalism," and now some two years after I wrote that, we find that a true faith must be enlisted in the struggle against revanchist neo-fascism as well. For we must "reject the Demiurge that is the Market, the Church, and the State and… return to a God who lives not within heaven but as allegory within every human's heart."

But why is it "America" and other fictions? The easiest answer is that I am an American, and I let nothing that is American be foreign to me. The more complicated answer is that I argue that the utopian, Enlightenment-era, secularized theology that we call "America" still has profound liberatory "semantic potential." Don't misinterpret me here; I am not claiming that America is a "Christian" nation. By any legal criteria such a claim is spurious at best. But, even with a firm belief in the importance of denominational disestablishmentarianism in American politics, an understanding of the complexities and contradictions in even the potential existence of "secularism" should demonstrate that the idea of "America" itself can't be untangled from theological concepts, language, and structures. Rather than saying that America is a Christian nation, more accurate to say that she was based in a non-Christian heresy, better to piss off both sides in that old, tired, ahistorical debate. For whether America is "Christian" or not, her history has always been recorded in mythic time. In 1552 the Spanish historian Francisco Lopez de Gomara wrote that "the discovery of the Indies" was "The greatest event since the creation of the world (excluding the incarnation and death of Him who created it)," and in many ways he wasn't wrong. Even excluding all of the literal significance of the event, from the ecological and economic effects of the Columbian exchange to the emergence of modern colonialism, the "invention of America" as historian Edmundo O'Gorman called it, introduced a fundamentally new image into human consciousness; a crucial entry in that encyclopedia of imaginary places.

This sense of wonder at the discovery of an entirely new world was not limited to the Spanish colonists; indeed English Protestant settlers understood the uncovering of America in particularly providential terms, with one theologian, William Twisse, writing in 1634 that considering "the opinion of many grave divines concerning the Gospel fleeing westward, sometimes I have such thoughts – why may not that be the place of the new Jerusalem?" As a locus of dreams and desires, and a place of projected aspirations, utopian promises, and millennial expectations, New Jerusalem was a city in America before America was even discovered. There are the North and South American continents, and then there is "America" as an imagined community. What America has meant has always been contradictory and ambiguous, and the actual history of the continents following that fateful "discovery" has certainly been a blood-soaked one of territorial expansion, warfare, ethnic cleansing, and genocide. And yet the image of "America" as paradisiacal realm where the individual is granted agency among the sovereignty of a new and constructed people still contains an evocative and enchanted power. This goes beyond any promises of the United States' Revolution, and gestures to a more mythic understanding of "America" as a theological construct, and in turn "America" is a type of religion which undergirds more traditionally defined faiths. Earliest among nation-states, American identity was able to at least intellectually subsume categories of race, ethnicity, language, and denomination into a group of new people who adhered to a covenantal understanding of nationality rather than one based in tribal geneology. That so much of American history is the deliberate subversion of that noble goal speaks to the central tragedy of this experiment, and that will be a prime theme of these essays. American civil religion, in some of its varieties, is an emancipatory political theology, and arguably the greatest of contributions birthed from the Reformation. Arguably the worst product of that historical epoch would be the cannibalistic machinations of totalizing capitalism, and both find their full contradictory synthesis upon this Hesperian landmass. Which is to say that that's a big part of what makes America fascinating to me, or as that other prophet Leonard Cohen says, America is "the cradle of the best and of the worst."

And so I return to Paine, who synthesizes the themes of *America and Other Fictions* in a perfect manner. He exhibits the acumen for theological rhetoric which is so desperately needed on the left today, not just for strategic reasons but for analytical ones. Despite his reputation for unmitigated secularism, the non-conformist child of Quakers was adept at speaking in a scriptural tongue and writing with a biblical pen; he who wrote that "We have it in our power to begin the world over again," unmistakably theological in its form, indispensably left in its implications. For the Englishmen Paine, this revolutionary nation was the cradle of these millennial expectations, for the "cause of America is in great measure the cause of all mankind," but that which began in America must by moral necessity end with all of humanity. As a citizen of any place which enshrines equality and liberty, Paine did not confuse "America" as mythic location with the prosaic political realities of a real country called "The United States" (a country which, incidentally, he coined the named for). Paine's revolution wasn't just in Philadelphia and Boston, but in London and Paris as well. To confuse the creed of an American religion with the United States must be the origin of our noxious nationalisms, it's an idolatry not befitting the nobility of the actual confession of the faith. Paine's faith, in both politics and religion, points beyond the mere words on a page. A radical theology can neither confuse the spoken God for the real God, nor befuddle the transcendent implications of "America" with the flawed and fallen history of the actual place. But just as radicals abandon the idea of Utopia at their own peril, so the idea of America, in all of its glorious paradoxes, must be similarly preserved in the revolutionary breast, not in spite of America's copious failures and brutalities, but precisely because of them. And so we return to those dark parlors in nineteenth-century America, where spiritualists claimed to have received celestial telegrams from the beyond, where an upstate New York lawyer by the name of Horace Wood received a missive from that ever-talkative corpse Thomas Paine. The old writer assured the attorney that "God is not a person, but a *principle*." Very true and good, and all the more accurate to remember that Paine's posthumous declaration is equally true about the nation that he christened. America, if there is to be anything redemptive or emancipatory in that old word, must not be confused for a country, but embraced first and foremost also as a principle. Now, like Paine, let's grab our crown and martial helmet and begin that necessary work of making our words glow once again.

An Augustinian Left

Save a few prayers for poor Pelagius, footnote to theological history, whose name mostly endures as an adjective of denigration among the orthodox. Save a few prayers for poor Pelagius because he is but a lowly sinner, like the rest of us, even if he thought he wasn't (or, more correctly, thought that all of us weren't condemned to be). And save a few prayers for poor Pelagius, not just for his dual exile from both Church and country, and not just because what scant record there is seems to indicate that he was a morally unassailable fellow, but also because he was author of a doctrine which seems so reasonable and humane in its inaccuracies.

Pelagius, a fifth-century patristic thinker from the cold shoals of a Britain that was rapidly descending into chaos, is often contrasted with his theological opponent, the far more influential Augustine. For Augustine, all of us were born with the stain of original sin on our white souls, and the descendants of the Latin Church (whether Catholic or Protestant) have largely agreed. His Celtic adversary however (whom he described as "saintly"), with perhaps a bit of paganism clinging to his theology, insisted that we are born into the world innocent of sin, and there is no reason that without vigilance we can't hold on to that innocence. For these sorts of claims, Jerome, another contemporary theologian, insisted that Pelagius was "stuffed with Irish porridge." In Augustine's understanding we were corrupted from womb to tomb, but for Pelagius, perfected sinlessness is there for those who want it. His disciples, who are almost never self-identified, are those who argue that humans themselves are not fallen but can in some way be perfectible in the here and now—through our own efforts.

Since the fourth century when they engaged in dueling diatribes against each other, Pelagius has seemingly existed only as a foil to Augustine, who in an appropriate demonstration of original sin's pettiness helped to have Pelagius fully excommunicated from the Catholic Church, which they were both devoted to. Pelagius, who lived a life of the utmost austerity and who once admonished, "We ought not to commit even very light offenses," and Augustine, who was a spiritual genius with terrible Greek, non-existent Hebrew, and who never in his lifetime was privy to a complete copy of the Bible (yet whose commentaries on that book are sublime). The pair are sort of an ironic inverse, "Goofus" and "Gallant," and the irony is that it is the whoring, thieving, sinful Augustine with his stolen pears and his bastard child who more completely embodies the paradoxical message of Christianity, not the steadfast, ascetic, and pious Goofus that was Pelagius. "Pelagian" was normally a slur, at least until most of us became Pelagians and forgot the heresy itself. The heresy is an innately attractive idea for obvious reasons; it has none of the dour, gloomy raininess of the heart or drizzly November of the soul that we associate with some black-clothed, prickly Puritan in a drafty New England room, or with a black-robed Jesuit mortifying himself with hair-shirt and whip of cords after preaching to natives who will bring his welcome martyrdom. But Pelagius' doctrine wasn't simply an "I'm OK, you're OK" worldview; no, far from it. Since Pelagianism regarded the role of individual works so highly in personal salvation there was little room for error (and, as Augustine would claim, no room for the saving grace of Jesus Christ). It was said that unlike Augustine, Pelagius conducted himself with the utmost morality, with the neurotic scrupulosity of those who are sure that any indiscretion will condemn them to hellfire. Though it's not a problem once you get rid of hell (or assume that everyone is going there but you).

In modern parlance, liberals assume that everyone is good and rational but just hasn't read the right *Mother Jones* article or heard the right NPR broadcast yet. Conservatives adopt a more pessimistic attitude, however, for they assume everyone to be bad, everyone but themselves. Indeed for as much as the exuberant fundamentalist likes to blame the liberal relativist or the New Age pluralist for the abolition of belief in sin, it is the reactionary himself who is arguably most responsible for incubating our new world, where the charge to responsibility is treated as anathema. I have in mind the anarcho-capitalist, the libertarian, those who idolize the myth of the "self-made man" when the only Man who can make Himself is not of this world. These ethical pip-squeaks have erroneously imagined that anyone can pull himself up by his bootstraps, or by his jackboots as the case increasingly seems to be. Let us not pretend that there is anything "Christian" in a worldview that lets children without insurance die or that is fine with men and women starving to death in the richest nation in history.

How do we explain such a tremendous self-regard that it would condemn anyone who looks, thinks, or acts differently than its holder, especially when this self-regard is often dressed in the sickening language of piety? Its adherents are parishioners in a heretical church, where a prosperity gospel begets the delusion of perfectibility. Belief in original sin keeps one honest, because you know you at least share a propensity to error with everyone, no matter how low. The market-fetishist forgets that the only universal pre-existing condition is fallenness. They say things like, "Why do I have to repent or ask for forgiveness if I don't make mistakes?" Contrast that to the humility of Augustine's "non possum non peccare," or "I cannot not sin." Say what you will about Augustine, I'd rather have someone with an awareness of his own inborn shortcomings occupying the highest position of power than someone who believes he never makes mistakes.

Pelagius' view, once you discount the neurotic moral austerity it actually requires, is congruous with how most of us wish to see ourselves: as basically good. Who admits to being bad, save for in the bromides of repentant justified sinners, or in the crocodile tears of politicians caught with their pants down (and that's very last-century these days)? We've come a long way from Puritans scouring the dark corners of their heart and putting pen to paper in acts of confession, or scrupulous Saints mortifying themselves for contrition. Pelagianism is unofficially the central heresy of our modern age, across the ideological spectrum. When Pelagius writes, "The best incentive for the mind consists in teaching it that it is possible to do anything which one really wants to do," do we not see the self-regard of the libertarian whose unfounded faith ultimately leads to nihilism? But we also see the danger on the left of always assuming humans tend towards that which is more just, free, and good. We are humans, and so we must be on guard against that which is human. A humanism which trusts too much in the innate goodness of people is a humanism which will ultimately fail the people.

For as appealing as Pelagianism may be, or at least as appealing as the cartoon version of it may be, a cursory reflection shows its theology to be a mirage. Contrast Pelagius' "I say that it is possible for a man to be without sin" with Augustine's bluntly honest "I became evil for no reason. I had no motive for my wickedness except wickedness itself. It was foul, and I loved it. I loved the self-destruction, I loved my fall," and ask yourself: which seems a more accurate description of human nature? Pelagianism may be a comforting myth, but watch children cruelly tease and fight one another (John Calvin called infants "seeds of sin" for a reason) and see how firmly you hold to the progressive given that "Children must be taught to hate." They seem to know how to hate pretty well already. It was a theologian, the celebrated Reinhold Niebuhr, who once claimed that "The doctrine of original sin is the only empirically verifiable doctrine of the Christian faith," and it was the psychologists Stanley Milgram and Philip Zambardo who proved that assertion with chart, data, and observation. Good people will brutalize underlings if given the chance, or electrocute strangers if told to by an authority. They proved what we can all observe with our eyes and what is confirmed by our experience: a deep malignancy seems programmed into the human soul. Evil may be banal, but it also comes easily.

A fundamental enough thing to remember, one would think, less than a century after Hiroshima and the Holocaust. The Romanian poet Paul Celan captured the dichotomy of humanity perfectly in "Todesfuge" when he described the German camp commander who at nightfall could lovingly write of "the gold of your hair Margarete" and then step outside where he "whistles his Jews off has them spade out a grave in the ground" and "orders us play up for the dance." Much can be made of the fact that the culture that produced Goethe and Bach also produced Hitler, but original sin and evil aren't German problems, they're human ones. Of course we're all human, we love our families, and we find joy and beauty in the world. Those facts don't eliminate the existence of sin in our world; our empathy makes an awareness of that fact all the more crucial if we're to resist oppression and injustice. That of course starts with the individual. The facts that I have written this encomium for belief in original sin on a computer built from tin, tantalum, and tungsten, minerals which fuel brutal insurrections in the African nations where they are mined, and that the coffee that I am drinking right now was harvested by the exploited labor of workers in Indonesia or Honduras, or that the clothes I am wearing were made in Malaysian or Indian sweatshops do not invalidate my claim or make me a hypocrite. No, rather my collaboration with such systems only more fully confirms my point.

The political-theological is the personal, as one might say. So, now, return to Augustine and Pelagius. Envision, for a moment, the world which birthed these two contraries, both, as all of us, products of their world (some call that insight social theory, but Augustine came to the same conclusion with a different vocabulary). Pelagius, proud son of the Britons, where Roman legionnaires had brought government and a Christian missionary had brought God. By the end of his life he would find himself chastised by the eternal Church. If he had returned to the "green & pleasant land" of his home he would have found it recently abandoned by civil authority; the Romans had left of their own accord, too weakened to bother defending their interests in the British Isles, ultimately leaving the Romanized Celts to Anglo-Saxon invaders in the coming centuries.

Now think of Augustine in the scorching brown Tunisian backwater of Hippo, completely aware that the social contract was fraying, that Rome was nearing its end. The boundaries of the imperial project may have been contracting, but as Gibbon explained, a great nation is only ever the victim of suicide, not murder (even if the Romans themselves feared a pernicious eastern influence). As decadent inequality rose and a sense of civic engagement fell, as aqueducts and roads crumbled, and as the arc of history only ever bends towards ultimate death, the sentence of Rome had been written when Romulus murdered his brother. Rome's chaos was, to Augustine, a demonstration of the intrinsic existence of humanity's total depravity. Hippo would eventually fall to the Goths (technically Christians themselves, albeit Arian ones), Augustine dying shortly before they would destroy the city. He who wrote thousands of pages, *The City of God* and *Confessions* and a stream of sermons, he who arguably wrote the first autobiography to convey any sense of the individual, perished in a world that had become so broken that we don't even know exactly how that life ended. Faced with the same dying world, Pelagius reacted with a consoling optimism about the goodness of humans, Augustine with an awareness of man's ever-present propensity for evil. Both, in their own ways, weren't wrong to react the way that they did.

So what use does original sin have today, after so many ideologically utopian children of the Enlightenment have rejected Augustine in favor of the perfectibility of society and man through reason, whether through socialism or libertarianism or fascism? What use do we have for the arguments between Augustine and Pelagius? They were both refugees from an age when everything solid dissolved as a morning mist, and where truth and fiction were confused for one another. Theirs was an era when a total civilization that had defined the values of the wider culture for centuries teetered on the edge of collapse because of its own selfish myopia. An age in which the public witnessed the ascendancies of effete, yet paradoxically rabble-rousing emperors who decreed from decadent and ugly golden gilt palaces with no sense of their own absurdity, nor any shame or humility. For them, the universe contracted in on itself; Pelagius' Britain separated from Europe. To make the parallels any more obvious would be heavy-handed (and we mustn't be that).

To be heavy-handed may not be a sin, but what is, is the absurd avarice which leads to the denial of evidence that an Antarctic ice shelf bigger than Rhode Island is about to break off into the ocean due to human-generated climate change, even as the former CEO of Exxon and the current Secretary of State, as well as his boss, the leader of the "free" world, both deny that global warming is real. Sinful is that the eight richest men in the world have a combined wealth equal to the bottom half of the entire planet. Sinful is that black mothers and fathers have to wonder if their children will be murdered, and the knowledge that the perpetrators of those murders will often not be brought to justice. Sinful is that for a shamefully large percentage of the Republic the assertion that "Black Lives Matter" is somehow debatable. Sinful is that humans who are incapable of ever being pregnant feel free to force woman into pregnancies that may kill them, either physically, spiritually, economically, or emotionally. Sinful is that we live in a culture that feels entitled to describe whole groups of humans as "illegal." Sinful is that so many men feel it their birthright to violate the bodies of women whether those women consent or not. Sinful is that Christian Pharisees feel free to deny their Muslim brothers and sisters the right to pray. Sinful is that a generation of children has been sacrificed to the Moloch of the firearms industry because some people have a hobby. Sinful is that so many reject the covenant of the commonwealth, of democracy, and are traitors to the democratic charge; so we remember that Dante tells us that the bottom circle is reserved for the traitors. Sinful is that the armies of intolerance and bigotry are waiting at the gates as surely as the Goths marched into Carthage.

The Greek poet Constantine Cavafy predicted as much when he wrote "Once the barbarians are here, they'll do the legislating." Do not mistake all of my glib God-talk for evidence of some deep faith (hypocritical or otherwise). I'm as agnostic as the rest of you faithless academics. And whether we have use of the God hypothesis or not is one question, but that we have to use the sin hypothesis strikes me as pragmatic truth. Much has been made of late about the language of engaged cultural studies, with its vocabulary of "privilege," "entitlement," and "intersectionality," a language which found itself migrating from the academy into regular political discourse and may have played a role in the defeat of liberalism in public opinion and at the polls. We're told that nobody appreciates being told that he has privilege, and that's true.

Most people don't appreciate being told that they are sinners either, though it comes down to pretty much the same thing. To benefit from things not of your own accord that were bought with the labor and pain of others is by definition a sin. But simply because people don't like to hear certain truths doesn't invalidate those truths. There is some truth to the claim that the terminology of cultural studies, especially when watered down by popular media, lacks in rhetorical power. Positivist inflected sociological terms don't exactly sound like Gabriel's trumpet. What is discussion about privilege but an acknowledgment of original sin translated into the disenchanted and anemic language of sociology? But trying to engage justice without the language of the sacred (and note that this is not the same as the language of God) is to remove the most potent rhetoric that we have. John Milton explained that "Law can discover sin, but not remove," just as surely as the language of identity politics can also discover sin, but often does little to alter it. That injustice, inequity, and bigotry are legally enshrined is manifestly a type of sin. I do not mean to suggest that fire-and-brimstone preaching will prove any more useful at the ballot box than cultural studies does; far from it. Yet I do think that the words we choose to describe the dark wood we find ourselves in are important, and any exorcist knows that you have to utter the demons' proper names to cast them out.

What we need is an engaged, radical, "left Augustinianism." We must recommit ourselves to the knowledge that a deep, irrational, immoral malignancy can influence politics. Both Marx and Smith, to varying degrees, inherited an Enlightenment faith in progress, where they believed that the individual was a rational agent. Now examine the behavior of those who are fully aware of, say, the apocalyptically pernicious effects of climate change on the world, yet who pursue financial gain by encouraging that very same climate change, and ask what is rational about such behavior? What does Rex Tillerson benefit by denying the existence of global warming, and in fact by drilling for oil exposed by the rapidly melting polar ice caps? One can psychologically and rationally understand the bank robber, but what of a man like Tillerson? What benefit does he have in losing his soul for a few billion barrels of Arctic crude? Does he need the money to pay for a nicer swimming pool? Men like him are already richer than Herod; they could retire to lives of inconceivable wealth and luxury. And as individual human comfort and material happiness are by necessity capped at a certain physical limit, how can we say that people such as him manifestly benefit by the movement of imaginary numbers on bankers' computer screens? No, the vocabulary of rational profit motive is inadequate when profit motive irrationally pushes us to the brink of collapse; a better language is that of the medieval schoolman. The best language to describe individuals like the former CEO is the language of greed, of avarice, of sin. It is consumption beyond reason, beyond mere logical explication. And we abandon a crucial aspect of our intellectual inheritance if we're not willing to use that language.

Because it's never just economics, stupid. Sometimes it's the dark corners of the human heart too. And sometimes the darkest corner of the human heart is also economic. But that's a positivist word; the one that the monks used, avarice, is often better. Let the secular draw from the wellspring of theology as suits the interests of justice. Let us engage a humanism that is also aware of the limitations of the human, of sin. Reason alone is toothless, even with all of the right information many of us will still do the wrong thing. This isn't about God, or someone dying for our sins. This is about people, and that people are capable of great evil can be easily confirmed. Acknowledging the presence of selfishness, cruelty, greed, rage, intolerance, and, in a word, sin (or evil), is that which makes the existence of good all the more obvious. Even if sometimes good only exists as a dim shaft of blurred light in our dark cell. I have written before, in seeming opposition to my argument here, that we must never stop sailing to Utopia. And I still believe that. Sailing toward what we pray is the direction of paradise must always be our charge, but thinking that we can ever arrive is the gravest error. Augustine said "Give me chastity, but not yet," to which I add "Give us utopia, but not yet." We once were lost, and still seem to be lost, perhaps with little hope of being found, save for the fellowship of others that gets us out of the prison of our skulls. If we're able to leave those prisons long enough, we are sometimes gifted that grace which relieves the tensions of sin and isolation even a little bit. And that little bit is enough to save the world. Our word for that concept is "love." The first charge in a new Augustinian radical left is understanding that revolution has to begin inside first, and the paradoxical admission that in powerlessness there can often be great power (something Augustine knew, that Calvin knew, hell, that the Zen Buddhists know). Seneca wrote, "We are all sinful. Therefore, whatever we blame in another we shall find in our own bosoms."

Sin, like life, is not our fault, but it is our responsibility. For we must understand that though we are fallen and though we are born between shit and piss, that we are all the more glorious for it. And as Pascal wrote, though we are but reeds, we are of course thinking reeds. A true humanism which embraces our fallenness necessitates it.

The Non-Apotheosis of Thomas Paine

For there's no gods/And there's precious few heroes.
Dick Gaughin

The King of England looking westward trembles at the vision.
William Blake

Since it became America's Bohemia, its "Republic of Dreams" as it's been called, many junkies and drunks have died anonymously in the tenement houses of Greenwich Village, but only one of them was a Founding Father of the United States of America. Before Andy Warhol and Bob Dylan, or Walt Whitman and Mark Twain walked Canal and Houston, there was Thomas Paine. Here the forgotten founder of America died alone of cirrhosis in a lower-Manhattan hovel with only six mourners at his funeral. His very body was absconded with and lost in transit to his native England. Regal George Washington lay in a massive mausoleum and a mural of his apotheosis looks out over the Capital (making him not just monarchical but divine); the silver-tongued hypocrite and patron of equality Thomas Jefferson's tomb is surrounded by the graves of anonymous slaves. But Tom Paine, most pious partisan and prophet of liberty, had his body mutilated, spread about, and lost. In myth-haunted America, land of the jeremiad, newest world based on some of the oldest legends, polemicists on both left and right treat our "Founding Fathers" as gods. Tom Paine, however, didn't believe in gods, and so he was just a man, sometimes a flawed one, and because of that he deserves our love.

Tom Paine did not have the aristocratic forbearance of Washington or Jefferson; he was an uncouth man, one of the roughs, an American. Born in Norfolk, he had a life-long working-class English accent. Rebellion was what he was raised on. It was not ideology; it was inheritance. Unlike Jefferson he needed no Locke and Bacon to convince him of man's natural state of liberty, and unlike Washington he had no need of a Jefferson to convince him of the same. His home village of Thetford was the site of Boudicca's royal residence, the raped Celtic queen who avenged her husband's death by descending on Roman Londinium and burning it to the ground, and it's that legacy he imbibed in youth. It's a historical slander of the English to say that they are a people of royal servitude, for Tom Paine demonstrated the deep sense of justice and equality which runs in the veins and sinews of those who belong to the radical English tradition. There is no understanding 1776 without understanding 1649, or 1381. His was not the England of Plantagenet, Tudor, Stuart, Hannover or Saxe-Coburg-Gotha. Tom Paine is of the England that gave us John Ball and Jack Straw, Gerard Winstanley and Abiezer Coppe, William Godwin and Mary Wollstonecraft. "When Adam delved and Eve span, /Who was then the gentleman?" is as if a nursery rhyme to the young Tom Paine, inheritor of radical religious non-conformism and theological dissension.

If Paine was an Englishman by birth, then he was an American by choice. For Paine "The cause of America is in great measure the cause of all mankind." Washington and Jefferson were wealthy plantation owners, but Paine's father was a corset-maker. Like his ally Benjamin Franklin, Paine was that most potent of American archetypes, the self-made man. He was the son of a woman's underwear maker who christened the thirteen colonies with his original name for them: "The United States of America." His parents were Quakers, followers of the radical tradition of George Fox and John Naylor and William Penn. It was the Quakers who took the Reformation tenant of a priesthood of all believers to its logical conclusion, rejecting even Luther's biblical "Pope of Paper" in favor of an "inner light." Because of his Age of Reason, he is often thought of as Theodor Roosevelt's "dirty little atheist" (the 26th president's estimation of Mr. Paine) but his convictions were forged in the kiln that is the hot and fiery inner light of the Society of Friends.

In England he failed at every task he tried: as a tobacco shop owner and a rope maker, as a town alderman and as a petitioner to Parliament. In 1774 he left his wife and escaped to London (can one see George walking out on Martha?) where he met the frontier physicist, the sage of Pennsylvania, the raccoon-fur clad guest of Europe's salons and courts: Benjamin Franklin. The printer wrote Paine a letter of recommendation. Five months later he was an immigrant in that apocalyptic-named Revelation city Philadelphia, sitting on the edge of the western horizon where the sun goes down on the last day of existence, but where Paine saw the sun rising in the west. It was the light marking the arrival of a "New Man," a Homo Novus, a millennial figure that would take at least a thousand years to truly develop: the American. And while Paine may have failed at his schemes in England, and he would die destitute and alone, forgotten and drunk in New York, it was for an act in that auspicious year of 1776 that he would be forever remembered, a little pamphlet with the humble title of *Common Sense*.

Paine was a pamphleteer, a journalist, a propagandist. And he was the product of a radical republican tradition that has existed in the shadow of Britain's royal absurdity for centuries. One could see him as in the tradition of that other revolutionary writer, John Milton. Like Paine, Milton had taken advantage of cheap print more than a century before (during the years of the English civil wars) to advocate for the ancient liberties of the Anglo-Saxon people. But where Milton was an educated man, a polyglot and a polymath, "the Lady of Cambridge," the author of the greatest epic poem in the English language, and the last of the Renaissance men, Tom Paine was but the son of a corset-maker. Milton's home was Trinity College; Paine's was a tavern in London or a bar in Philadelphia. That makes all the difference.

Milton – Thus did Dion Prusaeus, a stranger and a privat Orator counsell the Rhodians against a former Edict: and I abound with other like examples, which to set heer would be superfluous. But if from the industry of a life wholly dedicated to studious labours, and those naturall endowments haply not the worst for two and fifty degrees of northern latitude, so much must be derogated, as to count me not equall to any of those who had this priviledge, I would obtain to be thought not so inferior, as your selves are superior to the most of them who receiv'd their counsell: and how farre you excell them, be assur'd, Lords and Commons, there can no greater testimony appear, then when your prudent spirit acknowledges and obeyes the voice of reason from what quarter soever it be heard speaking; and renders ye as willing to repeal any Act of your own setting forth, as any set forth by your Predecessors.

Paine – These are the times that try men's souls. The summer soldier and the sunshine patriot will, in this crisis, shrink from the service of their country; but he that stands it now, deserves the love and thanks of men and women," and "If there must be trouble, let it be in my day, that my child may have peace," or "Tyranny, like hell, is not easily conquered," and maybe most amazingly "We have it within our power to begin the world anew."

This is not to defame or slander Milton. *Areopagetica* is one of the most potent defenses of free speech written, in *Eikonoklastes* and *The Tenure of Kings and Magistrates* he conceives of an inspiring radicalism, and of course the author of *Paradise Lost* could turn a phrase. And yet his political pamphlets when read today come across as stiff and scholarly, as arguments built on an edifice of the knowledge of the great classics. They ooze Latin and Greek. Milton can be stirring, he can be inspiring, he can light a love of liberty, but he can also be ponderous. Milton's Republic collapsed under Cromwell's Stalinist impulses; Paine's remains, shaken and often on the verge of collapse, yet somehow still standing. It would be hard to argue that it was the pure power of direct, simple, and angry rhetoric that stays the life-blood of a nation, but perhaps (or hopefully) some of that working-class rage of the dispossessed and ignored which threads its way through *Common Sense* is somehow to attribute to our survival. Milton was read widely, but he spoke in an educated tongue, a Cambridge man. Paine was a pub man; he spoke not to university dons but to the barkeep, the factory worker, the farmer. He has a rough language but it's the peoples' language. He wrote like an American. Paine's slight pamphlet sold half a million copies the year it was printed. Less than a year later, all thirteen colonies would declare their independence from Great Britain.

Americans were already fighting the British in a revolution, but Paine made it the Revolution. Like all true Revolutionaries he knew that America needed its Year Zero, and he reoriented and redefined what was at stake. No longer was this a small rebellion simply tied to anger over a few taxes here and there, petty grievances about expensive tea and playing cards to raise revenue to pay for a frontier war which in many ways the colonists started themselves. No, now this was about apocalypse, it was about Millennium, it was about making the world anew and redefining what it meant to be a person. In *Letters from an American Farmer*, written only a few years before by the Frenchman J. Hector St. John de Crevecoeur, the author asked "What then is the American, this new man?" Paine had an answer; the American was of no particular nationality, and of no particular faith. Rather his was a new creed, a new religion, for now the cause of America is the cause of all mankind.

It's important to remember that he was no provincial, his nationalism was cosmopolitanism. For Paine, "America" was but a synonym for the cause of liberty, wherever she may need to be liberated. It was Paine who coined the phrase that would be the official name of these fifty states, but in many ways there is a

distinction between "The United States" and "America." The former is a nation-state bordered to the north by Canada and to the
south by Mexico with the Atlantic on one side and the Pacific on
the other and a capital in Washington DC. Like all nations it has
its good and bad, its idealists and its corrupt. A country bound-
ed, like all nations, by a border of time and space. But "America"
is something different; if "The United States" is written in prose
then "America" is written in poetry. Its language is not that of
legislation and treaties, rules and laws, but rather of myth and
legend. "America" is the commonwealth, Arcadia, Eden. John
Locke wrote "In the beginning all the world was America." It's
synonymous with ancient and hopefully future freedoms. America is not a place, nor has it every really existed; it is merely
always in the process of coming into existence. That other destitute and drunk poet-prophet Oscar Wilde would write almost a
century after Paine's death that: "A map of the world that does
not include Utopia is not worth even glancing at, for it leaves
out the one country at which Humanity is always landing. And
when Humanity lands there, it looks out, and, seeing a better
country, sets sail." The United States is on the geographer's map,
but America is on the one composed by the utopian. America is
not found in the United States (alone) but she is found in Europe's revolutionary camps of 1848, in the Paris Commune of
1871, in the abolitionist's sermon, in the Union soldier's heart
at Gettysburg, at Seneca Falls and while marching in Selma, at
the Warsaw Ghetto uprising, in Ho Chi Minh's Declaration of
Independence and in Nelson Mandela's prison cell and inside
Vaclav Havel's type-writer, at Stonewall and Tiananmen Square.
Thomas Paine understood the crucial point that America must
never be a mere country, for it is much more; it is an idea, and a
potent one. The American is not a citizen of the United States or
an inhabitant of the western hemisphere; the American is "the
Adam of a New World."

In 1792 Paine found "America" in the streets of Paris, among the debates of Jacobins and Girondists. As he always maintained his cause was the cause of all mankind and his empire was Liberty's, so in France he took the banner of revolution up once again. It was the second time in his life he left his native England for radical causes across the sea. Left behind in Britain was the *Rights of Man,* which answered the objections to the revolution made by Edmund Burke, the comfortable father of contemporary conservatism. Burke may have maintained that the dead deserve a say in the present, but Paine was wise enough to know that the world is for the living, and he answered Burke's objections point by point. And he not only advocated the cause of revolution, he put his body "upon the gears and upon the wheels, upon the levers, upon all the apparatus to try and stop tyranny" (as Mario Savio put it in 1964). He was elected to the French Assembly, but his opposition to totalitarianism and his embrace of freedom was too consistent. He opposed the execution of the pustule rat-king Louis XVI, and Robespierre used the opportunity to have Paine imprisoned within de Sade's home, the supposedly liberated prison of Bastille.

But as they say, stone walls do not a prison make, nor iron bars a cage, and Paine found an America even within the Bastille. It was here that he wrote *The Age of Reason,* the book scandalous and heretical enough that the newly holy of Second Great Awakening America would turn their back on the man who baptized their nation, and whose political ethos made their faith even possible. "I do not believe in the creed professed by the Jewish church, by the Roman church, by the Greek church, by the Turkish church, by the Protestant church, nor by any church that I know of." Milton's rebellious and similarly exiled hero Lucifer taught us that the human mind can make of heaven a hell and of hell a heaven, and for Thomas Paine "My own mind is my own church." It only saw publication because his fellow American and member of the French Assembly Joel Barlow (who also gave this nation its first epic poem in *The Columbiad*) smuggled it out of prison. Paine's stay from execution was ironically perhaps more providential; all that saved him from the guillotine's blade was an improperly placed sign on his cell door. Thermidor and Robespierre's downfall awaited and James Monroe was able to secure his release. And this is how Thomas Paine found himself returned to the crooked streets of lower Manhattan, so different from the rational, rectilinear Enlightenment street grid of a few blocks north. But if America was an Arcadia then *Et in America Ego.*

Washington had his Mount Vernon, and Jefferson his Monticello, but Tom Paine just had 59 Grove Street. He died seemingly abandoned by all, with only Jefferson still supporting him but distancing himself at all costs, as the Federalists loved nothing more than to tout Paine's associations with the third president, like some eighteenth-century Weatherman. In 1799, when Washington died, Napoleon ordered ten days of mourning. Thousands of Americans felt intense grief at the death of their god, and they built an Egyptian pyramid to entomb him, after he lived through the construction of the capital which bared his name. Ten years later when Tom Paine died like a common drunk, most American newspapers merely reprinted the local obituary. There was no ceremony for Tom Paine; the Quakers wouldn't even allow him to be buried in their ground. Only six people came to mark the passing of the man who named the United States of America, including two nameless black freedmen. On the Mall of that right-angled city of Roman marble, there stands an occult obelisk in memory of Washington, and an American Pantheon holds a statue of Jefferson that is nineteen feet tall, but in the District of Columbia there is no memorial to Tom Paine. Washington and Jefferson are gods, but Paine is but a man, and the better for it. If you seek his memorial you must go to those places where people yearn for freedom, and are willing to fight for it. There if you seek his monument you must merely look and listen.

Scriptures for a Dead God (On the Occasion of the 150th Year of *Leaves of Grass*)

Walt! You should be living at this hour! America is in need of you.

America is in need of you because last month a man whose heart burnt with the disunity you deplored murdered nine men and women at prayer. And America is in need of you because last month our highest court sided with the better angels of our nature and recognized and legalized that persecuted love that you yourself knew. Walt, in your incarnational voice, your individual tongue which transubstantiates into all of ours, we need you once again to justify the ways of man to God, always a nobler task than the inverse.

Walt, America is in need of you because we are still large, we still contain multitudes. America is in need of you now more than ever because as in every moment we are the home of the best and of the worst. You have said that we but need only look under our boot soles to find you, well now is the time we must check our souls. We need you now so that you can mourn with us; we need you now so that you can celebrate with us. Do I contradict myself? Very well then...

In the 79th year of these states Walt Whitman received a revelation, and he recorded it in a book of sacred scripture he entitled *Leaves of Grass*. That we think of it as primarily a book of verse is a mistake of history, an interpretive error, for it is first and foremost a new gospel, a type of revelation that came from within, and has the wisdom to know that voice is the same as that which all other prophets thought they heard from the kosmos. For there is no moment any more sacred than that which is now. Whitman set the type himself and printed it at his own cost in a Brooklyn shop; he sold barely any copies of that first edition, that new birth of divinity on July 4th of 1855. He was an

American poet, New York born, but he was also of all time and for all ages. The child of Dutch and New English ancestry, raised on the preaching of Elias Hicks and inner light Quakerism, he spoke not just in a prophetic voice, but an individual one that reaches out across those chasms of time and which seeps into the lonely spaces between words, illuminating that which we've always known but don't have our own words to express. It sounds its barbaric yawps off the rooftops, unscrewing the locks from the doors, the very doors from their jambs.

Now in the 160th year of those leaves, we are desperately in need of Whitman's songs of himself (which are of course really songs of us all). Being a poet and a prophet need not be exclusive, indeed one thing those vocations (if we can use such a word, Whitman might) share is the understanding that rhetoric is reality. It's not so much that Whitman discovered a new doctrine, but that he defined it. The poet and the prophet are not scientists, rather they tell us the important things, which somehow we always knew but which we aren't eloquent enough to explain ourselves. The poet and the prophet are able to give breath to the ineffable, and to find the numinous in the material. The poet is the one who fashions and fuses the mirror and window together.

I would argue that *Leaves of Grass* is the first great work of scripture to be penned since modernity killed God. Copernicus and Newton, Nietzsche and Darwin signed the Lord's death certificate, but our most American of sages, Whitman, arranged the funeral service. The brilliance and importance of *Leaves of Grass* is that it has the bravery to acknowledge the current state of theological affairs, and the pragmatism to fashion an ethic of living in spite of it. Whitman told us to argue not concerning God, that he who was curious about each was not curious about God. Where the talkers of earlier faiths were always talking of the beginning or the end, Whitman did not talk of the beginning or the end. He admitted that he did not understand God in the least, but knew that there was nothing more wonderful than himself. "I find letters from God dropped in the street, and every one is signed, /by God's name. /And I leave them were they are, for I know that wherever I go, others will punctually come for ever and ever." Whitman teaches us not how to live without God so much as in spite of God. Like Spinoza, Whitman is either an atheist or the most God-intoxicated of prophets, or maybe something more; the rare figure who understands that neither of those categories exist, or that if they do they are synonyms.

Whitman's nineteenth-century colleague Dostoevsky supposedly said that if God did not exist, than all would be permitted, and Nietzsche observed that after God's murder life's meaning is irrevocably different. But where these old Europeans couldn't help but barely hide their despair at the divine theocide, Whitman constructed a new system and a new language with the gross practicality his carpenter father showed in building a house. Whitman's is the first great faith to incorporate the discoveries and the undeniable implications of positivist science and materialist philosophy – "A word of reality.... Materialism first and last imbuing" and "Hurrah for positive science! Long live exact demonstration!" – and he acknowledges that we must at least confront the fact that God's absence may alter how we live, how we organize our societies, how we face the finality of death. And where Dostoevsky feared the possibility of all being permitted, Whitman fashioned an antinomian morality of finding the theophanic in the moment, among the union of men and women, brothers and sisters. While those Europeans were still at the funeral, Whitman was enjoying a drink at God's wake, and making plans.

What Whitman understood is that the abolition of mere immortality allows for the liberation of eternity. Wittgenstein said that there was never any more eternity than now, something Whitman anticipated decades earlier. He writes "There was never any more inception than there is now, /nor any more youth or age than there is now; /and will never be any more perfection than there is now, /nor any more heaven or hell than there is now." In shining, luminescent verse, even when recounting his epic lists of anonymous nineteenth-century Americans from the president to the pimple-covered prostitute, the Missourian trapper to the Yankee girl at her loom, he crystalizes the sacredness of the moment—all moments.

For Whitman, each second is a portal through which the messiah or the devil may pass, which is in fact always what is happening. He writes that "The pleasures of heaven are with me, and the pains of hell are with me," echoing one of the truest and wisest lines in the old scripture when Isaiah has the Lord say "I form the light, and create darkness." There is no eternity in the hereafter, the hereafter is now; immortality is acquired by opening your eyes and clearing your ears. It is—to borrow the language of Whitman's older brother-prophet—an issue of cleansing the doors of perception. Infinity is not somewhere else—it is here. Eternity is not in the future—it is now. When Whitman looks out at the flows and eddies of the East River traversing the waters of his loved New York on the Brooklyn Ferry, thinking of us (he tells us that he thought of us!) and informing us that what he saw we will see, he understands that past, present, future are illusions. In collapsing them all together into that singularity he lets us know that it's not that death need not be proud, it's that death herself never existed anyhow. "The smallest sprout shows there is really no death."

Now, one must be clear, Whitman is agnostic on the issue of whether consciousness survives. He offers no consolation that there is life after death; what he offers is a vision of how to live as if the answer to that question didn't matter. In this way he matches the ancient Roman poet Lucretius, and *Leaves of Grass* is to us as his *De Rerum Natura* was to the classical Mediterranean. The gods are mute, and their pronouncements cannot be trusted. The only oracle who is still speaking after the great god Pan is dead necessarily speaks in our own accent. For Lucretius there were but atoms organized into matter, and our will was only expressed in the *clinamen,* in their random swerve. And for Whitman, he asked, "Who need be afraid of the merge?" The fear of death is an issue of ego. Lucretius said either there is a realm of the living dead or there is not; either way we should not be afraid, since either we will continue to be aware or we will not, in which case it doesn't matter. And for our American Lucretius, "the converging objects of the universe perpetually flow." Nothing truly dies because that smallest sprout's manure is us, we're never separate from that system, we're never divorced from the world, we're always a peninsula on the continent. "All goes onward and outward... And nothing collapses, /and to die is different from any one supposed, and luckier. /Has one supposed it lucky to be born? /I hasten to inform him or her it is just as lucky to die, and I know it."

It is my contention that all that one need know about either God, death, or America (which are all really the same thing anyhow) are contained within the complete works of the Sage of Camden and the Bard of Amherst. Both Whitman, who is the poet of the exclamation point! and of the ellipsis.... And Dickinson, who is the poet of the dash – are descendants of a culture that had at its center the elegant and parsimonious words of *The King James Bible* and of the *Book of Common Prayer.* And they took that rhetoric and saw no shame in pouring new wine into old casks. Whitman may have internalized the free verse of the *King James Bible* more than any other artist to speak English, yet his language was not marshaled in the service of God for James, England, and Saint George but rather for you, himself, and me. "We consider the bibles and religions divine...I do not say they are/not divine. /I say that they have all grown out of you and may grow out of you still, /It is not they who give the life...it is you who give the life."

His inspiration was that he crafted a narrative voice that speaks beyond the grave, which collapses distinction between people. It is the most vibrant literary voice I know of, which sounds like it is coming from inside your own head. In him we become not just his audience, but narrator as well. He is not a poet of egoism, far from it; rather he is the poet of the collapse between the listeners and listened, between reader and book, the singer and the song. When he addresses you directly he is literally addressing you directly, for Whitman the meaning of poems is that they convey immortality, not just because of posterity but because they are able to have almost a spooky presence in being able to communicate beyond the grave. "And that my soul embraces you this hour, and we affect each other, /without ever seeing each other, and never perhaps to see each/other, is every bit as wonderful."

Though he has the cadence, the chiasmus, the Hebraic and biblical parallelism of William Tyndale and Launcelot Andrews and Miles Coverdale and all the other English translators of the scriptures, he marshals that voice in the service of a different god, for as I have said Whitman was composing a new scripture for a new world:

> Taking myself the exact dimensions of Jehovah and laying them away,
> Lithographing Kronos and Zeus his son, and Hercules his grandson,
> Buying drafts of Osiris and Isis and Belus and Brahma and Adonis
> In my portfolio placing Manito loose, and Allah on a leaf, and the Crucifix engraved.
> With Odin and the hideous faced Mexitli, and all idols and images,
> Honestly taking them all for what they re worth, and not a cent more.
> Admitting they were alive and did the work of their day,
> Admitting they bore mites as for unfledged birds who have

now to rise and fly and sing for themselves,
Accepting the rough deific sketches to gill out better in my-
self...
Bestowing them freely on each man and woman I see.

Whitman's theology was large; it contained multitudes, and a characteristic American enthusiasm that is not only pluralistic, but also promiscuous, if not queer. We do not reject these past gods; Whitman did not. We take what is useful in them and we discard the rest. From the detritus of their pronouncements he fashions a new system, lest we be enslaved by those of another man. The great "I AM!" may now be silent, the fiery Tetragrammaton's voice now mute and silent, but Whitman has proven that it is still possible to write scripture. This fact alone may be *Leaves of Grass's* most important lesson, that the oracles need not be dumb even if God is dead, that we may still deliver supplication even if the kosmos is silent, a lesson that in and of itself may be as important as anything contained in scriptures new or old. Walt Whitman was a christ, for he taught us that we are all christs.

I have said that Whitman provides us with an ethic from this new metaphysic; how do we live in light of the seeming moral irrelevance of the transcendent? Yes, perhaps we can experience the infinite in an object, or eternity in a second, and maybe we can collapse the sacred into the profane. But why care for our brothers and sisters in a world without the threat of reward or punishment? But Whitman is a great mystic. Like the Sufi nun who wished she could burn heaven down with the flames of hell so that one worshiped God only to worship God, Whitman knew that an ethic predicated on apple and lash was no ethic at all. Rather, like a good democrat, his was a system of how to live, and it did not just logically flow from his ontology like some Euclidian syllogism. Instead, his metaphysics and his ethics were simply identical. Much as the founding document of Whitman's

Holy Land claimed that human rights were "self evident," Whitman's ethic of brotherly affection and democratic egalitarianism was similarly so.

Democracy need not have a recourse to those transcendent signifieds that theocracy must prop itself with. The principle is simple: there is nobody, no matter how talented, rich, or brilliant, who as a matter of principle has the right to control another capable person without that person's consent. And this simple ideal is what the society we strive for should be built on, and it's what must be celebrated. "It is also not consistent with the reality of the soul to admit that there is anything in the known universe more divine than men and women." Our union is not just mystical, it is literal, and our systems of governance must reflect that. But unlike that cynic Churchill, Whitman knew that democracy isn't simply the worst form of government that happens to be better than all other forms; democracy is a faith as vibrant and strong as that of the prophets who came before him. It is not simply a way of organizing our government; it is a way of organizing ourselves. He famously begins "Song of Myself" (in the superior, 1855 edition) with "I celebrate myself, /and what I assume you shall assume, /for every atom belonging to me as good belongs to you." This is the first principle of Whitman's democratic faith. It is not a mere principle of equivalence, and it is not the show of egoism his readers often misinterpret it to be. It is rather a radical, theological assertion on the commonality of all of us; it is the foundation for his anarchic democratic vision. This, in our year of "owning our privilege" and intersectionality, of trigger warning and microaggressions, contains the radical core of the most simple of progressive messages: "For every atom belonging to me as good belongs to you." Nothing is sacred because everything is sacred; this is the basis of both his religion and his politics, which are identical. This is the fundamental truth of Whitman's bible; the rest is but commentary. Now go, and learn.

Despite my apparent declarations, Whitman was neither god nor messiah but a man, and inheritor of all the petty bigotries, small-mindedness, and prejudice of his era, even if in verse he could be visionary. He of course knew this himself, the man who not only placed a line-drawing of himself (with a purposefully enhanced crotch bulge) in lieu of a byline on his book of poetry's first edition, and who felt no shame in composing "advertisements for myself" was no hypocrite in admitting his own deficiencies – it was only consistent with his poetic vision. And he admitted that when he composed those lines, about the non-existence of death, the love between citizens, the simple ethic of kindness and embrace, that these were more theoretical than lived for him.

A parable: In 1862 the poet was worried that his brother who was serving the Union cause was among the fallen at Fredericksburg, and he journeyed to the capital to discover what he could. His brother was fine, but in that city he found the moaning body of America's youth, and for the next three years he would attend to the thousands of wounded and dying who clogged the makeshift hospitals of Washington DC. Whitman's Civil War-time service was true to his Quaker roots, where the bearded man looking older than his 43 years consoled the maimed and dying sons of both North and South. He would sit by their side, talk to them in their infirmity, read to them from a Bible that he did not believe (understanding that the essence of religion need not be belief), and distribute candy to the men who were scarcely older than boys.

Shortly after May 1, 1865, the mother of one of those boys, a Mrs. Irwin of Pennsylvania, opened a letter postmarked Washington DC. There is little doubt that she would not have recognized the signatory's name, a name that would fill anthologies and book titles, syllabi and monuments. The name "Walt Whitman" would have been just the name of a stranger. He writes, "No doubt you and Frank's friends have heard the sad fact of his death...I will write you a few lines – as a casual friend that sat by his death bed." Whitman goes on to recount the wound Frank Irwin received in Virginia a month before, the pain her son went through, his amputation. He recounts the fever that Frank suffered, and that he passed on May Day, the year the Civil War ended.

Whitman writes, "I was in the habit of coming in afternoons and sitting by him, and soothing him, and he liked to have me... Toward the last he was more restless and flighty at night....I do not know his past life, but I feel as if it must have been good...I can say that he behaved so brave, so composed, and so sweet and affectionate, it could not be surpass'd.... I thought perhaps a few words, though from a stranger, about your son, from one who was with him at the last, might be worthwhile – for I loved the young man, though I but saw him immediately to lose him." Whitman did not give Mrs. Irwin a gift of verse, but rather the knowledge that her son did not die alone, that though she could not be there with him he still had consolation and love in his last moments.

In his introduction to *Leaves of Grass*, Whitman writes that to internalize its teachings is to live as if "your very flesh shall be a great poem and have the richest fluency not only in its words but in the silent lines of your lips and face and between the lashes of your eyes and in every motion and joint of your body." In consoling this mother, in consoling her dying son, we see how one's very life can be as of the greatest of poems. Even after a millennium we may not deserve one as holy as Whitman, but grace, like love, is undeserved and still given freely. Walt Whitman's kiss is still on America's lips, like that undeserved gift.

Walt, we have need of you. And we pray. He stops somewhere waiting for us.

Daddy, What Did You Do in the Culture Wars?

It would be easy for conservative "culture wars" diatribes to be penned by an artificial intelligence. One imagines that it wouldn't be too hard to come up with a rough outline of how the standard literary-critical jeremiad is composed, and to develop the software necessary to replicate it.

Bemoaning the current state of academic literary study, and blaming it for the supposed collapse of the humanities has been a cottage industry since the so-called "Culture Wars" of the 1980s when fashionable French Theory was supposedly responsible for the degeneration of everything holy. The contours of this genre are fairly standardized. The writer is either a conservative academic comfortably imprisoned within the belly of the beast, wailing about the machinations of pernicious radicalism permeating higher education; or they are a traditionalist minded journalist working at the right-wing press (*The Week*, *The National Review*, and *First Things* are prime databases for this kind of rhetoric) sharing with their audience the horrors of tenured radicals who have discarded Shakespeare in favor of Inuit lesbian slam-poetry, or whatever imaginary subject du jour is enraging the author.

After the perfunctory anecdote is dealt with, there is a listing of works which are supposedly under attack (the Bard, of course, who has more readers now than at any point in his reception history, is often a prime example), a fulmination about "political correctness," and finally some kind of impassioned plea for a nostalgic and imaginary return to traditional humanistic values. A recurring theme is that partisans, of what Harold Bloom called "the schools of resentment" (that is, any scholar who interprets literature through the lens of race, class, or gender), secretly hate literature. That any individual would possess the psychology that would lead them to choose the not particularly lucrative career of professionally studying literature because they secretly harbor hatred towards that subject seems absurd, much less that this would be an en masse phenomenon.

Yet as moribund as the humanities have supposedly been (according to positivist scientists, economics majors, and higher education administrators) the "Culture Wars" have surely blazed a bright path across the consciousness of any literature, history, philosophy, theology, or cultural studies major. Columnists from William Safire to David Brooks have bemoaned the supposed death of the humanities (while conveniently ignoring how supply-side economics has had a hearty role in that) identifying a "post-modern bogeyman" as being responsible for the murder. In an era of limitless adjuncts, directionless theory, and little respect for the humanities, where does the issue of the "Culture Wars" stand now? In an era of trigger warnings, blogs like *Thought Catalog* and *Buzz Feed* mindlessly parrot the language of privilege as appropriated from cultural studies while universities cut classes and limit the number of tenure track appointments. Whither does the culture wars rage when the university is closed for business?

Of course the cause for there being fewer majors in the humanities (and even this can be disputed) is ascribed by the conservative critic to the influence of "Theory," and not say, the octopus-like reach of corporatization within the university. But it's an uncomfortable fact for market-fundamentalist periodicals like *The National Review* to acknowledge that if students are indeed taking less English, history, and philosophy classes, it may have less to do with Michel Foucault, Jacques Derrida, and Edward Said than it does with the obscene cost of higher education, the permeating and often anti-intellectual rhetoric of corporate logic in the academy, and the assault on tenure led by many on the right, like David Horowitz. The values of genuine humanistic inquiry are often at odds with the gods of the marketplace, yet the conservative culture warrior finds himself in the unhappy position of trying to serve both God and Mammon. That these sorts of reactionary diatribes with their stock figure of the radical black studies or women's studies professor trying to destroy the canon are so common doesn't change the fact that they're taking part in a debate that is not just old, but passé. And boring.

Allan Bloom in his classic (and delusional) *The Closing of the American Mind* was enraged by academe at the time. It's not even that our culture today is different from Bloom's in 1987; it's that Bloom wasn't even accurate then. The "Theory Wars" of the 1980s could indeed be divisive within literature departments, but it's a period of academic history that belongs to the past, and it doesn't reflect the reality of graduate students and young faculty who have indeed absorbed the critical lessons of that period, but who have also moved on into different, and sometimes more important and exciting, avenues of scholarship than either merely worrying about who is or is not on an accepted, canonical list of authors and works, or on the contrary supposedly drafting the fall of Western civilization. Most of us are too busy trying to find any kind of employment instead of doing either. And yet *The National Review* still warns about "The looming cul-de-sacs of postmodernism, diversity and revisionism," as if diversity was de facto and obviously bad and that the critical faculties of revision are not the central project of humanistic thinking. Also note the borderline anachronistic insertion of the word "postmodernism" which increasingly seems less like a real thing and more as if something from a Harold Bloom fever-dream. Gilbert T. Sewall, the author of the piece from which I quoted, makes one point which I do find interesting, and worth analyzing more. In critiquing a report released by the National Endowment for the Humanities about the state of the liberal arts, he writes that its authors "steer away from any concrete definition, standard, or design of excellence, thought, or beauty."

Here, I think, is a potentially legitimate criticism of the state of the humanities today, though perhaps not in the way that Sewall thinks it is, and perhaps in a way that has more to do with perception than reality. What Sewall's sentiment gets to is a function of the humanities which I do think (in some form) is central to literary, philosophical, and historical experience, but which we on the left have ceded ownership of to our conservative critics. Too often when in a defensive posture we seem to legitimize that they are the ones who take Literature (with a capital "L"...) seriously, that it's true that they are the gate-keepers of culture. But is this fair? Might our own "revisionism" be more authentically in line with the Western liberal arts (for who was more revisionist than that old gadfly Socrates)? Note that Sewall has an obsession with "concrete" definitions, with standards and design. The public, and perhaps we on the left (internalizing the rhetoric of the right), take the traditionalist as if anything a lover of literature, but I find their arguments about canonicity to be profoundly cynical and disingenuous. I do not doubt that many of them love the humanities (a consideration that they too often do not give to the rest of us), but I find their language to be that of the anatomist, or the classifier, and not of the poet. Sewall sees the humanities as handmaiden to politics; he writes that its function is "refinements of character, morality, and ethics." And while the didactic justification for literature has a venerable critical history (and it should be pointed out is pretty much the same argument that those on the social justice left are making about literature's utility), it's also not one that particularly privileges literature as itself a different mode of being.

Certainly at his best, Harold Bloom, who is the veritable master of this type of critique, conveys the sublime power of literature in works like *The Anxiety of Influence,* or even his criminally underrated *The American Religion.* Bloom sometimes has the sort of transcendent, almost sacred love of the transformative power of poetry and prose that should indeed (in part) be the birthright of those who wish to learn about the humanities. But as Terry

Eagleton cattily, but accurately, said about Bloom, he "was once an interesting critic." Perhaps starting with *The Western Canon* we've had a Bloom who seems primarily interested in showing his readers all the very interesting and important stuff he has read, and then even more crudely listing and ranking them. This type of discourse, popularized by the Blooms, William J. Bennett, Lynn Cheney and so on, take it as a given that it is their side which sees literature as important, and the rest of us let them make that argument too often. That the question of "Who is the better writer, Marlowe or Goethe?" doesn't really make sense and isn't even that interesting, doesn't seem to cross the mind of commentators who fume about the supposed abolition of the canon. These questions of aesthetic value are, contrary to the critics who obsess over the apparent abandonment of such concerns in the academy, questions that aren't even particularly serious about literature.

Indeed one repeatedly sees that this conservatism isn't even particularly humanistic. As both a term of derision, but also as a reclaimed designation of pride, these critics proudly celebrate the "Dead White Men" whom they see as composing sacrosanct, eternal, platonic canon of "Great Books." That some authors on this list like St. Augustine were not white, or that others like Emily Dickinson were not men is of no accord (finding a living person on the required reading list of St. John's College is another issue entirely). Yet this proud touting of the values of the "Dead White Men" is not just profoundly illiberal (in both the classical and current sense of that word), but also completely antithetical to the spirit of humanism. Since the Renaissance (the period which I study) it has been a creedal belief of the humanist to find wisdom where one does. In their snarky and fussy condemnations of my previously mentioned hypothetical (and honestly sort of awesome sounding) lesbian Inuit slam-poetry, the conservative critic has barred himself from finding the wisdom which may well lie within literature which they refuse to read for its not being adequately dead, white, and male. This is not an approach which celebrates literature, rather it is a method which puts it on ice, or locks it away, or preserves it in amber, as good as something dead in a jar of formaldehyde. To assume that these are the critics who have an authentic love of literature is to abdicate our own responsibilities to defend precisely what the value of literature is.

In Bloom and his compatriots' formulation the canon is an Arnoldian repository of the sweetness and the light, and it is under attack by an aggrieved collection of feminists, black activists, and gay rights groups who would abandon universal literary greatness in favor of winning points for political correctness. As a vision it is attractive to the wider public, not used to the jargon-heavy prose of theoretical writing and the progressive politics of many in academe. For defenders of both cultural studies, but who also believe that literature is a generically unique textual medium, it is a frustrating state of affairs. But again, those of us on the left have ceded too much ground to figures like Harold and Allan Bloom and E.D. Hirsch (and in all fairness, I should point out that Harold Bloom considers himself to be part of the socialist left), taking it as a given that their view of literature somehow does take literature more seriously than the rest of us. And yet what does an analysis of books like Harold Bloom's *The Western Canon* demonstrate? What we see is the obsessive listing, categorization, and borderline crass ranking of books where he falsely claims objectivity for matters of personal taste; a sort of thinking-man's *BuzzFeed* listicle. In the conservative canon warriors' obsession with which books are great, which ones aren't, and which ones are greater than others, we see a reaffirmation of a type of competitive blood-sport which far from taking literature seriously, simply reduces it to a matter of demonstrating an individual's superior taste. If the theory-generation proved that canon-based thinking is undeniably biased and reaffirms certain social strictures, then the irony is that nobody demonstrates this more than Harold Bloom. And yet it's impossible to not have sympathy for wanting to embrace a critic who at least superficially takes literature seriously.

The "school of aggrievement" that is composed of critics like the Blooms, Hirsh, Cheney and so on is in a way not wrong that Theory did in part iron out some of what makes literature so profound, and different from other linguistic forms. Cultural materialism, New Historicism, cultural studies and so on provided us with a partial critical service in removing the special status of the literary text. In opening up all of written language to the hermeneutics of interpretation they helped us to understand how literature is formulated within given cultural and material contexts. But as an exorcist casts out demons, she must also be careful not to cast out angels. In expanding the canon there has been a necessary democratization of texts, voices once mute now sing with the inclusion of those who were too often ignored. That is not a cause to abandon the special power and significance of literature however, far from it; it is a call to do the exact opposite, to reaffirm the written word's immense and almost supernatural significance, and to reclaim the concept of literature back from the traditionalists. In reducing all works, be they Chekhov or VCR manuals, to the status of "text," cultural studies damaged the unique qualities that make literature itself important. There should be no shame in the charge that we need to re-enchant the world a bit. But the solution should not be Bloom's masculine ranking of books, but rather a consideration of precisely what is important about literature itself. We need a new and engaged mode of criticism that is true to the vision of Kafka who claimed that "A book must be the axe for the frozen sea within us," or Dickinson who said "If I physically feel as if the top of my head was taken off, I know that is poetry." But the canon-obsessives, in forcing something as wild, untamable, profound, and powerful as literature into the straight-jacket of anal retentive lists and evaluations of "greatness," also did a profound disservice to literature. The conservative defense of the canon is so often a celebration of mere wallpaper, a means of demonstrating one's education, pedigree, or wealth. If the humanities now take on an existential, if not spiritual, import than we must reject this suburban ranking of texts. The ranking of "the best which has been thought and said" is an affectation – it's literary Fantasy Football. In short, we need to stop asking which literature is great, and reinvestigate why literature is great.

The Death of God, Again

A young, attractive blonde woman with a fashionable pixie haircut sits anxiously in the waiting room of her exclusive Upper West Side gynecologist's office. She is a few months into her first pregnancy, and she fidgets nervously as she waits to see the doctor, as she has felt increasingly isolated since moving to the city with her actor husband.

Recently she has had a series of recurring nightmares, and she has become paranoid about the smothering attention she has been receiving from her wealthy neighbors in the Dakota. There has, she thinks to herself, been a feeling of the demonic as of late.

To distract herself she reaches for a copy of *Time Magazine* sitting on the office's coffee-table. There, on the cover, in stark blood-red words against a black background is the question "Is God Dead?"

Many will recognize this scene from Roman Polanski's 1968 horror classic *Rosemary's Baby*, but though the title character's satanic pregnancy is fictional, the magazine used as a prop is not. For audiences watching Polanski's film, the magazine would be instantly recognizable, a dark joke. Indeed that cover would go on to become iconic, repeatedly listed by designers as one of the most provocative of the twentieth century, though the contents of the article have been less discussed, both then and now.

The piece "Towards a Hidden God" by John Elson, and edited by the otherwise staid, conservative Otto Fuerbringer, was *Time Magazine*'s cover story appropriately enough around Easter of 1966, and it was released to immediate public backlash, as was a previous article published in October 1965 entitled "The Death of God Movement." Though this April marked the fiftieth anniversary of its release, "Is God Dead?" remains that periodical's bestselling issue.

In that precursor article, Elson wrote about a group of theologians who "say that it is no longer possible to think about or believe in a transcendent God who acts in human history, and that Christianity will have to survive, if at all, without him."

The Death of God movement found a home, however controversial, in some of the liberal Protestant seminaries that were once a mainstay of American intellectual life, as well as at secular universities. Since the rise of the religious right in the last generation and a half, we have become accustomed to thinking of issues surrounding faith as dividing easily between traditionalists and the secular. But as the scholar William R. Hutchinson made clear, many mainstream American Protestants starting in the nineteenth century encouraged seminaries to develop an approach to religion that went "beyond Christianity," setting the groundwork for the paradox of "atheist theology" being developed at those same seminaries a half-century later. In short profiles Elson considered the philosophy of scholars like "Paul van Buren of Temple University, William Hamilton of Colgate Rochester Divinity School, and Gabriel Vahanian of Syracuse University" as well as Thomas J.J. Altizer at Emory University, a Methodist school.

The earlier article begins with a quote from Altizer, where he says "We must recognize that the death of God is a historical event: God has died in our time, in our history, in our existence." For Altizer it was the task of the worshiper to understand what it meant to be a "Christian atheist," and to perhaps move towards what the German theologian Dietrich Bonhoeffer, martyred at the Flossenbürg concentration camp two decades before, meant when he wrote of a "religionless Christianity."

The four thinkers profiled, to whom Rabbi Richard Rubenstein could be added, represented a diversity of thought drawing from eclectic sources, including (perhaps obviously considering the movement's name) most prominently Friedrich Nietzsche. In short, the Death of God movement broadly believed that Nietzsche's infamous declaration in *Thus Spake Zarathustra* was not a nihilistic challenge but rather a prophetic injunction.

The general reading public in the mid-century United States did not agree, and the four profiled theologians were subject to denunciations from pulpit and press, and the target of scorn, derision, and threats. The reaction is not surprising, for even though progressive seminaries were willing to entertain these sort of provocative theologies, historian David Hollinger has pointed out how many within the mainstream had derided liberalizing Protestants as "too worldy." Indeed what shocked many of *Time Magazine*'s readers was the perception that when it came to their seminaries and universities (be they Methodist, Baptist, or Episcopal) that it seemed as if it was the right hand that didn't know what the left was doing.

This backlash, which was arguably equally against the provocative cover, ironed out the stirring, radical, and in many ways profoundly moving interpretation of the gospels that the Death of God movement was exploring. These assorted thinkers faced the silent ineffable with not a spirit of defeated skepticism but rather existential responsibility. As Elson explained "The current death-of-God group believes that God is indeed absolutely dead, but proposes to carry on and write a theology without theos, without God."

Death of God theology was in part developed as a response to the twin specters of Auschwitz and Hiroshima, the Holocaust and the bomb. Yet the question of theodicy, the "problem of evil," appears as far back as Job's anguished cries unto the whirlwind. Dostoevsky's *Ivan Karamazov* may maintain that the suffering of a single innocent child makes God's existence untenable and the Death of God theologians may have agreed, but like the Russian novelist they weren't quite done with God either.

John Caputo is one contemporary theologian who has frequently engaged with Death of God theology, especially in his own work that draws connections between deconstruction and post-structuralism with radical theology. In an exchange with me where I asked him what role he felt the death of God could play in our contemporary moment, he answered "I do not think that God exists (my death of God), but that God insists, and calls for our response, which gives birth to God in the world."

Echoing Marx, he continued by explaining that radical theology is "the heart of a heatless world, and offers an alternative to the greed, narcissism and self-aggrandizement of a purely secular culture which prizes nothing other than its stock portfolio," and that radical theology does this by "formulating the notion of something of unconditional worth that lays claim to us unconditionally."

While modernity may have posed new circumstances on which to contemplate God's death, a crisis of faith has supposedly haunted the West since the sixteenth century. God's metaphysical status was called into question by the scientific revolution, his ontological definition was disrupted by the fracturing of Christendom during the reformations, and his ethical justification was confused by the bloody wars of religion during early modernity up unto the hideous atrocities which marked our own era. There were many pallbearers at God's funeral.

Indeed the perennial nature of theodicy is seen in the author Elie Wiesel's brilliant 1979 play *The Trial of God*. The play is set in the mid-seventeenth century during the Khmelnytsky Uprising, which was a period of far-reaching and bloody anti-Jewish violence. In his play, a rabbinical tribunal charges and condemns God as guilty for His crimes. In setting his play in the distant past, Wiesel reminds us that the issues of theodicy are not a purely modern problem; indeed our days have always been a shadow upon the Earth. Wiesel witnessed a similar rabbinical tribunal while in Auschwitz. At a Holocaust Educational Trust dinner in 2008, the author recounted that upon delivering their verdict there was an "infinity of silence" after which all of the rabbis broke for evening prayers to the God whom they had just convicted.

It's an existentialist parable that was particularly true to the Jewish Death of God theologian Rubenstein (indeed the movement was by necessity and definition ecumenical), for this theology allows us to worship a God whom we have condemned. The insight of this movement was that faith is not mere affirmation of a positivist claim that is subject to empirical verification, but rather how to ethically live in spite of nothingness' reality. That is to say that true faith (as opposed to the "cheap grace" which Bonhoeffer wrote against) is not to live ethically because God exists, but in such a way that it doesn't matter if He exists or not.

It's this profound critical vocabulary offered by theologians like Rubenstein, van Buren, Hamilton, Vanahain, and Altizer that, a half-century after they briefly entered popular culture, reminds us that we still need this mode of thought. It is a sentiment that Altizer still agrees with, undaunted and still working fifty years after the *Time Magazine* article. He wrote to me that "contemporary scholarship is alienated from theology itself, and my real hope is for a rebirth of theology." Or as Caputo told me, this type of thought is the "last, best hope for making theology believable in the world." We have a need for the death of God, again.

This may seem untenable to some, after all the new millennium saw religion return with an apocalyptic fervor in politics, both domestic and foreign. The "secularization hypothesis" that religion would slowly die out has been delayed as long as Christ's return. And yet this is precisely why we need Death of God theology right now. It may be cliché to argue that the "New Atheists" and religious fundamentalism are necessarily similar, and yet both largely trade in anemic thought, empty creedal recitation, and anti-intellectualism. If atheism is what we deserve, and it may be, then at least we deserve a better class of atheist than Richard Dawkins. Death of God theology offers us a means to admit the importance of existential questions while avoiding the Scylla and Charybdis of the positivist pair of religious literalism and boring suburban New Atheism.

While it's true that "Is God dead?" has seemingly been answered in the negative from a sociological perspective, the philosophical questions that it addresses stubbornly remain an undeniable aspect of modernity, no matter how many people tell pollsters they attend church (or don't attend church).

Death of God theology raises questions that are important to many of us for whom the massive poetic, metaphorical, literary, and cultural edifice which constitutes religion is still a narrative vocabulary for expressing these questions, but for whom modern orthodox faith can seem hollow. It is the "better atheism" we have needed, since the Flying Spaghetti Monster is not as profound as his followers may think. It is a movement that recognizes both the ontological realities of modernity, but also the profound beauty and power of religious mythopoesis; it is a way of pouring new wine into old skins.

The thinkers profiled by Elson a half-century ago saw themselves not as abolishing Christianity, but rather fulfilling it. In their writings they sometimes drew on radical currents within orthodox Christianity, and many of these thinkers (including Altizer and Caputo) constitute the syllabus of contemporary Northern Irish theologian Peter Rollins' cheekily, yet brilliantly named "Atheism for Lent" digital course, which provides a model for how complex radical theology can be conceptualized in an iconoclastically devotional way. Atheism for Lent presents a series of readings over the Lenten season which engage first with philosophical and then theological atheism. As its website explains, the course "seeks to use some of the most potent critiques of Christianity as a type of purifying fire that might help us appreciate and understand Christ's cry of dereliction on the Cross in a new way."

Rollins explained to me that radical theology "could capture the popular imagination and potentially coalesce into a practice and influence the way Christianity was approached and acted out." One of the founders of "pyrotheology," Rollins envisions a "religionless Christianity" along Bonhoeffer's lines, and has organized faith communities in Europe and the United States, such as ikonNYC in Brooklyn.

"My own vocation is to set up communities that attempt to be faithful to the disruptive event that Death of God theology articulates," Rollins explained to me. That he has helped to found a community of atheist Christians worshiping in Brooklyn need not be confusing, after all the earliest Christians were accused of atheism by classical pagan writers. It's part of a venerable tradition.

Indeed Christian atheism drew upon the radical philosophy of the religion it originated from. With the incarnation, Trinity, and crucifixion, Christianity was always comfortable with paradox. In its origins Christianity was always an oppositional and counter-cultural faith; Death of God theology is in many ways the rightful inheritor of that as a tradition.

Rollins sees this as central to Christianity being understood as a "rupturing of worldview" rather than a worldview in itself. In this way Christ's promise is that He "lends an ear to the liberating potentials promised in, but not delivered by, our religious, political and cultural realities."

Much as Christianity understands God to be incarnated as a simple man, the death of God is a divine theophany. It reminds us that that which is the least can be the highest, and where it is the darkest there is hope. It is not simple atheism; it is a divine atheism that understands that it's possible that the fullest affirmation of God comes in His denial. If central to some religious practice is a stripping away of all idols to get closer to the ineffable, than an iconoclasm of language, even belief, is paradoxically that which brings one closest to God, since the spoken God is not the real God.

For the Death of God movement, a dead God was not a repudiation of Christianity, but rather the strongest affirmation about what precisely made that religion so beautiful in a fallen world. To paraphrase a later Jewish prophet, it is a testament written in the language of a broken and holy hallelujah. The central insight of the Death of God theologians, needed now more than ever, is that even if God isn't real, His love very much is.

Apocalypse is the Mother of Beauty

Consider, Boethius. He was a descendent of a noble Italian family, a beneficiary of a classical education, and in some ways the last of the Romans. In the sixth century, he found himself accused of treason in a Lombardy prison. To console himself as he awaited execution, he synthesized all of his philosophical knowledge, and attempted to still his mind even as fortune's wheel turned. In his *De Consolatione Philosophiae* he lamented "Mad fortune sweeps along in wanton pride…Now tramples mighty kings beneath her feet." He was executed in 524 AD, supposedly with a rope around his head pulled so tightly that his eyes popped out.

In this world of entropy, Boethius' task was both personal and communal, for in stoically embracing the decisions of the goddess Fortuna he admitted that death would soon come. But as he was also a refugee from a world that was dying, his manuscript served as an *ars moriendi* for culture, too. And in subsequent centuries his accomplishment was steadfastly maintained by fellow humanists, laboring in monasteries and libraries dotting Europe, making *The Consolations of Philosophy* one of the most copied texts of late antiquity, a capsule from one culture's final moments through the eclipse of the next centuries.

In not unrelated news, it was above freezing at the North Pole last New Year's Eve. We may not be so different from Boethius. It's worth thinking about him, and how he faced extinction both personal and communal, and what exactly his and our humanities are good for as we face our own civilization's possibly approaching conclusion. A rough contemporary of Boethius noted that "in the middle of the debris of the great city, only scattered groups of wretched peoples, witnesses to past calamities, still attest to us the names of an earlier age." For UCLA professor Linda Marsh, that description of the distant past sounds similar to one of the near future. In her essay "Scorched Earth, 2200 AD" she describes "Once-teeming metropolises … [that are now] watery ghost towns … sparsely populated colonies of hardy survivors who eke out vampire-like subterranean existences, emerging only at night when the temperatures dip into the low-triple digits." As we face potential climate apocalypse, the question we must ask is: what are the humanities for?

It's an interesting question how much someone like Boethius could anticipate that their world was coming to an end; it's an important question to ask if we are adequately anticipating it right now. There is a story that upon the legionnaires leaving Britain, the Romanized Celts sent a request to the Emperor asking for the army's return. Instead they found themselves waiting for the barbarians. A few centuries later and an Anglo-Saxon poet wondered if Roman stonewalls had been built by giants who once populated the island, memories of technologically advanced civilization now no longer history, but legend. Both the monasteries of the Middle Ages as well as scholars in the Islamic east preserved the classical knowledge that they could, how would things have been different had the Romans more fully seen collapse coming?

We have a benefit in being able to anticipate and plan for the possibility of our civilization's collapse, a luxury Boethius didn't exactly have. Roy Scranton in *Learning to Die in the Anthropocene* explains "even if we banned dumping CO_2 right now … we would still be facing serious climate impacts for centuries." He writes that with this rise in temperature we will face "the imminent collapse of the agricultural, shipping, and energy networks upon which the global economy depends, a large-scale die-off in the biosphere that's already well under way, and our own possible extinction." Harvard professor Naomi Oreskes and Erik Conway agree with Scranton that coming "losses — social, cultural, economic, and demographic" may be "greater than any in recorded history." Humanity after all survived the fall of Rome; it's a sunny assumption that we will make it through this time.

To quote Dr. Johnson, "Nothing focuses the mind like a hanging." Well it's time for us to focus our minds.

If science's role in all of this is to try and save the world, the humanists' is in part to preserve it. If there are future historians, they may be as befuddled with our "culture wars" as we are with the scholastic abstractions of ancient church councils. This is not to say that our "culture wars" are unimportant — or indeed that what those church councils debated was unimportant either. But perhaps it's time for a détente, or a treaty of some sort. These arguments will seem less significant once the West Antarctic ice-sheet has collapsed into the ocean. But let us not doubt the importance of what it is that we could offer the world, as Scranton writes "The fate of the humanities, as we confront the end of modern civilization, is the fate of humanity itself." The humanities provide a methodology for critical analysis, and also an approach to preservation.

Both of these roles are crucial as we decide what material to save, and how to save it.

As we face collapse we must initiate a "New Curating" to preserve what could be lost in the coming darkness. If everything else closes, some of us would do well to try and man the library. Think of what we've lost from the past. Unless a dutiful archeologist finds some preserved papyrus in the desert, you will never read Aristotle's second book of the Poetics (on comedy). Only six of the ninety plays of Aeschylus survive. Aristophanes faired a bit better, of forty written we have eleven. Or of scripture that no one shall ever preach from, we have, or rather, do not have, the *Acts of Uziah, Laments for Josiah,* or the *Story of the Prophet Iddo.* Closer to our own time and, considering the subject at hand, a particularly poignant book that none of us can ever read is the thirteenth-century travelogue *Inventio Fortunata* in which the Franciscan author describes the North Atlantic — which was cold, once. Of that most prolific author who goes by the name "Anonymous" we have even less. No doubt works of incomparable beauty and truth were spoken and penned by those on the margins — many of them women, slaves, and the conquered — and the bulk of these sit in no library.

The vast majority of our culture, Western and Eastern, has been lost. It has been victim to war, weather, entropy, disinterest, and decay. What we think of as the canon sometimes often survived more due to the inscrutable turning of Boethius' wheel. It was humanists in the past who preserved these works, copying down manuscript to manuscript, in a thread connecting antiquity to their moment to our own day. We must be new monastics, preparing what we can to endure the interim, which we may shortly face. Scholars at places like the Long Now Foundation and Oxford University's Future of Humanity Institute are asking for us to reorient our perspective, and eco-critical scholars have been asking similar questions as well. Perhaps the humanities train people how to be more innovative thinkers in a market economy, and that might be fine justification in the short run to keep classes full, but in the "long now" the importance of the humanities takes on an obvious and profound import — that is nothing less than ensuring the preservation of our voices and thoughts unto the next generation. And we must consider that since so much of what we think of as the "canon" are works which survived because of the relative prestige of their authors, that we may now have the chance to curate a more democratic list of artists; ones that reflect a diversity of human experience that was erased in the past, but whose current voices we have a responsibility to preserve for the future.

We need to ensure that scholars on the other side of the darkness are able to read Walt Whitman, Langston Hughes, or Emily Dickinson as we wish we could read the lost plays of Aristophanes. Will people be able to listen to rock and hip-hop, or watch Kubrick, Scorsese, and Kurosawa? That so much of our crucial digital culture may be impossible to preserve is the sort of central problem that a New Curating must address.

In speaking of why we must curate such an ark of culture, we must remember precisely why it is that the humanities are important. Perhaps apocalypse can help us to clarify that mission in the same way that Wallace Stevens claimed "Death is the mother of beauty." At the risk of tautology, what is important about the humanities is the human; the survival of these texts is the survival of humanity.

In the present day we also must undertake this New Curating in part for our own selfish reasons — so that the future may remember us, what was important in our lives, what our experiences were. And what shall be lost, that our monks must copy into codices for future humans to recite? In the future there may be no summer trips down the canals of the Dutch capital, her colorful, resplendent tulip markets long since sunk. The dodge's palace and St. Mark's Square shall slide into the Adriatic who will finally be victorious in her war of attrition against the most serene republic. Autumnal Central Park may well sit under Atlantic waves, the Empire State Building and World Trade Center rising up out of turbulent, warm waters.

Envision a hypothetical anthology of literature based around the seasons: the frozen landscape of an Alice Munro short story, the melancholic autumn chill of Washington Irving, the Chilean spring of a Neruda love sonnet, or even the frantic, Jersey summer of a Bruce Springsteen song. Now, as climate change becomes more extreme and unpredictable, as a chaos erases those formerly independent, sovereign nations that were the seasons, consider how alien such an anthology's recorded experiences will seem to your grandchildren, and their grandchildren. That such a hypothetical anthology might seem so foreign to them is all the more reason to press the flowers of culture in a New Curating.

Our grandchildren and their grandchildren may not remember the seasons. For our and their sakes the ark must not merely make room for Shakespeare and Goethe, but for the experiential specificity of what it was like to see the leaves change color, or the first snowfall of early winter, or the cool breeze of spring as the ice started to melt. Because it is so omnipresent we do not appreciate the sacred power of the calendar. The twelve months are a liturgy of everyday life, still patterned, structured, and punctuated by the rhythms of temperature and the cycles of seasonal transition. We must resolve to remember what it was like when it still existed. In her beautiful *Elegy for a Country's Seasons* Zadie Smith wrote of the newly erratic weather, an increasing abolition of the seasons which we've all noticed by now. "In the end, the only thing that could create the necessary traction in our minds was the intimate loss of the things we loved."

By the waters of the Atlantic, and the Pacific, and the Indian we shall lie down and weep, for how shall we remember you Amsterdam, Venice, New York, in this brave new world, with so few people in it? Our tongues should cleave to the roof of our mouths, and our hands should wither, for we did not save you when we could. Memory is but a veil of shadows, but it may be all that we have left, and it is the job of the humanist to preserve these songs, it is to record testimony and to bear witness for the coming wars, and genocides, and collapses. As the humanities had to face apocalypse before, so shall she have to face it again. Let us begin.

New Jerusalem in the Alleghenies; or, the Madman of Bedford County

Herman Husband – itinerant preacher, politician, regulator, radical – would amble among the woods surrounding Pittsburgh. Here on the trans-Appalachian frontier, the native North Carolinian with his shoddy patchwork clothes and with his biblically long beard either echoed the prophet Jeremiah or prefigured John Brown. Amongst the cleared gun smoke of the Seven Years War and the American Revolution and the Whiskey Rebellion he had visions, visions of that western frontier that stretched epically on to Drake's millennial Nova Albion on the Pacific coast. For Husband, the unbridled promise of this western world – and the Appalachians were the west before they'd ever be split between north and south – was of an Empire of Liberty where those old dreams of the Earth being a common treasury for all could be realized (of course the fact that those lands were already occupied was another issue). Boston has its conservative Adams, Philadelphia her innovative Franklin, New York the self-invented Hamilton, and Virginia of course dignified Washington and intellectual Jefferson. Pittsburgh, she does not have any founding fathers; but, if we are to declare there to be one, let us make it the madman Herman Husband.

Husband believed that it was in this "western country" that humanity would "produce an everlasting peace on Earth," that Christ would return and that this would be the "glorious land of New Jerusalem." But he was no simple fundamentalist theocrat, Christ was coming to inaugurate a Godly communist state where work was for the common good, for "God sent the true Republican form of Right Government... in which the body of the People will have Supreme Power to choose [the] Supreme Law of the Land." An illegitimate king sat on a throne in London, so the rebels of the thirteen colonies were divinely charged to spread not salvation but liberty through this country. Where he prophesized that one day a fully formed, golden Jerusalem would descend here among the Alleghenies, a Hesperian utopia, a westerly millennium. The Bible speaks of paradise, but Husband preached of Pittsburgh.

For Husband, the American Revolution was not interpreted through Enlightenment rationalism, but rather with a type of religious mysticism. He was a radical in the mold of his contemporary William Blake, who wished to break our "mind forg'd manacles," for whom a cleansing of the doors of perception would make everything appear infinite. Husband's was an anarchist's gospel, with a golden thread linking him back to the non-conformist dissenters of the English Revolution a century before, like the great Leveler Gerard Winstanly, or even further back to the medieval Peasant's Rebellion when the radical priest John Ball asked "When Adam delved and Eve span, /Who then was the gentlemen?" For these Christian anarchists, rejection of Mammon was to worship God; to fight our economic order was to enter heaven. For Husband, this creed first manifested itself with his participation in the North Carolina Regulator's Rebellion, then his embrace of the American Revolutionary ideal (including an unlikely friendly correspondence with Benjamin Franklin) and finally with his disillusionment with the Constitutional Convention, and an embrace of the French Revolution while becoming a major participant in the Whiskey Rebellion. Ultimately Husband would, like many a broken-hearted romantic, come to see his past heroes like Washington and Franklin as participants in the same Babylonian corruptions as the British aristocracy.

Despite his unconventionality as a political thinker, he was elected twice to the state legislature, was a participant in the 1790 Pennsylvania state constitutional convention, and as Wythe Holt points out in his indispensable article about him, Husband was also "constable, township tax assessor, auditor of road-maintenance accounts, and county commissioner." Rarely have misty-eyed utopian mystics also been such dutiful bureaucrats. And after the assembly at Parkinson's Ferry in 1791 he became the people's representative to what would be remembered as the Whiskey Rebellion. Despite the relative local esteem he was held in, his apocalyptic preaching led to James Madison and Jefferson calling him the "mad man of Bedford County."

While the Whiskey Rebellion is sometimes misremembered as simply a tax protest that prefigures some sort of American libertarianism, the reality is a bit more complicated. Dissent arose after the first federal tax leveled against a domestic product was enacted; the legislation was conceived of by Secretary of the Treasury Hamilton as a way to pay down the national debt incurred as a result of the War of Independence. What might seem estimably fair today was viewed as anything but on the western frontier from New York to Tennessee, where the law was seen as an unfair imposition on poor farmers (many of whom used non-perishable liquor as a type of currency), as being passed without proper legislative representation from the west (which after all, the Revolution itself was fought over), and with its flat-rate excise clause an undue burden on small distillers. The flat-rate was an option for those mostly eastern distilleries who were able to pay it, and was not unfairly seen as a means of promoting the growth of massive business on the coast at the expense of individuals in the west. And so taxes went unpaid; armed resistance was organized.

As the first major constitutional crisis following that convention a few years before in Philadelphia, the federal government's ultimate victory in western Pennsylvania signaled the strength of the new political order. Far from being some sort of Ayn Rand libertarian rebellion, the insurrection was against a regressive tax whose goal was the consolidation of a private economic oligarchy among an entitled few. The Whiskey Rebels themselves knew this of course, with Jacobin Liberty Polls raised throughout western Pennsylvania, as heads to the east worried about guillotines. Far from being a Howard Roark-style revolt of the wealthy, the Whiskey Rebellion was a good old-fashioned uprising of the poor and oppressed. In Pittsburgh the spirit of 1791 was the same as that which motivated other battles in the perennial Manichean war between the classes. It was the spirit of the Peasant's Revolt of 1381, or the English Revolution of 1640, or the French Revolution of 1789, or yes, of 1776. It was said that David Bradford, the eventual radical leader of the rebellion, viewed himself as a type of Pennsylvanian Robespierre, the cockcrow red of the Phrygian cap sitting metaphorically upon his head.

The theater of the rebellion was the frayed palimpsest that is the terrain of western Pennsylvania; a rebellion that was barely a rebellion was fought on a landscape where space can be collapsed into time. This country evidences the strange synchronicity and correspondences of history, where the significance of place can be excavated like relics from the strata. It was the chief executive himself, Washington, who marched on the region (the only time a sitting president has done so) across a topography he knew well from his days as a British officer in the French and Indian War. The radicals had once met at a meadow of English loss from that war known as Braddock's Field, where one day Andrew Carnegie's Edgar Thompson Steel Works would rise. Husband had himself raised one of those liberty polls (with the phrase "Liberty, but no Excise") at the town of Summerset, near where a hijacked airplane on its way to Washington DC would one day crash. The drafted militiamen who would march on Pittsburgh were enlisted from Philadelphia, as indeed they would be again during the Great Railroad Strike of 1877 when a national paper said that Pittsburgh was in the deathly grip of red Communism. Ultimately the march on western Pennsylvania was a victory for the government, and thus a demonstration of the power of the Constitution that was after all in large part designed to reduce the rank and base democracy, which the framers saw as threatening the power of the nation during the years of the Articles of Confederation.

The end result of the uprising was that twenty-four men would be charged with treason, only ten would actually stand trial (including Husband), and only two convicted, both of those ultimately pardoned. More sober representatives for the rebel cause such as Hugh Henry Brackenridge, novelist, lawyer, and founder of what would become the University of Pittsburgh, found their respectability restored with the ascent of the Democratic Party upon Jefferson's election to the presidency. Even the more radical leaders of the movement would find a type of exoneration; Bradford would escape only later to find himself pardoned by Adams. Husband, however, was brought back in chains to the east, where he was held in a Philadelphia prison. It was said that Husband's Jacobin preaching had been so affective that the president mentioned his capture as specifically paramount. Eventually the magnanimous victor Washington had the preacher's charges dropped, but not before the now elderly Husband caught a chill, dying on his way back west where he believed his New Jerusalem would yet descend, ultimately one of the few people to actually lose his life as a result of the rebellion.

Husband may have died for an idea, but more importantly he lived for one, and it was a concept germinated in those groves he used to wander. The Arcadian visions of the man are inseparable from the geography of his life. In short, this liminal land between the civilized east and the western frontier was the progenitor for his utopian thought. Husband's Pittsburgh was the first metropolis of the western frontier; its history is comparatively short when compared to those cities on the east coast. Part of France for longer than it was ever a British colony, Pittsburgh signaled the limits of Anglophone expansion in the eighteenth century. In Boston, or Philadelphia, or even in construction-heavy New York there are traces of a colonial past that almost abut against the European Renaissance; Pittsburgh's history seems much shorter. But brevity of the place is illusory, there has long been a charged, spiritual power, perhaps generated by those shrouded green hills or the rivers cutting through them. Husband was not even the first to dream of paradise here; in the twelfth century the Huron Great Peacemaker and his follower Hiawatha traveled through what was then a destitute country and formed the Iroquois Confederacy. And Husband would not be the last to dream of Eden in western Pennsylvania, as indeed in the early-nineteenth century the Seneca Prophet Handsome Lake would receive similar apocalyptic visions while in Pittsburgh, or as with the sages of the Second Great Awakening who witnessed revivals firing down the Allegheny line, making the whole country glow with the fervor of faith, like heated coals.

The Appalachians run like a crooked spine parallel to the Atlantic coast. White settlers – mostly Scots-Irish – wished to populate the fertile Ohio River Valley but were prohibited by the Crown, a sticking-point in the Revolution of course. Pittsburgh may have been young, but as the gateway to that new frontier it was the locus of so many American dreams, and from the violence between settler and native of so many American nightmares. But Husband was not originally of this land; he had been born in the east, in the Piedmont country where a motley assortment of English, Scots-Irish, and even heretical Italian Waldensians existed. In his home country, Husband first began that task of forging an Apocalyptic American Adam, a New Man here in the New World. Once a Presbyterian, then a Baptist, eventually a Quaker and finally a Church of no man but only God. He would, true to the customs of the Friends, doff his cap to nobody. He took his hat off to nothing known or unknown, whether English or American, and he recognized no kings, whether one in London or a thousand in Philadelphia. His was a gospel of individuality, but also of community. Husband may have supremely believed in a literal God, but that being was identically with the conscience of man. For Husband felt that the Inner Light of man was conversant and equivalent to the Holy Spirit of the Lord; he knew, lived, and exhaled that perennial philosophy which is threaded through everything from the Upanishads, to Spinoza, and to Blake. But Blake had his Lambeth; here Husband had his Pittsburgh.

Husband's radicalism came from his readings of Christ, not Cato; as was the case with those rational deists who would meet in Philadelphia. But he was no pious theocrat; rather his politics came from reading the Bible in its infernal or diabolical sense as that contemporary and spiritual compatriot Blake may have put it. For Husband the great code of the scripture was not a system of binding and social control, rather if read askance or upside down it provided a manual for the destruction of Babylon, and everything could be Babylon. He certainly didn't first acquire this belief from his family; they were High Church Episcopalians from that Cavalier colony of Maryland, slave owners too. But, during those years when a gospel fire burnt down the Atlantic coast from Boston, Massachusetts to Savannah, Georgia, years known as the First Great Awakening, he heard the pulpit preaching of a minister named George Whitfield. Many men had heard Whitfield preach, indeed sometimes crowds of 30,000 on at least 18,000 separate occasions, from Jonathan Edwards who shared the preacher's deep sense of sin and salvation, to that old devil Benjamin Franklin who couldn't help but respect the minister.

For Husband, Whitfield affected a deep change; he imparted God's gift of grace to the young farmer. He could never stay within one church though; Husband found himself moving from the incense and bells of his family's Anglicanism, to the fervency of Whitfield, to that of the "New Light" Presbyterians, and finally to those most radical of non-conformists, the Quakers. Their sect was viewed with suspicion in England, and they were barred from all sorts of offices, but the laissez-faire religious attitude of the New World largely left them unmolested, except when it didn't. A Quaker family just north of the Mason-Dixon line in a mythic place called Pennsylvania may have owned the largest private landholding in the world; but the radical pacifism and the implications of non-allegiance to any government still made these Christians suspect to Church and State alike. During the Reformation the schismatics may have called for a "Priesthood of all Believers," and a *sola Scriptura* understanding of God's word, but only the Quakers were radical enough to say that the inner light is that voice of God dwelling in all people's chests, that in silence the divine's voice can be heard over the dun of life. For Husband the idea that all people were equal was not an abstraction, and it was not a convenient legal fiction. The equality of all before the Lord was deeply, intuitively, fundamentally *true*.

We can see the disappointment of failed prophets and revolutionaries (which is all of them). Yes, to be alive is bliss, and to be young is very heaven, but the revolutionaries who don't have the dignity to die in their wars will inevitably see their compatriots sell out. So that spirit of liberty (if any such thing exists) left England (if ever it did dwell there) and came to find itself among the cedars and poplars and pines of the Carolina coast where young Husband learned the lessons of a radical gospel (which is just to say the regular gospel as it is given to us), and it then found itself at his Pennsylvania country homestead. Husband's premonitions of a coming apocalyptic rebellion against the Beast of Babylon never came to pass; if anything the Moloch of industry was enshrined in that very place he saw New Jerusalem as descending, but for a short time this man could see the bright burning apocalyptic ribbon of the frontier spreading not commerce and capitalism but rather the radical equality of man from sea-to-shining-sea.

There is no monument to Husband and his name is not known to schoolchildren. There is no Paul Revere trail for Husband, no signs affixed to inns and taverns that read, "Herman Husband slept here," and his face is not on currency. He is not a founding father, but he lived in their world, and he envisioned one more perfect than they did. He was one of the roughs, a cosmos, an American. Herman Husband deserves our respect not because he forged a new nation, because he didn't, and not because he was a coherent political thinker, because he wasn't. But in that perennial dream, whether born of faith or reason, which posits that a better world isn't just possible but also that men and women deserve it, he may as well be Thomas Jefferson. Husband's gospel was one of radical egalitarianism, and he knew deep in his very sinews and joints and ligaments that apocalypse is the working man's utopia, that there is a field on the other side of what is right and wrong, a garden on the west shore of that river, and its name is "Millennium." Husband's very life was a scripture, his actions and his preaching its sacred words, and he breathed that foolish truth that knows that the earth belongs to the meek, the Kingdom of heaven to the poor, and that the peacemakers are the children of God. When Husband stood at that confluence of the Allegheny and Monongahela, facing that westward Ohio which bifurcates this nation between North and South, he saw what should have happened, not what did.

In reality that push to the west dragged across the continent, despoiling and murdering, and perhaps there was no version of history where this wouldn't have happened. But, at least for a brief period, in Husband's brain he envisioned an ecumenical, egalitarian, democratic utopia spreading west to the blue waters of California. Before there really was an America, Husband envisioned a more perfect union. There was radical potential in those years of the Articles of Confederation, and perhaps the historians are right, the Constitution needed to be drafted to consolidate power, that the weak country would never have survived without the centralization of federal power. And maybe Hamilton was correct; men are not angels, and citizens certainly never are. Maybe the Federalists were right; too much democracy is a dangerous thing; the crowd quickly becomes a mob. But even if Husband was a fool, or if Husband was crazy, there is poignancy in those liberty dreams he had; for the farmer understood that the United States is a human construction, imperfect and finite, but that America, well America is different. She is a mythic concept, as perfect and imaginary as Utopia, or Cockaigne, or the Hesperides, or Ultima Thule, or any of the other imagined nations in that atlas of perfect places. Husband was a citizen of that nation, and so he can be perfect in a way that Washington, or Jefferson, or Franklin, or Hamilton never can be; for the poor men and women who hungered for a new gospel, not of chapter and verse that act as ball and chain reconciling the oppressed to the needs of their masters, but rather of the emancipatory potential hidden within those words. Holt writes that "They had no difficulty understanding the New Jerusalem because it was what they needed and longed for." Husband's New Jerusalem may have never descended, but in his dreams and words, he was already an inhabitant of that city.

The Bondsman's Years

In 1676 an English aristocrat named Nathaniel Bacon led a group of about 500 protesters into the Virginian capital of Jamestown. Agitating against the incompetent colonial governor, William Berkeley, who had seemingly done little to militarily protect the Virginians, the motley assortment of working class rebels ultimately burned the capital to the ground. The Virginian leadership was horrified, not just because of Berkeley's mishandling of the situation, but also because Bacon's ersatz army was composed of not just white indentured servants, but African slaves as well.

It was an example of early modern, working class solidarity (though academic honesty forces me to admit that one of the causes which unified the diverse assembly was a noxious anti-Indian agenda). Commitment to collective power distributed across the bottom rungs of the economic order did not see a black-white color line, which was dangerous to the ruling colonial elite for whom it was in their best interest for the white working class not to acknowledge their shared interest with African slaves.

In 1741 a series of fires broke out in lower Manhattan, and a paranoia began to grip the minds of local government that the city's large slave population (the second biggest in British North America) was conspiring with poor Irish Catholic indentured servants to burn New York down as Jamestown had been burnt down 65 years before. Historians have compared the mass panic surrounding this mysterious "Negro Plot" to the Salem witch trials, with the existence of an actual conspiracy to destroy the city about as real as the supernatural was in Massachusetts. Trials of suspected conspirators were held, and over a hundred white and black "arsonists" were executed, some of them burnt at the stake in emulation of a practice which Americans associate with the barbarity of the medieval past and not our own national history. The two accused ringleaders of the non-existent plot, an African slave named Caesar and a white tavern owner named John Hughson, were killed and hung from gibbets to rot in the open air, only a short distance from where the Freedom Tower would one day rise.

In both Jamestown and New York, south and north, country and city, there would be repercussions for both the real and perceived allegiance between blacks and poor whites. In the south it would lead to the strict Virginia Slave Codes of 1705, ratified in part due to events like Bacon's Rebellion, and leading to a hardening of the legal distinctions between black slaves and their poor white allies. It was, in short, a solution to the ruling class's problem; creating artificial distinctions of race would eliminate the potential of solidarity between the proletariat of various racial and ethnic groups.

It is a sobering reminder of our shameful legacy concerning race in America. The Pilgrims landed at Plymouth Rock in 1620, but a year before that the Jamestown colonists first purchased African slaves. The slaves were men and women who had experienced the unimaginably horrific degradations of the Middle Passage. There was slavery and racism in America before there was an America. Before the inauguration of the trans-Atlantic slave trade, early modern Europeans had a very different conception of race than subsequent generations did. It was at least initially more accommodating toward racial difference, for early modern Europeans it was religious otherness that concerned them.

But the mass importation of forcibly captured Africans began to necessitate rationalization, and so pseudo-scientific biological-based racism backed by the force of law began to coalesce as a means of justifying the slave trade. Conveniently it was also a way to prevent insurrections like the one in Jamestown, by making poor whites think of themselves as different and superior to black slaves who would have been their natural allies. From our origins, Americans were sold a bill of goods, and it does us no good to pretend that the past is simply the past. Those lynched bodies rotting in the open Atlantic air in lower Manhattan are not so far removed from Eric Garner being murdered by the police.

It is common for defensive white apologists to justify away privilege by making the point that they were not directly involved in the slave trade or its associated injustices as if that were some sort of profundity. This is, of course, a cop out and obfuscation. When the very material wealth of the nation itself (in antebellum America slaves were economically the most valuable commodity) was structured and built on black bondage, it is our spiritual imperative not to close our eyes and deny that heinous fact.

Charles II was the monarch who recalled Governor Berkeley from Virginia after the embarrassment of Bacon's Rebellion. He was also the king who charted the Royal African Company (RAC) and gave it a monopoly on the English trade in African slaves, handing the reins over to his brother and the future King James II; many of the slaves imported by the RAC would be branded with "DY" for "Duke of York." James would ultimately also give his name to that captured Dutch city at the tip of Manhattan Island. It is imperative to understand that racism in our nation has never been just a southern problem, but always an American problem.

It can sometimes seem as if the charters granted to those early slaving companies have never expired. Many Americans, whether willfully or not, refuse to grasp the full scope of slavery as it legally existed from the seventeenth to the nineteenth century, and the ways in which it mutated but affectively survived Reconstruction and how it continues its legacy today. And it is true that in many ways institutional racism was born out of economic justification, but the reality of racism both personal and structural cannot be reduced to economic analysis. Even if disparities in wealth were completely eliminated, and we lived in an economically just society, the original sin of racism would still sadly endure. It may have been birthed out of political expediency, but now racism is a spiritual malignancy that must be addressed as a related but distinct problem to economic injustice. This is one of the many points which Black Lives Matter, the preeminent moral movement of our era, has tried to address on the left. Again, it does us no good to deny history. We cannot abolish this cursed legacy if we refuse to even see it.

The greatest theological mind to ever occupy the office of the presidency was Abraham Lincoln, and he succinctly expressed the debts politically, economically, and spiritually accrued over the course of legal slavery. At his second inaugural address he forlornly conjectured whether the violence of the Civil War was part of America's atonement for the introduction of race-based slavery; he said of the discord:

> if God wills that it continue until all the wealth piled by the bondsman's two hundred and fifty years of unrequited toil shall be sunk, and until every drop of blood drawn with the lash shall be paid by another drawn with the sword, as was said three thousand years ago, so still it must be said "the judgements of the Lord are true and righteous altogether."

A hundred years of those 250 have expired since Appomattox; I pray that we do not have to wait another 150 to see a society which lives to the best ideals of racial reconciliation. But it is for this reason that it is our moral duty to bear witness to all that was involved in the founding of this nation, and all which came after it as a result. And it is not merely to bear witness, for acknowledgment with no action is toothless, but rather it is to use our bodies and our minds as the brick and mortar for a new and just civilization. If we must work for 150 years, we will work; if we must work for a millennium, we will work. For as another American theological genius, Martin Luther King Jr., said, "The moral arc of the universe is long, but it bends towards justice."

Chair'd in the Adamant of Time: On "America" and Other Fictions

Time's Noblest Offspring is its Last
George Berkeley

Visitors to the magnificent Jefferson Building of the Library of Congress in Washington, D.C. can ascend her rococo double stairway, turn to the left past the opulent green wallpapered reading gallery, and into an exhibit hall filled with Mesoamerican urns, acid etched copper Renaissance globes, and framed coffee-colored maps which line a serene and almost melancholically dark room.

On one wall, at the very back of this room, encased in a climate-controlled chamber filled with argon gas, is an impressively large, brittle, and browning map of the world from 1507, printed in Alsace-Lorraine by the formidable and respected German mapmaker Martin Waldseemüller and his friend, the poet Mathias Ringmann. Committed humanists, the men who produced the map were cartographers who heard stories of the new discoveries being made by sailors and merchants for the Spanish and Portuguese. Across twelve separate panels, the map depicts a huge heart-shaped cartouche in which the entire geographic knowledge of the world up until the early sixteenth century could be presented in an expression of completest ardor, a new *Universalis Cosmographia*. The accuracy of the map is superior to the so-called medieval T-O maps (named as such for envisioning the world as effectively a perfect letter T inscribed within an equivalently perfect circle), for unlike those maps charted in the mathematics of myth, Waldseemüller and Ringman attempted to draft a diagram according to the particulars of fact. Their universal map was the most accurate of the era, but to a modern audience, the *Universalis Cosmographia* is shockingly erroneous.

The cartographers' home continent may be the most accurately represented, with the Mediterranean and the Levant roughly as they are in reality, but the British Isles still appear a long skinny smear at the northwestern corner of Europe. The orient suffers from a deficit of correct charting; China melts into the Indian subcontinent, an archipelago based on Dutch reports from Indonesia uncertainly ringing down the Indian Ocean to the still undiscovered antipodes of *terra Australis*. At the Hesperian edge, there is a long ribbon of land stretching between the poles, a region that until Waldseemüller's map was assumed to be but a peninsula of Asia. This long stretch of earth, whittled to an ephemeral gossamer thinness, was almost completely unknown, its width was a knowing fiction for the cartographers who were aware that the landmass must extend many miles, perhaps thousands, beyond the strands of the coastline which alone had been observed. At this Occidental extreme, they noted down the details and particulars of various exploratory missions which had been dispatched and returned from what the necessity of incomplete knowledge had forced them to depict as a sort of hemispheric isthmus. In the middle panel of the far western edge, there is a drawing of some sort of tropical bird, probably a parrot, who looks slightly bemused. And in the panel at the bottom left, in slightly larger print than the rest of the geographic information which surrounds it, is a word that was here printed for the first time in history: "America."

Out of a thousand printed, the map in the Jefferson Building is the only copy which survives; five gores (a type of map cut in a way so as to be attached to a round wooden globe) and this original are all that remain of the earliest usage of the word "America." Those of a romantic bent have referred to the Waldseemüller map as a "birth certificate" for the continents, although strictly speaking North America had yet to be officially discovered, and the northern ribbon of land the German drew was a hypothetical *terra Incognita*. That was certainly the language used by the Library of Congress when in 2003 it completed negotiations with German Prince Waldburg-Wolfegg to purchase the Waldseemüller for $10 million dollars; the document was discovered by a Jesuit cartographer in the early twentieth century, having survived four centuries as a complete portfolio in the prince's ancestral castle in Upper Swabia. Money was exchanged, speeches were given, Angela Merkel came to a ceremony.

Despite the fact that later editions of the Waldseemüller map deleted the word "America," the decision to name the new continents after the Italian Amerigo Vespucci endured, even as some preferred the name "Columbia," which had an antique ring to it even then. Vespucci had the rare and singular honor to be the only person in history to have such a large portion of the world christened in his honor while he was still alive. "Europe" of course named for a mythic Phoenician princess, "Africa" from a Latin name for a Libyan tribe, and "Asia" a name so ancient that not even Herodotus knew its etymology for certain. But this new word "America," as mystical sounding as those that designate the three parts of that previous world, found its provenance in the Christian name of an Italian from Florence.

As Ringman wrote, "There is a fourth quarter of the world ... we can call 'America' or the land of Americus ...We do not see why the name of the man of genius, Amerigo, who has discovered them, should not be given to these lands, as Europe and Asia have adopted the names of women." Vespucci lived for six more years after his name was given to that fourth part of the globe, dying a year after that stout Balboa with eagle eyes that first stared at the Pacific, even though Waldseemüller had logically predicted that ocean's eventual discovery and placed it on the map. This new world upset the Trinitarian balance of those continents of old, where Shem, Ham, and Japeth had once descended, dwelled and multiplied. Here now, was a new continent which did not fit into the schema of tradition, and the name on it was Amerigo's. Envision what it was like to be this man who had knowledge of this brave new world with such people in it, and envision being Waldseemüller and Ringman having the strange authority to baptize this place.

It's a name that has always worked well, because independent of its provenance it aurally conveys a certain power implicit in the very sounds of the word itself. "Columbia" of course has a particular, regal stateliness, and though it finds itself used in certain official capacities from "The District of Columbia," to the South American nation of different spelling, and the university on New York's Upper West Side, that name still has a bit of fussy antiquarianism about it. One sees "Columbia" as a dignified older woman in Phrygian cap, or as some sort of feminine spirit of liberty motivating pioneers to move ever westward; but "America" in its strange mysteriousness conjures up mythic associations to words like "Hesperides," "Eden," and "Utopia." Partially, this is due to the simple fact that though Vespucci got the continent named after him, he's not as famous as Columbus, and as such his name need not be associated with him but can rather float as free signifier for the land itself alone. The word-magic implicit in the name is also in part onomatopoeic. Depending on one's dialect, the word is either a gentle, lilting iambic bimeter that you could envision hearing as a whispered promise, or a forceful, rhotic trochee that in some western accents sounds almost indistinguishable from the word "miracle."

The name of the country is not the only one which has a certain power of conjuring transcendent evocations. Certainly, "Britain" with its Arthurian connotations can sound similarly mythic. Counterintuitively, Britain is in many ways even more of a constructed identity, first born out of Tudor propaganda calling back to the Celtic past of the ancient Britons, which James I attempted to impose as an identity on the diverse kingdoms of England, Wales, and Scotland, and not legally made the name of those nations until a century later. This was a national myth of political expediency, when Scotland was wed to England following the former's inglorious economic degradations in Panama requiring a union whose sutures may yet be removed. But as mystical as the green and pleasant lands of Britain may be, "America" as a word seems to be used even more commonly as a type of incantation, as witnessed by how frequently it appears as an adjective modifying a noun in the title of a work of literature, film, or music.

The word "American" is meant to convey a certain power, grandeur, or seriousness. We're in the realm of the Great American Novel, epic narratives heralding the endlessly mercurial and tough paradise that the country is supposed to be – or on the contrary, the word "American" serves to demonstrate reality's ironic distance from those things promised in the title, as an act of blaspheming jeremiad. To wit, the following terms have had the word "American" placed in front of them in the titles of films of varying degrees of critical and commercial acclaim: Beauty, Gangster, Pie, Graffiti, Hustle, Psycho, Buffalo, Haunting, Rhapsody, Summer, Terror, Fetish, Gigolo, Pop, President, Virgin, and Splendor. There is something more charged about the word "American," for who has seen *Belgian Psycho* or *Canadian Beauty*? As a word "America" is both dangerous and consoling in its promises – false and otherwise. Rarely does a single word seem to have such implicit potential drama, a latent atomic energy contained in such a tiny nucleus, an unexploded gun always waiting to be discharged.

Of course, nativists have not always thrilled to the fact that "America" is an Italian name which ends in a vowel, and so alternative explanations of the name's origins have periodically arisen. In the early twentieth century one historian claimed that "America" took its name not from Vespucci, but rather from a certain Bristol merchant, trader, and sheriff named Richard Amerike, who owned the *Matthew* upon which John Cabot sailed. According to Bristol resident Alfred Fudd, the name "Amerike" was well known in the port at the turn of the sixteenth century, and

Waldseemüller and Ringman simply made a transcription error on their map by assuming that the name "America" must come from Vespucci and not from the solidly Anglo-Saxon Amerike.

English-enthusiasts of this theory must overlook the fact that he who gave America an English name wasn't originally John Cabot but was rather Giovanni Caboto. A few decades after Fudd's conjecture, a Scandinavian historian claimed that the Norse word for district, "Amt," was added to Erik the Red's name to produce "Amterik," or "America." Etymologists of an equivalently Nordic supremacist character have claimed that the name really comes from the Norse "Ommerike," which translates as "farthest outland." There are other (almost certainly untrue) assertions that the name of the continents can be originally derived from the Anglo-Saxon kingdom, Mercia. Fanciful etymologies are not limited to northern European attempts to usurp the swarthy Vespucci from his position of pride; there are also examples of claimants that "America" as a word is American in origin. These theories elevate not nativists but natives, seeing the name of the country as having a solidly domestic origin. One French scholar in the nineteenth century claimed that Vespucci actually changed his name from "Alberto" to "Amerigo" so that it would more closely match the name of the Amerique tribe of Nicaragua, who would thus be the true originators of their own continents' name. Others have claimed that the name has its origins among the languages of the Carib, Mayan, or Algonquin Indians. While such claims are often grounded in little more evidence than that which posits Richard Amerike as he who granted his name to the baptism of the nation, there are some evocative and compelling indications that such stories could possibly have a bit of the truth about them.

The question of the origin of the name itself enacts one of the central tensions of who gets to be called an American. After all, the word could be applied to any of thirty-five nations in the Western Hemisphere, where the overwhelmingly most popular language is not English, but Spanish. Indeed of the five largest cities in the Americas, only New York City (which is the third largest) is primarily English speaking, while also having an English name. It was of course founded by the Dutch. Over a billion people live in North and South America, dwarfing the slightly over 300 million who live in the United States, making palpable the general annoyance directed at that minority who feel entitled to the exclusive rights of the designation "American." I have heard it only slightly jokingly said that a more apt designation for the citizens of that land which runs from the Atlantic to the Pacific, and from the Gulf to the Canadian border, should be "United Statesian," but that of course gives short shrift to the inhabitants of Estados Unidos Mexicanos.

As jingoistic and obnoxious as it might be that inhabitants of the United States claim a monopoly on the term "American" – as if Canadians, Mexicans, Hondurans, Brazilians, Guatemalans, Argentinians, Chileans, Uruguayans, Bolivians, Nicaraguans and so on aren't really in the Americas – there is some historical justification for their claimant. The word "American" may have originally come from Vespucci's baptism, but as a term applied to a group of people it was almost exclusively used to differentiate the Indian inhabitants of the continents during the colonial era. Spanish, French, Dutch, and even English colonists in what would be the southern United States never referred to themselves as "American," but rather only thought of themselves as Spanish, French, Dutch, and English. "American" and "Indian" were synonyms, it was unthinkable that the term "American" could ever be used for a person of European descent, even if they had never been anywhere other than America.

This started to change at a very particular point in time: the late-seventeenth century; and in a very particular place: New England. Following the degradations of Stuart Restoration after the fall of the godly Puritan Commonwealth in England, and the royal abandonment of the colonists during the unspeakable violence of King Philip's War, writers began to appropriate the term "American" for themselves. In the late-seventeenth century, the Puritan divine Cotton Mather seemed to prefigure other advocates for Americanness when he wrote in a sermon that "I that am an American," a self-declaration which would be impossible to envision a Spaniard, Frenchman, Dutchman, or even a Cavalier planter of the Southern colonies as making during the same time period. Ultimately the Confederate descendants of that Cavalier planter were so uncomfortable with the adjective "American" that in negotiations with potential French and British allies they took pains to differentiate themselves from an American identity that they identified as a symptom of Puritan heresy, preferring rather to see themselves as colonial representatives of European civilization on the American continent, rather than as Americans themselves.

The American Civil War is a convenient locus for seeing how the implications of the word "American" have changed over the generations and centuries. Not only did partisans of the Confederate States of America see themselves as representatives of European civilization (normally as Anglo-Saxons or Scots-Irish) who simply happened to live in the Americas, but they had no compunctions about rejecting "America" as any kind of universal identity, as would indeed make sense for advocates of schism and disunion. Yet the rejection of "America" as some kind of transcendent or universal signifier was not limited to the South; regional identity was not subsumed under any kind of national one until well after the Civil War, something that can be demonstrated by the grammatical construction of how Americans talked about the country. A reading of books, articles, essays, newspapers. and pamphlets from both before and after the war show a shift from the plural to the singular, that is from speaking of "The united states are," to "The United States is." A Washington Post editorial from 1887 noticed the transition; the writer remarked that, "Along the line of fire from the Chesapeake to

Sabine Pass was settled forever the question of grammar...The surrender of Mr. Davis and Gen. Lee meant a transition from the plural to the singular." A similarly rapid shift can be seen in the abandonment of "These united states of America" in favor of the definite article of "The United States of America," alongside attendant alterations in capitalization. The popular historian Shelby Foote explained that the Civil War was the event which "made us an is."

I argue that the word "America" often functions as what the literary critic Stanley Fish has called a "self-consuming artifact." Fish was writing of the Renaissance verse of English poets like George Herbert, John Bunyan, and John Milton, but what is the word "America" other than its own minimalist Renaissance sound-poem? In his analysis of seventeenth-century poetry, Fish argues that the most profound of devotional verse from the most profound of devotional centuries is often structured around a process of self-consuming. That is to say that the poems allude to something beyond language, and even in their technical acumen they point to something transcendent of words, and that as part of their design they fail in their task of trying to correspond to this reality. The language of the poems unravels, they are unable to encapsulate or express the divine experience, which was their task. But in doing so, they function as profound theological expressions of the very ineffability of language which is their medium. The self-consuming artifact is a genre of negation, a method of paradox, but so too then is "America," which has come to mean everything from the City on a Hill to Moloch's Babylon. As a word it can refer to a particular time and place (though as we've seen a wide variety of particular times and places), legally binding as a definite location but also as a quasi-mythical realm, and it can function as the grammatical intensifier of "America!" That process of the name being shouted out as mere orgasmic intensifier is what lends itself to being utilized in hawking beer under the brand name "America", to the charlatan's call to "Make America Great Again." Used cynically, the word "America" is conceptualized not as that undiscovered country yet to be born on maps yet printed, but rather it is to employ the word as simple superstitious talisman. They take the Lord's name in vain.

Orthodox Jews write the name of "G-d" with a dash of negation, a type of apophatic punctuation that acknowledges that the written Lord is never the real Lord. The stipulation on taking great care in writing the Hebrew letters of the Tetragrammaton was in part so that the pious were careful not to see mere crafting of ink and manuscript as replacement for ultimate reality. Without suggesting that "America" is an equivalently mystical word, I do wish to propose that it's a term which endlessly defers and gestures towards something much greater than and beyond itself. "The United States" may be a country bound in history and time, and by space and geography, like all countries which exist before it and which will exist after it.

That "America" is in her title is a function of historical contingency, but we should be careful not to reduce that particularly mythic place to simply the nation which most prominently displays her in her title. Do not misread this as pedantic argument that the word "America" also encompasses a variety of other places, for as true as that may be, it is not the focus of what I claim here. Rather it is that the word "America" may be decoration or adornment for the names of various historical polities, but the actual location of a place called "America" is in a Republic not of this world. There is the semantic meaning of the word, and then true to a four-fold hermeneutic there is an anagogic meaning of the word. "America" may have first been printed on Waldseemüller and Ringman's map, but its truest location is in an atlas not available in our reality, for "America" is a place as mythic as the previously mentioned Eden or Utopia. But though she may not truly exist, this understanding of a New World that is full of equality, liberty, and freedom is an Arcadian belief which not only can, but must structure our own yearnings towards a more perfect union. This America is not on any map, and yet necessity requires us to set our course towards her and sail in that direction regardless. America may not be real, but we must always be in the process of discovering, and more importantly creating her.

The Crucified God

That we are sound, substantial flesh and blood –
Again, in spite of that, we call this Friday good."
T.S. Eliot, The Four Quartets (1940)

If Jesus had been killed twenty years ago, Catholic school children
would be wearing little electric chairs around their necks instead
of crosses.
Lenny Bruce, How to Talk Dirty and Influence People (1967)

I have, perhaps due to an innate inclination towards the macabre, always appreciated the crucifix more than the cross. The
crucifix and the cross are certainly not contradictory, and obviously the latter is the ultimate narrative conclusion of the former. But in its sanitized abstraction, the cross seems to me to be
eliminating the most crucial part of the story, and in the modern
era of the Death of God I don't think the story Sunday tells is as
important as the one that Friday does. While Christians of all
denominations wear crosses, for the most part only Catholics
embrace the crucifix. Interpreting a crucifix as an important part
of religious material culture conceptualizes the object as a symbol of group allegiance, one advertising its wearer not as a member of the United States' traditional Protestant ruling classes. In
popular culture it is the shriveled Irish nun, the Italian boxer,
the Hispanic laborer, who wears the crucifix, while the cross is
worn by the WASPy suburban couple, the campus Christian, or
the cheerful door-to-door missionary. As a matter of semiotics,
a crucifix has different connotations than a cross does. But this
perspective has more to do with sociology than theology, and
for me the fact remains that my attraction to the crucifix has a
noumenal element about it as well. Perhaps it is simply because I
grew up Roman Catholic, but the crucifix—whether a cruciform

Christ punctuating the ring of rosary beads, a termite-feasted medieval church artifact, or a neon kitsch relic—seems to state a truth more real than the cross. Independent of the vagaries of orthodoxy, filtered through the interpretive lens of my own belief (or disbelief), I still accept the story the crucifix tells; but when the tomb is empty, I'm not so sure I buy that story anymore. Friday tells the truth, the jury is still out on Sunday.

There are other Christian symbols of course; the cross and the crucifix being only two. There is the Ichthys, a simple hieroglyph of a fish: the word is an acrostic in Greek meaning "Jesus Christ, Son of God, Savior," and the symbol evokes Christ as the "fisherman of men." It once adorned dark Roman catacombs, understood only by the elect. Now it is affixed proudly to car bumpers, spreading the good news at stoplights. There are the Greek letters Alpha and Omega, the Staurogram, the Chi Rho and so on. There are the allegorical symbols of Christianity: Christ as shepherd, or sheep, or even pelican (for men once believed that creature nourished its young with her own blood). But in the popular imagination, the cross reigns as triumphant as it did when, according to the Church father Eusebius, on the eve of battle the Emperor Constantine had a vision of a cross in the sun and heard a voice proclaiming "with this sign, you will conquer." The cross is as universally recognized as a symbol of Christianity as the Crescent is of Islam, or the Star of David, of Judaism. While the cross is frequently understood as the general symbol of the faith, the crucifix is perhaps a more exotic version of its less disturbing relative. There is something stranger, odder, and kinkier about the crucifix when compared to the cross, which can easily look like a lower-case t (or as the famously eccentric mathematician Paul Erdos once mistook it, a plus sign). That is to say that a cross can easily make one forget what it is you're actually looking at – a representation of a purposefully disgraceful instrument of state-sanctioned murder. A crucifix never lets you forget that fact.

Reformation-era critics of Catholicism took "Scripture Alone!" as one of their rallying cries, but the specifics of Christ's crucifixion are fairly minimal in the biblical account, to the point where there is uncertainty as to what the actual instrument of his death even looked like, or how he was affixed to it. One needs few details to understand what was at stake in a process that Cicero described as "a most cruel and disgusting punishment." The common medieval depiction of the stigmata indicates that two of the spikes used to crucify Christ were hammered through his palms, though this is based upon a mistranslation of John. Nailing through the palms is an anatomical impossibility (at least without additional support) and it is now commonly thought that stakes were most likely driven between the radius and ulna of the wrist. Medically speaking, what finally killed the punished wasn't blood loss so much as suffocation: the condemned's lungs compressed as he hung from the cross. While details of the crucifixion are sometimes amended in contemporary depictions of Christ's crucifixion, what is less commented on is that the traditional shape of the cross is also a bit of extra-biblical elaboration, one based in tradition, not scripture. Crucifixion as employed by Roman authorities encompassed a wide variety of practices, including impalement, nailing the victim to two cross-beams attached as if an uppercase T, nailing the victim to a simple upright pole (appropriately known as crux simplex), or to a tree. The latter possibility, when applied to Christ, has a nice typological symmetry, evoking as it does the Tree of the Knowledge of Good and Evil. It was the transgression of that mythic tree that necessitated Christ's sacrifice in the first place. That is the tradition John Donne was working in when he wrote in 1613 "We think that Paradise and Calvary, /Christ's Cross and Adam's tree, stood in one place." Whether tree, pole, or the more traditional cross, the Bible is spare on details as to what the actual apparatus looked like, but that has not stopped supposedly *sola Scriptura* Protestants from relying on tradition to embrace the cross as symbol of their denominations.

Artistically speaking, a cross is no more difficult to draw than a pole. Only two intersecting lines are required to depict the set for the central drama of the Christian faith. But a crucifix requires a much higher degree of artistic aptitude. It's probably more for this reason than any other that the cross (along with similarly minimalist images like the Icthys) was common in the early centuries of Christianity, and that the crucifix first began to appear half a millennium after Jesus lived. The cross is simply geometrical, whereas the crucifix's vocabulary is not rectilinear, but positively biological. The manufacture of a crucifix is not a question of right angles, but a question of flesh, bone, and wound. When Christians came out of the catacombs the more complex symbol could flourish, but in the West the crucifix didn't become common until the end of the first millennium.

Possibly the earliest surviving example of a representation of the crucified Christ was made not to glorify him, but rather to mock. Near the Palatine Hill in Rome during the early third century, some wise-ass drew a crude representation of a supplicant praying to a donkey-headed man strung up on a cross with the Greek header "Alexamenos worships his God." Resembling a mixture of Christ and Bottom the weaver from *A Midsummer's Night's Dream*, the ass-headed Jesus dimly and dumbly would have looked out from marble at Romans going about their day; Romans who paused perhaps to chuckle at the expense of poor Alexamenos (whoever he was).

No amount of creative explication can claim this image is meant to be anything but demeaning. Do not look for ways to interpret the bestial donkey-man dying upon his cross as a reference to Christ's triumphant entry into Jerusalem on Palm Sunday; this picture has one simple meaning: that Christianity is absurd. No less than Paul said that Christ crucified was "foolishness to the Greeks." And indeed this was true; inheritors of classical paganism saw Christianity as just one more exotic, oriental cult and they believed any number of slanders against the religion. Around the same time that some ancient tagger chiseled his little joke on that wall, the respected philosopher Porphyry of Tyre offered a more academic critique of the Nazarene's religion, commenting that "the Christians are a confused and vicious sect." Roman authors accused early Christians of orgiastic night rituals, of human sacrifice, and of the use of human blood in the performance of the Eucharist. That Christians worshiped a blood sacrifice as supreme God, and that they claimed to ingest his flesh and blood no doubt contributed to a misunderstanding that this was a literal act of cannibalism (the vagaries of transubstantiation – which had yet to be explicated – not withstanding). No doubt there is an irony in the Roman slander against the Christians that claimed they murdered pagan children and used their blood in the production of communion; it is an exact parallel to the medieval Christian blood libel against the Jews. The latter reflects the profound internalization and projection that can result when the persecuted become those that persecute. But in the third century, Christians were still the Other, and the Alexamenos graffito reflects that status, that Christians lacked social capital and as a faith they were associated with women and slaves who venerated an executed criminal born to an ethnically marginalized people. There is something sobering and fully appropriate in remembering that the first crucifix was crafted to demean Christ, as if the humiliation of his passion continued centuries after his death. One of the innate powers of Christianity is that it is, in a sense, impossible to mock in any effective way. The fundamentalists' anger over so-called blasphemous art evidences not the possibility of blasphemy, but only the fundamentalists' anxious faith. It would do them well to remember that centuries before *Piss Christ*, the very first depiction of their crucified Lord was meant to offend (although the former was not meant to), and that those images only serve to confirm faith, not deny it. One of the lessons of the crucifix is that God died not just a human death, but also a particularly painful and shameful one. The Alexemanos graffito, contrary to the wishes of its sarcastic author, confirms that central Christian teaching more than any jewel-encrusted artifact ever could.

Crucifixes became predictably more elaborate as they became central to Christian devotions. It was the Roman Rite of the fourteenth century that required that "either on the altar or near it, there is to be a cross, with the figure of Christ crucified upon it, a cross clearly visible to the assembled people." Byzantine Christians, with their different ordering of the Decalogue, had a stricter prohibition on sculpture, and despite their own iconoclastic convulsions over flat images, they ultimately embraced icons. The sculpted or carved crucifix is therefore a Western tradition, and technically the term can only apply to a representation of the crucifixion that is three-dimensional; in Orthodox churches the representation normally takes the form of a flat painting. Orthodox conceptions of Christ tend to emphasize the divine aspect of his hypostatic union, and as such depictions of his crucifixion can be otherworldly or alien. During the Western Carolingian renaissance of the Middle Ages, European artists embraced what became a tradition of depicting Jesus in all of his humanity as man of sorrows, a trend that only accelerated over the centuries into the early modern period. A particularly stunning example is the celebrated Gero Cross of the Cologne Cathedral, a large colorful carving of the crucifixion from tenth-century Germany, commissioned by the archbishop who gives it his name. The Gero Cross is the largest and oldest of its kind, chiseled from a massive oak that once grew in those cold lands north of the Alps. Carved by anonymous and forgotten hands, this oak calls to mind that tree from which sin first emanated, or perhaps the defeated Yggdrasil the Germans had exchanged for a crucified Jew. Standing over six feet tall, Christ is depicted for the first time as no longer in the process of dying, but as now unequivocally dead. The Gero Christ's paint has been retouched over the years; his skin remains the rich coffee nut-brown of the oak, and the blond Teutons who carved him made his hair dark, a surprising instance of historical accuracy. He reminds me of the black Madonnas which proliferated in medieval Europe from Iberia to Poland, and which must have served as uncomfortable reminders about the specific corporeality of the Lord to the descendants of those who had carved them, those later Germans who had embraced the fallacy of idolatrizing phenotypical difference.

In the late-seventeenth century the Gero Cross was placed at the center of a triumphant golden sun, one that with its curved rays almost recalls Guadalupe. Baroque aesthetics were a direct rebuke to Protestant iconoclasm, and here in the birthplace of the Reformation the Gero Cross stands as a testament to the Catholic embrace of the image (though Luther was himself fine with artistic depictions of biblical subjects). Not for nothing have Americans tended to understand Puritan minimalism to define good taste, while the busy, crowded, or colorful is dismissed as too tacky, too kitschy, too ethnic, too *Catholic*. Archbishop Gero's crucifix gets a pass because it's old, but let there be no mistake, it is tacky. Of course it's also beautiful. The road from the Alexemanos graffito with its scatological, obscene donkey god to the triumphant sun-emblazoned God of the Gero Cross was a long one, but one still marked by the humiliating nature of Christ's execution. And in its willingness finally to depict something that seems so paradoxical – the dead God – the Gero Cross, for all of its technical magnificence, still gestures to the fundamentally radical message of Christianity. Echoing Adorno, the poet W. H. Auden once remarked, "Christmas and Easter can be subjects for poetry, but Good Friday, like Auschwitz, cannot. The reality is so horrible, it is not surprising that people should have found it a stumbling block to faith." If there is scandal in a dying God, how much more so in one who is now dead?

The Germans have always been grand masters in depicting the deadness of the savior, for the Gero Cross' representation of a deceased Lord is only the first in a long line of crucifixes that meditate, sometimes gruesomely, with agonizing, if not sadistic, precision. Any cradle Catholic knows that there are only catholicisms, and that they often have a national character. At the risk of essentializing, I'll claim that German Catholicism is not Italian Catholicism, or Mexican or Irish. And if a certain melancholic disposition has been inculcated in the morbid ruminations of German Catholicism, this is not a new phenomenon. Some of the most stunning examples of this obsession with death are the paintings of the crucifixion by the great Matthias Grünewald, who, though possibly a Protestant himself, was the inheritor of the German Catholic artistic tradition.

Grünewald's Christ is not just dead, but in the process of decomposing. Tortured, twisted, ripped, and torn, he bears a multitude of purple scars that almost evoke Kaposi's sarcoma; they spread across his emaciated body. His fingers are curved towards the stigmata wound, as if he has failed to close his hand, and his head hangs in an exhausted, aching defeat. The undeniably paradoxical message of Christianity is that this defeat is an ultimate victory, as expressed in John 19:30 when Christ (ambiguously?) says, "It is finished." Do not mistake what I'm saying; calling Christ's sacrifice a paradox is not meant to cast aspersions on the sacrifice; it's rather to sanctify the idea of paradox. Look at Grünewald's painting, which in its violence to the body recalls a horror story or an etiological account of disease, and realize the terrifying, fundamental truth it tells about death – that death is rarely glorious. Beautiful deaths are for pagan gods and Romantic poets; real deaths for you, me, and everyone else are almost always a different ordeal. If Christ is to share in the pain of being a human then the depiction of a beautiful death only lessens that sharing.

For the most radical of reformers the crucifix served not just as a reminder of death, but also indeed as an occasion to violate the commandment against graven images. The cross of Sunday was a reminder of the resurrection, while the intricate crucifix of Friday displayed a fundamentally morbid obsession with death. As aesthetic critique it arguably has its justification in a variant of orthodoxy, but it's ironically not dissimilar to the smug pagans who mocked Christians worshiping their dead ass-god. Rather than necessarily reflecting the glory of the resurrection (which we're all still awaiting) the cross demonstrates a fundamental fear of death (which we're all guaranteed to experience). Such a position demonstrates an unwillingness to see in the crucifix our image, our fate. But the evangelicals obviously didn't adopt that perspective, seeing instead crucifixes as idolatrous examples of rank Romish superstition. Indeed they made great hay of monastic chicanery when it came to supposedly miraculous crucifixes, such as the famous Rood of Grace kept at the Cistercian Abby located in Boxley, England. Throughout the Middle Ages pilgrims journeyed to witness the Rood of Grace, whose figure of Christ was known to open and close his eyes, and to move his jaw as if talking. In 1538, an official who was taking part in Thomas Cromwell's project to dissolve the monasteries discovered that the monks, through a complex set of wires and levers, mechanically operated the Rood of Grace. And thus the Rood of Grace was demonstrated to be robotic, a terrifyingly macabre Puppet of Horror (even though scholars have convincingly argued that the Rood of Grace's mechanism was always fully known by its audience). The crucifix was exhibited in the local marketplace as part of the Protestant policy of disenchantment, and Geoffrey Chamber, the bureaucrat responsible for its confiscation, claimed that the populace reacted with "wondrous detestation and hatred so that if the monastery had to be defaced again they would pluck it down or burn it." Ultimately the Rood of Grace was sent to London where it was burned in effigy, a type of second crucifixion, which forever stalled its gears and levers (and which also unfortunately means I have no photo of what must have been an undeniably weird object).

What all of those previous examples demonstrate are the ways in which crucifixes enact Thanatos, what Sigmund Freud described as our innate "pressure towards death." But as Freud (more than all others) reminds us, human desires aren't just pushed by the death impulse, but of course by Eros as well. Sex and death are twinned, the first is the reason why we're all here and the latter is the place that we're all going. If the spiritual power of the crucifix is that it depicts God fully as man at his most vulnerable, then it can also depict him at his most intimate. Death is only the most obvious subject of the crucifixion, but some of the most beautiful and moving depictions of that event have an undeniably charged and latent erotic energy as well, one that fully reconciles the twin poles of what it means to be human. Consider the seventeenth-century Spanish Baroque master Diego Velázquez's masterful *Christ Crucified,* painted in 1632 after the artist's return from Italy.

While he was in Italy, Velázquez clearly imbibed the techniques of the brilliant queer painter Caravaggio, dramatically using the latter's method of chiaroscuro to frame the beautiful body of Christ in the center of a striking field of black – Christ as a spark of charged erotic electricity lighting up the infinite abyss. The Spaniard's Christ is feminine, beautiful with his thin waist and hips, arched back, and flawless skin. A feminized God is not foreign or incidental to biblical language; the Hebrew word for God's indwelling presence, *Shekhina,* is grammatically feminine, and even dour Puritans like Peter Sterry in the seventeenth century could write "Lay the mouth of your soul by faith to the breasts of the Godhead ... spouting forth their milky streams into your face and bosom." Or even more radically, consider the eighteenth-century Moravian leader Christian Renatus von Zinzendorf, who expanded on the relatively conventional tradition which saw Christ's side-wounds in explicitly vaginal terms, developing a wound-mysticism which surpassed that of German Catholicism, and certainly that of his fellow Protestants in both Europe and Pennsylvania. Zinzendorf's idiosyncratic teaching went beyond writing hymns to a specifically androgynous savior. As Aaron Spencer Fogelman argued in his 2008 *Jesus is Female: Moravians and Radical Religion in Early America,* Zinzendorf and his coreligionists had developed a devotional theology of "sensual and for some even sexual spiritual relations" with Christ. That eroticization of Christ surprisingly cuts across denominational affiliation, with Velázquez's painting being of a time and place whose greatest works, such as Teresa of Avila's mystical writings, were able to fuse Eros and Thanatos into an approach towards the transcendent. It was Teresa who, after all, described her mystical union with God by saying that He "appeared to me to be thrusting [a spear] at times into my heart, and to pierce my very entrails; when he drew it out, he seemed to draw them out also, and to leave me all on fire with a great love of God. The pain was so great, that it made me moan; and yet so surpassing was the sweetness of this excessive pain, that I could not wish to be rid of it."

Since the thirteenth century it has been a Franciscan principle "nudus nudum Christum sequi," that is, we must all "follow naked the naked Christ." The art historian Leo Steinberg argued in 1983 that the Franciscan creed encouraged not just taking an oath of poverty, but that it also refocused the religious imagination upon nakedness as a conduit for understanding what is human about God (and perhaps what is godly about humans). This renewed attention manifested itself in a focus on not just the naked Christ, but indeed on the penis of the naked Christ. In his *The Sexuality of Christ in Renaissance Art and Modern Oblivion,* Steinberg painstakingly demonstrates how common Christ's nudity, and indeed sexualization (including depictions of the divine erection), were in medieval art, and the way in which prudish moderns subsequently censored the godly priapus. Steinberg admits that these images made a "disturbing connection of godhead with sexuality," but he also brilliantly demonstrates how our squeamishness over sexualized images of Christ reflects not a latent anti-eroticism in Christianity, but rather a post-Victorian priggishness, which still manifests itself in our supremely un-erotic but consummately pornographic culture. We should not be surprised that the penis was important in classical Christian art, whether through artistically exploring the themes of circumcision or as an additional "humanation" (as Steinberg calls it) of the godhead – I'll refrain from punning on the latter. Renaissance Italians, however, had no problem employing the word "resurrection" as a double entendre for erection (as Boccaccio does). The tradition of depicting both the crucified and resurrected Christ with an erection, known as *ostentatio genitalium,* only sounds shocking to moderns thoroughly disenchanted by the Reformation and modernity, but for the German Hans Schäufelein painting two years before the 95 *Theses,* there was neither titillation nor obscenity in presenting a well-hung Christ upon the cross with a bulging erection. Victorians supposedly suppressed sexuality in the subconscious; we've not totally excavated such repression, but we've also pushed the religious impulse down there, too, making it doubly impossible for some to interpret these images as anything but upsetting. We need not be squeamish about the phallic Christ, however; just as we shouldn't be about Velázquez's feminine Christ.

Eros and Thanatos are connected throughout the two broader themes found in representations of the crucifixion: the duel intermingling of both immanence and transcendence. Critic Regina Schwartz has referred to a type of "sacramental poetics" which permeates English Renaissance poetry, whose authors were reacting to the traumas of disenchantment that signaled the arrival of modernity. She writes in 2008's *Sacramental Poetics at the Dawn of Secularism: When God Left the World* "A sacramental poetry is a poetry that signifies more than it says, that creates more than its signs, yet does so, like liturgy, through image, sound, and time, in language that takes the hearer beyond each of those elements." If Christianity has a particular genius it's in that mixture of the sacred and profane, of spirit and matter, which marks God as neither completely Other, nor the human as completely material. No doubt Christianity through its Platonism and its dualism has often had a fundamental anxiety about physicality, but the crucifixion as subject explores this central creative tension about God's corporeality. Examine the previously mentioned photograph of Andres Serrano, one of the so-called "NEA Four," whose *Piss Christ* (1987) came in for special censure by conservatives in Congress for its apparently sacrilegious meaning.

If viewed for the first time, free of the knowledge of its medium (a photograph of a crucifix submerged in the artist's urine), many viewers might see the image as strikingly, almost ethereally, beautiful. Christ seems to pulse with an inner orangish-red luminescence. Critic Lucy R. Lippard described *Piss Christ* as "a darkly beautiful photographic image ... the small wood and plastic crucifix becomes virtually monumental as it floats, photographically enlarged, in a deep rosy glow that is both ominous and glorious." New York Senator Al D'Amato disagreed, calling Serrano's piece a "deplorable, despicable display of vulgarity." Fellow Republican legislators like Jesse Helms were outraged that the artist received federal funding from the National Endowment for the Arts. Incidentally, Serrano, who was predictably raised as a strict Catholic and who still considers himself a Christian, defended his piece as a critique on the commercialization of Christ, an interpretation shared by none other than amateur art critic and Roman Catholic nun Sister Wendy Beckett. While admitting that the title is obviously intended to generate a rise in people, I think that *Piss Christ* can be defended as Christian art, which consummately presents the immanence of Christ, a visual explication of incarnational poetics. What Serrano provocatively reminds us of is that Christ was not just God, but equally man, and just as humans piss so must Christ. It's an uncomfortable thought perhaps, but a supremely orthodox one.

Piss Christ is in the same tradition as Schäufelein; if Christ sometimes had to piss then he also sometimes had erections, just as surely as sometimes he had to shit, or sleep, or eat, or cry, or do any of the other things that make humans human. To be horrified by Christ pissing is to be horrified by Christ; to be horrified by piss is to deny all that makes us human. Christ crucified is Christ human, and as surely as the former was a stumbling block to Gentiles in Paul's day, then by the transitive property so must have been the later. And not just in Paul's writing to the Corinthians, but in 1987 as well, when Christ human was a stumbling block to ostensible Christians like Helms and D'Amato. Not unsurprisingly, *Piss Christ* came in for an ending not dissimilar to the poor puppet of Boxely Abby, when in 2011 an enraged museumgoer attacked a print of the photograph in a pique of iconoclastic fervor at an exhibit in Avignon, France.

The personal, physical, intimate, corporeal immanence of Christ isn't the only attribute of the hypostatic union that can offend, however. Indeed, somewhat counterintuitively, transcendence can as well. In 1961, a stone-throwing museum visitor to the Kelvingrove Art Gallery in Glasgow attacked the Spanish surrealist painter Salvador Dali's *Christ of Saint John of the Cross*. Reflecting the artist's ever-mercurial politics and conservative Catholicism, Dali claimed that the heightened perspective of a levitating Christ, looking down upon presumably the Sea of Galilee, came to him in a dream. But a stranger and more beautiful crucifixion of Dali's is his *Crucifixion (Corpus Hypercubus)* displayed at the Metropolitan Museum of Art in New York, and which the painter claimed was an example of his "nuclear mysticism."

Dali presents a hairless, perfected Christ as held by unseen nails not to a cruciform, but rather on an unfolded tesseract; that is, a polyhedron network of hypercubes, the four-dimensional analog of the cube. Composed in light of both Hiroshima and Einstein's general theory of relativity, Dali's Crucifixion may be kitsch, but it is also a sublime evocation of Christ's transcendence, removing the event of his death from the realm of normal space and time and into that of infinity and eternity.

That *Piss Christ* and *Corpus Hypercubus* are both legitimate expressions of Christian theology, strung as it is between the extremes of cosmology and anthropology, speaks to the profundity of said Christology (regardless of whether it is an accurate description of reality or not). The crucifix is the great aesthetic representation of the central tension of Christian metaphysics, a creative tension that is also its central message. The body of the tortured Christ is not just displayed between two thieves, but indeed hangs between the poles of Eros and Thanatos; the body of the murdered Christ is not just hung on a cross, but indeed hangs between immanence and transcendence. Do not take any of this as a work of apologetics as much as an extended critical appreciation of a theme explored through art and culture. The profundity of Christianity is its scandal, and that is expressed through the enigma of the death of God.

No doubt you may have a skeptical friend who can go through a litany of dead and resurrected near eastern gods, lumping Christ into a tradition that includes Osiris, Dionysius, Orpheus, Mithras, and so on. Such archetypal criticism (provided that it's not there to supply a mythic "Gotcha!") has more utility than depth. Categorizing deities in this way might be satisfying to our inner stamp collector, but it brings us no closer to the paradoxical novelty of Christianity. I do not mean to suggest that Christianity is "a true myth," as C. S. Lewis claimed (a formulation that I find singularly unsatisfying). Whether true or not, the dead God of Christianity is categorically different than an Osiris. The great French theorist of violence, René Girard, wrote in 2007 that in contrast to the superficially similar resurrected pagan deities, "The God of Christianity isn't the violent God of archaic religion, but the non-violent God who willingly becomes a victim in order to free us from our violence." Where the polytheistic gods are like us, only bigger; Christianity posits the death of that which is the fundamental Ground of all Being. Christianity implicates reality in a fundamental way, for it claims that that which is the most radically different, foreign, alien, and Other can actually become us and die, subsequently altering existence as a result. With that perspective, the crucifix is actually enchanted, for it lets us look upon God even if he is a dead God, for in his physicality there is still a presence. The cross, by comparison, with its absence, may find itself less a promise than an empty one. A crucifix, with its strained muscles, its bloody wounds, its punctured brow and tortured face, forces you to consider having a body in all of its horror and glory. Theologian Paul Tillich wrote "The reality of death is excluded from daily life to the highest possible degree. The dead are not allowed to show that they are dead; they are transformed into a mask of the living." In our culture where awareness of death is as repressed as sex was to the Victorian, the crucifix has an important role—not to act as Tillich's mask but rather to function as a mirror. A crucifix is holy because it does not look holy. A crucifix is holy because it tells a truth. A crucifix is holy because it does not sanitize, clean, erase, obscure, or deny the trauma – or the majesty – of being a human, even if that human happens to be God. Or not.

Philadelphia, West of Babylon and East of Paradise

"And to the angel of the church in Philadelphia write; These things saith he that is holy, he that is true..."
Revelation 3:7

"Kelpius from his hermit den/By Wissahickon, maddest of good men, /Dreamed o'er the Chiliast dreams... Shall bid all flesh await, on land or ships, /The warning trump of the Apocalypse."
John Greenleaf Whittier *Pennsylvania Pilgrim* (1872)

In the mid-seventeenth century a religious mystic, seeker, and occultist named Johannes Kelpius laid in his bed in Transylvania, and he dreamt of Philadelphia, Pennsylvania. And so, he went.

In 2016 in the neighborhood of Germantown, a few miles north of Center City with her wedding cake City Hall and the gleaming Comcast Tower from which William Penn once again has the highest vantage point, you can see where Kelpius would eventually live and die. By the Wissahickon Creek in Fairmont Park you can enter the cave that the largely forgotten Kelpius called his home. Here, amongst broken beer bottles and graffiti, is what was once the anchorite's cell where Kelpius and his band of mystical minded, radically Protestant "monks" studied the Christian kabbalah, astrology, and magic.

They awaited the apocalypse that they believed *Revelation* had foretold as beginning in this new city in a New World, on the western edge of everything, and east of Judgment Day. And while they waited that date (a 1694 which came and went without the end of the world) they prayed, they divinated, they meditated, they wrote, and they supposedly discovered occult secrets here by the shores of the Schuylkill. For John Greenleaf Whittier, the Fireside Poet of the nineteenth-century, Kelpius was "Weird as a wizard" with command "over arts forbid."

Kelpius was born in 1667, only one year after a diabolically and auspiciously apocalyptic year, which saw widespread millennial excitement throughout Europe. He was raised amongst the German minority of Transylvania, then an independent kingdom known for both its religious freedom and heterodoxy (as Kelpius' future home of Pennsylvania would be as well). Though his life reflected the intellectual diversity of early modern Europe, it would become a characteristically American one as well, as he and his followers searched for utopia in America. Kelpius was no simple wild-eyed zealot; he was a consummate scholar, a philologist and scientist. As a student at the University of Altdorf near Nuremberg Germany, Kelpius devoted himself to the study of theology, mathematics, and music. But the sober principles of mainstream Lutheranism didn't move him, for he was attracted to the ecstatic and transcendent worship style of Pietism, as well as the more esoteric conjectures of kabbalah and Rosicrucianism. He was influenced by that perennial philosophy of mystical union which threads through thinkers ranging from Pythagoras to Bruno; that hermeticism which claims that the world is not as it seems, but that the higher intellect can brush back that veil to see the bride's face laid bare.

While at Altdorf he read the works of the Pietist Jakob Böhme, who was also a firm believer in the coming apocalypse. Based on both his reading of *Revelation* which spoke of an exilic remnant of the faithful that was as a "woman in the wilderness," as well as glowing accounts of the colony of Pennsylvania, Kelpius became convinced that the "Philadelphia" which John of Patmos wrote of was not the historical settlement in Asia Minor, but rather this new metropolis on the American frontier. What the men he convinced to travel with him to this New World found was perhaps not the Millennium, but they did find that divine experiment of Pennsylvania with its unprecedented degree of religious freedom.

This proprietary English colony was the largest private land holding on Earth; it was also marked by an exceptional ethnic, linguistic, and religious diversity, truly a remnant of the varied faithful in this wilderness .Welcomed by that similarly religious non-conformist Penn (even though Kelpius' private diaries could be scathing to the point of ingratitude when discussing the Quaker), Kelpius would make his home among the growing German population around Philadelphia, such as Daniel Falckner who was advocate for the colony in his pamphlet *Curieuse Nachrischt von Pensylvania,* and the brilliant polymath Daniel Pastorius who functioned as the *de facto* leader of the German community. Yet Kelpius and his fellow pilgrims were as men apart from Pennsylvania German society, true to the principles living in the wilderness of the forest with natural caves as their cells, awaiting the breaking of the seals and the end of the world. It was also where Kelpius, a musical prodigy, would compose New World hymns in the tongue of his fathers. It was where he and his fellow initiates would use the divine numerology of gemetria to try and ascertain scripture's sacred secrets. It was where these hermits charted the stars, attempting to divinate a future they thought was rapidly depleting. And it is where he and his oddly named "Society of the Women in the Wilderness" tried to create what was not just a new and perfect communal society, but also indeed the last society on Earth before the end of the world.

But the world did not end in 1694, though it did end for Kelpius when he died in 1708. As a bit of local lore has it, that alchemist discovered the mythic "Philosopher's Stone" capable of transmuting base metals into gold, only to toss it into the river before he died – even though some followers claimed that Kelpius never really did expire, rather elevating to a higher realm like the biblical prophet Enoch. Whittier wrote that Kelpius "saw the visions man shall see no more...The warning trump of the Apocalypse, /Shattering the heavens before the dread eclipse." Here in Philadelphia, at the ends of the world, and awaiting the end of the world, Kelpius was one of many who saw a paradisiacal promise here in Pennsylvania. For him, this was not just a place to await apocalypse, but a place to attend its perfection before that event as well.

The utopian religious freedom promised by Pennsylvania would attract other pilgrims. Kelpius came in the seventeenth-century, and then more of his countrymen came with the great migrations of utopian religious groups like the Amish, the Mennonites, and the Moravians in the eighteenth-century. The nineteenth-century would see a young Joseph Smith believing that he had restored the Aaronic line upon the Susquehanna River, as well as other attempts to build a perfect society such as those at New Harmony and Ephrata. And the twentieth-century would see the arrival of the utopian Bruderhof as refugees from Hitler's Germany. Over more than three centuries the state has been a haven for the searchers, the seekers, the eccentric, the dreamers, the divinators. He was simply an early one.

Kelpius may have hoped for a Peaceable Kingdom in the wilderness, though paradise did not descend his hoped-for year. That is not justification for turning one's face away from Eden (or Philadelphia). Yet though he is obscure, having learned of his story, why not hope that on a clear night you may yet see the gentle glow of the Philosopher's Stone at the bottom of the Schuylkill River?

The Page to Damascus

In the beginning there was the Word, and the Word was printed. In 1836 a provincial man of 21 years of age named Hong Huoxio came across some poorly translated Chinese-language pamphlets and Bibles left by visiting American Methodist missionaries. Ultimately, his reading of this material convinced Hong that he was the heavenly half-brother of Jesus Christ, and that it was his sacred duty to liberate his Hakka people from imperial oppression, and to purge China of the "demon worship" that he associated with Confucianism and Buddhism. Starting in 1850, and going on for fourteen more years, Hong (who had now taken the new name Xiuquan) fought what was called the Taiping Rebellion against the Qing dynasty. In that decade and a half of fighting, as many as thirty million people lost their lives, making it thirty times bloodier than that other civil war being fought at the same time in the United States. There were many causes for the Taiping Rebellion of course, but it arguably began with a conversion of sorts. And that conversion began with an act of reading. Popular culture often dramatizes conversion as always being a Road to Damascus moment, but Hong's conversion, and then all the drama which resulted from it, was enabled not by a shining light but by a smudgy pamphlet.

Before he read them, Hong had heard the gospels, as preached by the Connecticut-born missionary Edwin Stevens. But it was only upon seeing with his eyes the print of *hanzi* logograms that there began a turning of his soul, this embrace of an unknown god. In Reformation Europe, on fire with the philological ambitions of the great Bible translators like Erasmus, Luther, and Tyndale, there were debates as to whether the gospel was sufficient if only heard preached, or whether the gift of grace required one to actually read the written words of scripture as well. Does God enter the soul only through the ears, or does he

113

require the portal of the eyes as well?

Three-and-a-score centuries before Hong would be converted by reading, Martin Luther's soul was turned in a similar way. Despite the reputation of his thundering-yet-calming, apocalyptic-yet-funny, colloquial-yet-moving German preaching, the Augustinian monk who is popularly taken as the initiator of that Reformation was also converted through the eyes and not the ears. His hot personality and modest background notwithstanding, Luther was of a scholarly temperament. As with Jerome and his lion at foot, or Luther's contemporary Erasmus, faith was not just a thing of the heart and blood, but of the book and ink as well. Luther used the writer's tool of the inkwell to chase out the devil, and with those tools he consolidated the maxims of what is a profoundly textual way of living religion. As he recounts, it was a passage of Paul, Romans 1:17, which was to him "a gate of heaven." In studying a book that as a monk he was of course intimately familiar with, he affected a conversion: "Thereupon I felt myself to be reborn and to have through open doors into paradise. The whole of Scripture took on a new meaning."

Notice the organic metaphors, whereby the anthology which is the Bible is conflated with the garden of paradise (The Greek root for anthology after all means "flower pressing"). The regenerative nature of Edenic restoration and salvation are superimposed upon the pages of the volume, paper being both from and in and of itself a type of leaf. For Luther, the Book is not just metaphor for the Garden of Heaven, but indeed it is the thing itself.

But the anachronistic triumphalism that takes the Reformation to be the child of Guttenberg's machine should be avoided, for this new textuality of conversion was not limited to Protestants; indeed it preceded them. We should be suspicious of the commonplace knowledge that the Catholic Church abjured the printing press. Despite the anecdote that recounts a crimson-clad Prince of the Church who felt the press must be destroyed lest it destroy them, the Magisterium was actually a fervent enthusiast for the new technology. Before Luther would become the multimedia juggernaut of sixteenth-century Germany, the most commonly printed material was not the Protestant Bible, but rather fill-in-the-blank forms to administer indulgences.

Luther's pamphlets and translations were sold in all of the printing capitals of Europe, from Frankfurt to even Venice, in the hope that the printed Word could affect conversions as fully as the gift of grace had been imparted to him. But indeed if Luther would ultimately become the great evangelist for printed redemption in the form of read scripture, then his nemesis Johan Tetzel offered his own form of printed salvation in the indulgence forms he offered throughout the German countryside. Whether a form of conversion affected through reading, as with Luther, or written contract, as with Tetzel, the printed word was what was important. Neither listened sermon nor spoken oath was permanent enough to turn one's soul.

One thousand, four hundred and fifty years before Hong read that Methodist missionary Bible in Guangzhou, and 6,000 miles to the west in north Africa, another man a decade older than Hong would be when he had his religious visions, heard a voice that similarly affected him. After years of sinning, whoring, drinking, and blaspheming, the 31-year-old man sat in his mother's paradisiacal garden underneath a fig tree, and heard a child's voice imploring him "tolle, lege," that is to "take up and read" (I like to think this happened while he was hung over, but future Saint Augustine doesn't say). The former Manichean, fornicator, and repentant thief of pears was compelled to grab his mother's Bible. In a pique of bibliomancy, the man's book fell open to Romans 13:13-14, where he read, "put on the Lord Jesus Christ, and make no provision for the flesh to fulfill the lusts thereof." By an act of reading, the man who had once asked the Lord to grant him chastity, "but not yet," was suddenly converted. In his *Confessions* he records, "No further would I read, nor did I need; for instantly, as the sentence ended—by a light, as it were, of security infused into my heart." The English translation conflates the end of the "sentence," as in penitential time served, and the completion of the syntactical unit — a connection again between the magic of reading and conversion. A year later, Ambrose, whom, the penitent would marvel, could read the *scripto continua* silently to himself, would baptize Augustine in Milan, taking him from being the son of a strange god to one of the living God. Augustine, who would arguably become the most central western Christian figure, after Christ and Paul, had, his entire life, heard his mother Monica adjure him to convert, but it was the injunction "to read," and its completion, that had final efficacy.

The words of the resisting prophets are among the most potent stories of occasionally violent transformation. The prophets believed the very act of writing, and consequently reading, to be divinely inspired, enchanted with a sacred power, so that spiritual transformation becomes a profoundly textual act. Of course, how conversion is conceptualized differs broadly across Christian denominations, not to speak of how it would be understood by an Axial Age prophet. Luther conceived of his conversion as being "born again." Some speak of "getting right with God." Both Luther and Calvin, upon their conversions, felt a release from the anxieties associated with their lives before their religious awakening. One presumes that Hong perhaps felt consolation upon his conversion, or at least the palliative that comes with being given a mission — or upon discovering that Christ is your half-brother. But not all moments of theophany provide succor. Indeed, being called by the Lord, whether you are Muhammad or Joseph Smith, was often an event of sublime terror. But both of those initially reluctant prophets still had their calling intimately tied up with issues of textuality — Muhammad's transcription of the Archangel Gabriel's divine recitation of the Qur'an, and Joseph Smith's discovery of the angel Moroni's tablets. Again, reading, writing, listening, is all tied to religious transformation.

Before Hong, before Luther, before Augustine, and even before Paul, he who was converted by the Euripides-quoting-Christ, there was the prophet Ezekiel. If Luther felt a pacific mood descend upon reading Romans, and if that same epistle quelled Augustine's internal turmoil, the Jewish prophet's godly encounters were more ambivalent, and bluntly strange, compared to those later men—if just as profoundly textual as theirs was. If the reformers disputed whether the word of God entered the soul of man through eyes or ears, then Ezekiel knew that it sometimes entered through the mouth. Ezekiel 3:1-3: "Moreover He said to me, 'Son of man, eat what you find; eat this scroll, and go, speak to the house of Israel.' So I opened my mouth, and He caused me to eat that scroll. And He said to me, 'Son of man, feed your belly, and fill your stomach with this scroll that I give you.' So I ate, and it was in my mouth like honey in sweetness." And so, with not just his head and his heart newly filled with the word of God, but his belly too, Ezekiel could bear witness and hold accountable the House of Israel.

God's love of Ezekiel often seemed troubling, such as the time He forced him to lay for 390 days on his side, and then to reverse position and lie for another 40 on the other. But the ingestion of the very physical manifestation of His words seems particularly odd; one can't help but try and imagine the feel of tough, fibrous, stringy, bitter papyrus being slowly chewed and roughly swallowed, and count it as miracle enough that it somehow tasted sweet to the prophet. His fellow biblical eater-of-text John of Patmos was less fortunate; for him, God warns in the Book of Revelation, that the scroll shall "turn your stomach sour." For the earlier prophet, one wonders of the contents of this ingested scroll. In a fit of metaleptic symmetry, did he eat the Book of Ezekiel itself? If Augustine allowed for the magic of bibliomancy to turn him into an instrument of the Lord, than how all-the-more radical that Ezekiel committed an act of bibliophagy?

As strange as it is, the actual consumption of books for spiritual purposes is not unheard of. For what embrace of textuality is more complete than to literally make ink and fiber part of your flesh and blood, a type of readerly Eucharist? This is perhaps an extreme form of the Benedictine *lecto divina,* whereby scripture is not to be examined by the hermeneutic mind, but rather to be digested by the pious intestine. Origen believed that scripture was a sacrament; it is not so extreme to imagine actually swallowing the word of God as one does the communion wafer. This way one is all the more holy, God's letters and words and punctuation flowing in your very bloodstream. Examine the washed-out letters of gnostic gospels and illuminated manuscripts and medieval grimoires, and wonder: how many of these physical texts have been diluted and mixed with holy water, to be drunk by the penitent as the soul's curative, as did the Ethiopian king Menelik II? Derrida tells us that "There is no outside text." How to make that pronouncement more certain than to place that text inside of yourself? If our converts had their moment of illumination while reading, imagine how much more full that transformation is to make those very words part of your physical body. What more profound textuality could there be than that?

That's at least one radical option. The converse to making the book a part of yourself is to make yourself part of the book. Only a year after Hong's conversion, another man but a few miles from where Hong's evangelist would be born had his own turn of the soul. Witness the repentant nineteenth-century American cutpurse James Allen, alias Jonas Pierce, alias James H. York, alias Burley Grove. He chose his Christian name for the *Narrative of the Life of James Allen, the Highwayman,* a deathbed confession to the warden of the Massachusetts State Prison in 1837. The conversion narrative is a popular genre, especially in these pious United States of America, where we thrill to the tales of degenerate thieves, drunks, and whores who once were blind but now can see. But seldom has a story of contrite redemption been presented quite like that of the highwayman James Allen, who had his account bound in his own flesh upon his execution, and presented to a brave man whom he respected for successfully resisting Allen's attempt at robbery. Today, Allen's cemetery plot is a bookshelf, his graveyard the Boston Athenaeum, where, presumably, he cannot be checked out (Whether Allen is slated for republication is known only to his Author).

Whether seen, heard, eaten, or ourselves bound, reading and conversion describe remarkably similar processes of absorption and reaction. The narrative of conversion may be a genre; and indeed reading of scripture may occasion conversion itself, but reading itself is also a type of conversion. As the conversion narrative is printed, print itself often enacts the conversion. For the act of reading is also a transcendent experience, whereby the prosaic, material world of faded paper and smudged print abuts the eternal world of hidden sacred things. Christ became flesh, but the printing of books is all the more representative of an incarnational poetics whereby the sacred book is also a material embodiment of more noumenal things. This type of material object is one whose existence any of us can confirm, as surely as Thomas could place his finger in Christ's wound. The word "conversion" comes from the Latin *conversio,* which literally means "to turn," as the word "translation" from *translatio* mean "transfer." Both enact spatial metaphors. To convert is to turn, to face God or the Truth, and to translate is to also move something, in this case meaning. In reading, there is a transformation that acts on the individual as surely as conversion can act on the soul. In *A History of Reading* Alberto Manguel writes, "Nothing moves except my eyes and my hand occasionally turning a page, and yet something not exactly defined by the word 'text' unfurls, progresses, grows and takes root as I read." Not all conversions need be as dramatic as that on the road to Damascus. For both good and bad, think of Hong's Methodist pamphlets, or of Luther and Augustine reading their Paul. Sometimes the turn of a soul is as subtle as the turn of a page.

For Sister Frances Carr

On January 2nd, 2017, a small, distinctive, and beautiful world in our midst moved a bit closer to its own end. The first Monday of the New Year saw the passing of Sister Frances Carr, one of the last three remaining Shakers.

Sister Frances was a member of the Sabbathday Lake Shaker Village in New Gloucester, Maine, who spent her life teaching and writing about her experiences as a member of the ever-dwindling, idiosyncratic Protestant denomination. Brother Arnold Hadd, one of those who survive her, reported that Sister Frances died "surrounded in love, tears and Shaker songs."

A Shaker since the age of 10, Sister Frances converted to the faith with her mother after her father's death. As the sect practices complete celibacy, no Shaker is born into the faith. With her death, a small, but significant, part of America's religious ancestry moves closer to its extinction. To paraphrase John Donne, as the death of any person diminishes the individual, so of course does the death of Sister Frances diminish our world a bit—and so much more so because she was a refugee of a counter-cultural tradition that held a bit of utopian promise against the machinery of state and industry.

Often confused with the far larger denomination of the Quakers (though itself a relatively small sect), the Shakers came from the same milieu of dissenting, radical religious traditions that emerged in seventeenth- and eighteenth-century Britain. Ann Lee, the religion's founder, was the daughter of a Manchester, England blacksmith. In 1774 she set out to the wilds of America with the promise of establishing a godly community in the New World. Mother Ann's experiment became an important chapter in American utopianism, which included groups as varied as the Oneida Community, the Fourierists, the pilgrims at Ephrata, and the social experiments of the 1960s. For Mother Ann, the New

World was an opportunity to make the world new. As Mother Ann would reflect on her new home in upstate New York, "I saw a large tree, every leaf of which shone with such brightness as made it appear like a burning torch, representing the Church of Christ, which will yet be established in this land."

Like so many other heterodox religious communities that proliferated in early America, Lee saw in the continent an opportunity for remaking society in a more just, egalitarian, and equitable way, including the radical equality of the sexes. Indeed the Shakers understood Christ's return as being in a feminine form, and they understood their founder to be a messianic "manifestation of divine light." For the Shakers, God's gender was always understood as dualistic, as containing both the masculine and the feminine, and leadership was often matriarchal.

The cultural context that birthed the group was the same that led to the emergence of other exotic non-conformist sects in seventeenth-century England. Groups with strange names like the Ranters, the Seekers, and the Muggletonians have already disappeared. Others, like the Baptists and Methodists, are still around (if now less radical than they once were). Mother Ann's role as the founder of the Shakers mirrored other women prophets like Jane Leade, Jane Wardley, and Anna Trapnell who proliferated in the years around the English civil wars and after. Their theological origins stem from the inventive dynamism of the English civil wars, but they branch into the equally inspired decades of the American First and Second Great Awakening, as such they are an important part of the most theologically creative periods in Christian history.

Groups like the Shakers represented a sort of "Second Reformation" in the seventeenth century, one that took Luther's injunction of a priesthood of all believers to its anarchic conclusion. Rejecting the conservatism of the magisterial Reformation, these non-conformist groups (so-called in England for refusing to conform to the official ecclesiastical settlement of the State) derived an even more revolutionary understanding of religious experience than the older Reformation's call to reading scripture alone. Where Luther, Calvin, Zwingli and so on may have had *sola Scriptura* as an anti-traditionalist rallying cry, the dissenting churches of the English Revolution often claimed that it was human conscience, or the "Inner Light" as Quakers called it, that was the ultimate arbiter of God's voice.

Officially known as "The United Society of Believers in Christ's Second Appearing," the Shakers have never had membership numbers on their side. At their height there were dozens of communities throughout New England, the Mid-Atlantic, and the Midwest. Despite always being relatively small (as the rigors of their religious vocation, not to mention the imperative to celibacy was not widely attractive), the Shakers have had an outside influence on American culture. One can see it in the almost modernist minimalism of their furniture design that defined wood-working style of the nineteenth and twentieth centuries, to their hymnology that influenced Aaron Copeland's magisterial orchestral suite *Appalachian Spring*.

But even more crucial than their rich cultural traditions is their witnessing to the possibility of legitimate counter-culture within the machinery of capitalist America. Like the Amish, the Shakers have represented an American counter-tradition that uses the vocabulary and experience of faith as a bulwark against systems of oppression. The Shakers were among the first conscientious objectors to compulsory military service in US history.

That the Shakers, with their pacifism, their communal living, and perhaps most of all their celibacy, seem weird to us is precisely the point. As in the tradition of the radical Reformation they don't just believe in separation of church and state; they see any collusion between religion and government as a profound rejection of Christ, as rendering all unto Caesar. For the Shakers, Constantine's cross makes the shadow of a sword; it is only by setting themselves apart in a type of simple purity that the hypocrisies, violence, and oppression of the wider world can be demonstrated to the rest of us.

The Shakers, in their pious oddity and their strange holiness, remain, however small, a crack in the wall that divides us in this increasingly insular, hierarchical, and oppressive era. They rejected the apparatus of state, economy, industry, and military. Theirs was a pacifist army against Moloch's minions. In offering us difference they enacted the possibility and promise of that difference.

Religions are intellectual ecosystems, and like biological ecosystems they are threatened by war, commerce, and the pernicious promises offered by oppressive normalcy. This century will most likely see the extinction of the Shakers, along with so many other groups like the Mandaeans, the Zoroastrians, the Yazidis and so on.

As I have written elsewhere, "Every religion is a world, every person is a world, and the destruction of either is a type of irredeemable apocalypse." Individual religions are composed of their own unique metaphysics, ethics, cosmologies, and theologies. The death of a religion is as the extinction of an entire world; the loss of a religion is the end of an entire universe. But we must remember that religions are not simply built out of metaphysics, ethics, cosmology, and theology. They are built out of men and women.

Sister Frances is survived by Brother Arnold and Sister June Carpenter. And so we mourn.

Speaking in Tongues of Fire

"I thank my God, I speak with tongues more than ye all."
Corinthians 14:18

"Mystery, I'd read somewhere, is not the absence of meaning, but the presence of more meaning than we can comprehend."
Dennis Covington, Salvation on Sand Mountain

Nobody can know what that initial cacophony of babel sounded like. Supposedly, fifty days after the resurrection, and some ten after Christ ascended bodily into heaven, the apostles gathered to observe Shavuot, that other holiday of the indwelling presence of the Lord amongst men. That day was when "cloven tongues as of like fire... sat upon each of them." The author of Acts reports that "they were all filled with the Holy Ghost, and began to speak with other tongues, as the Spirit gave them utterance."

What were the actual sounds like? The soft sensuous vowels of the Romance languages, or the alliterative accentuation of English, with its guttural staccato syllables that ping out like rapid Gatling-gun fire? Or the polysyllabic sesquipedalian rumblings of German, a language for which speaking feels more like chewing? Most likely, as Hebrew speakers, even their gibberish would share the strangely beautiful throat gutturals of their native tongue. Indeed, those modern penitents who claim to share such gifts of the spirit speak their nonsense in a pitch and tenor in keeping with whatever their regular language is; speaking in tongues done by Swedes sounding more like Swedish than the speaking of tongues in English, which sounds like English, and so on. But whatever the details, it was a "sound from heaven as of a rushing mighty wind."

The Philistines who witnessed the Pentecost believed the

apostles to be "full of new wine," a slur that has been leveled for eons against those who are so full of words that they burst at the very seams. Intoxicated ecstasy like this–the maenads knew it, the Sufi dervishes knew it, and so the Apostles knew it. Such is the nature of being visited by that inscrutable "other one," the Holy Spirit, forgotten partner in the Trinity, whether she comes under the guise of God, muse, daemon, or some other form. This event, the Pentecost, is recognized by all Christians, whether metaphorically or literally. In the compendium of strangeness that is the Bible, with tales ranging from the Bridegroom of Blood to Jacob's tussle with the angel, Pentecost preserves its mysteriousness, even for those who turn from the wild and untamable God to a respectable god, those for whom the Bible is prosaically transformed into moneymaking guide, boring collection of obvious moral platitudes, or incorrect science textbook.

The difference between these two deities is that the respectable god's name can be written; the untamable God's name is in a language never heard before, only to be uttered innumerable times in different ways, each one unique and forever to disappear like some quantum fluctuation–a foolish wisdom known by those penitents, at that Shavuot (Luke doesn't record what exactly was said in the mad chorus of burbling tongues in a Palestinian attic some two millennia ago. Perhaps it was everything that was ever needed to be known by anyone, but the frequency was simply too high to hear it?).

And the particularity of the burbling tongues is, however, as close to universal a phenomenon as one could find, and pre-Christian. Between Pentecost and Pentecostalism there is a rich history of others speaking in tongues, or glossolalia, as linguists and theologians call it, whether by a Gnostic bigamist named Montanus, the medieval mystic Hildegard von Bingen, or pagan shamans chanting on the Russian steppes. In many instances, tongue-speaking is strangely, almost mythically, connected to the Ouroboros handling of dangerous snakes. There is a direct line from the tongue-speaker Alexander of Abono-teichus, with his snake-puppet named Glycon, to Appalachian Holy Rollers, the Islamic musicians of Jajouka, Morocco (who some believe are the last Maenads in the world), and the Italian Catholics of Cocullo, Abruzzi, who adorn a statue of Saint Domenico with snakes during the *Festa dei Serpari*. But square society mostly associates glossolalia with Pentecostalism, with those "Holy Rollers," what literary critic Harold Bloom called the "pure version of an American shamanism." The golden thread which connects all different manifestations of tongue-speaking is thicker than might be presumed. Medical doctor E. Mansell Pattison, in his 1968 article "Behavioral Science Research on the Nature of Glossolalia," notes that it is practiced by:

...the Peyote cult among the North American Indians, the Haida Indians of the Pacific Northwest, Shamans in the Sudan, the Shango cult of the West Coast of Africa, the Shago cult in Trinidad, the Voodoo cult in Haiti, the Aborigines of South America and Australia, the Eskimos of the subarctic regions of North America and Asia, the Shamans in Greenland, the Dyaks of Borneo, the Zor cult of Ethiopia, the Siberian shamans, the Chaco Indians of South America, the Curanderos of the Andes, the Kinka in the African Sudan, the Thonga shamans of Africa, and the Tibetan monks.

And yet most people, when they hear "speaking in tongues," don't envision the Dyaks of Borneo, but rather the all-American Holy Roller, all sweat and strychnine and Southern fried snake-handling. We think of weird babbling of nonsense phonemes and nonsense words, bubbling up out of the throat of mad believers. Eyes orgasmically rolled back in their skull, arms and legs twitching like some ergot-poisoned peasant, tongue unhinged from the mouth, meaning unhinged from language.

Charitably speaking, that's not too far off from how many

charismatics might describe the experience itself; travelling Bible salesman A.J. Tomlinson, sanctified in the spirit on January 12, 1908, described how "my body was rolled and tossed about beyond my control, and finally while lying on my back, my feet were raised up several times, and my tongue would stick out of my mouth in spite of my efforts to keep it inside my mouth." The condemnation of this sort of thing by the majority of Protestants, who reject modern-day "gifts of the spirit," is even more damning than the secular skeptic's scorn.

But we abandon speaking in tongues at our own spiritual peril. I do not mean this literally, of course; I'm not going to head to the front of the tent, hands aloft and offer to do that service myself. I'm much too High Church for that sort of thing. I am, however, going to consider the cultural contributions and the cracked brilliance of the Pentecostals, our own homegrown Gnostics, and to argue that the practice of speaking in tongues is one that has an innate, charged, dangerous, anarchic, powerful, liberatory, profound, and strange potential to it. It is, in short, "meaningful nonsense." Despite its lack of grammatical, syntactical, or semantic organization, Canadian linguist William J. Samarin observed in his seminal 1972 investigation of the phenomenon, "word-like and sentence-like units" emerge in tongue-speaking, "because of realistic, language-like rhythm and melody." It is this tension that lends glossolalia the quality of meaningful nonsense. Speaking in tongues is neither actual language nor a cacophony of random sounds; it is something different. It can sound terrifying, the purview of hypnotists and voudon witch doctors. Linguist Felicity D. Goodman in her 1969 study writes that "the glossolalist often does not hear himself ... does not afterwards remember what he said, and thus cannot repeat it." The worshiper acts as "an artifact of the trance; it is generated by it." Fearful or not, glossolalia is far too common to be written off as unimportant, some pre-modern artifact to be exoticized and made into anthropological curio (though of course I'll hypocritically do a bit of that too).

Speaking in tongues is not an exhibit to put in the metaphorical formaldehyde jar of past religious superstitions–it's too important for that. In Euripides' *Bacchae,* that proto-Pentecostal rock star Dionysius says to the square mayor of Athens that "He who believes needs no explanation." Pentheus asks, "What's the worth in believing worthless things?,," to which our rock star responds, "Much worth, but not worth telling you it seems." Despite the god's admonishment, let's see if we can muster a little bit of an explanation of the worthiness of worthless things, to anatomize the tongues of fire.

What are the nerves which connect the divine intoxicated brain to the mouth loosed of conventional syntax, of the tongue which now only wags in the language of God? Is there any wisdom, foolish or otherwise, to be gained from parsing the strange grammar of the Holy Roller? This "gift of the spirit" is a strange present indeed. There is, theologically speaking, a difference of opinion as to whether the gifts of that ancient event are still accessible to humans today; those who assent are "continuationists" and those that deny are "cessasionists." For continuationists, glossolalia represented, to some worshipers, direct contact with the divine, like that of a saint. But historically, most Christians have been cessasionists, emphatically believing that such gifts are no longer accessible. Charismatic revivals and tongue-speakers in the first decades of the twentieth century were denounced as superstitious, insane, or diabolical.

One of the supposed results of Reformation half-a-millennium ago was a certain disenchantment, but gifts of the spirit seem to be something more primal, more Maenad ripping Pentheus apart at a Bacchic orgy than sober Protestant banker for whom it's all early to bed and early to rise. The project of modernity, of which the Reformation was in many ways a cause, is supposedly one of cool rectilinear rationality, of logic and sensibleness. And yet, our designated straw-penitent Holy Roller is still the strange step-child of the magisterial Reformation. Like other radically innovative sects of the priesthood of all believers, such as the Quakers of the English civil wars, or the Millerites who blanketed the burnt-over-country of the American Second Great Awakening, both of whom had their own flirtations with glossolalia, the Holy Roller is a renegade from the staid, scriptural conservatism of normative Protestantism.

As with all things radical, many denominations moved through their adolescent speaking-in-tongues phase. Now Methodism is all church pot-luck dinners, but once, it was metal. The Methodist revival preachers amongst the tent cities such as Kentucky's Cane Ridge could speak tongues with the best of them. That is, of course, assuming that it's fair to even classify more obvious tongue-speaking groups like the Pentecostals as even being Protestants in any conventional sense. For in speaking a divine language of their own invention they perhaps depart as far from Luther's scriptural inerrancy as Quakers and Shakers did when they made an "inner light" the primary judge over the text of the Bible. For these God-intoxicated Protestants, the logic of a priesthood of all believers was taken to its inevitable conclusion, one where every man can be a denomination and every prophetic utterance a new gospel. Religious ecstasy knows no denomination, enrapturement no theology; they are, rather, a facet of what it means for some humans to be in prayer. Indeed, Christianity has always had the strangeness of meaningful nonsense at its very core. The word may become flesh, but being able to define that word has always been the central enigma of the faith.

As universal as the practice is though, Pentecostalism's entry onto the scene did represent an abrupt explosion in religious history, as decisive as Luther's nailing of the *95 Theses* to that Wittenberg door on a Halloween in 1517. Pentecostalism's reformation can be decisively dated to April 9th, 1906, when the gifts of the Holy Spirit were restored to the earth, descending this time not unto dusty Judea, but onto the overwhelmingly American city of sunny Los Angeles, California. Though plenty of pyrotechnic preparation had been made for tongue-speaking in American religious history, from Jonathan Edwards to Joseph Smith to the Indian prophet Handsome Lake and the Ghost Dancers of the native insurgencies across the prairies and plains, it was an itinerant black preacher named William J. Seymour who lit the fuse on that spring day in Los Angeles, initiating what has come to be known as the Azusa Street Revival.

The Kansas-based son of former slaves, Reverend Seymour, was invited to preach in Los Angeles by Neely Terry, a member of a local "holiness" church, pastored by Julia Hutchins, at the corner of Ninth and Santa Fe. Seymour had been a student of the then-respected Pentecostal minister Charles Parham, but when preaching to Hutchins's flock in California, he taught that to speak in tongues was to display modern-day gifts of the spirit. Hutchins rejected Seymour's heterodox teaching, and the minister ultimately found himself and his followers conducting their services out of a house on North Bonnie Brae Street. Though Seymour had attested to the possibility of gifts of the spirit, they had yet to be made manifest, until that April 9th, when one Edward Lee began to speak in tongues among the assembled worshipers. Seymour's future wife Jennie Moore was the next to be visited by the spirit. Seymour himself wouldn't experience glossolalia until three days later, when on April 12th that spontaneous overflow of divine intoxication passed up through his throat and out of his mouth unto the assembled congregation. News of the event spread throughout the working-class communities of Los Angeles, and soon Seymour was leading a revival of not just black worshippers, but white and Hispanic ones, who flocked to North Bonnie Brae Street so that they, too, could be filled with the spirit. Eventually that modest family home where the spirit had first visited Lee, Moore, and Seymour was so full of the writhing body of the Church Militant that the porch collapsed in on itself, and the ersatz congregation found itself relocated to a dilapidated former African Methodist Episcopal Church on Azusa Street. From its new headquarters, Seymour's preaching became a movement.

At Azusa Street, Seymour's flock was racially integrated, much to the outrage of both conservative Los Angeles and also Seymour's mentor, Parham, who would later be felled in a gay sex scandal. The congregation was theologically diverse as well, initially drawing Quakers, Presbyterians, and Mennonites, in addition to members of the Wesleyan Holiness Movement that served as the germinating seed of Pentecostalism. During the revival–which has operated continually for the last 111 years– there were reports of not just glossolalia, but xenoglossy and faith healing as well. Though the church itself only ever accommodated a few dozen people at a time, hundreds of thousands of pilgrims made their way to the Los Angeles ghetto so that they, too, could drink in the spirit that had once descended upon the Apostles of Christ. One participant in the earliest days of the Azusa Street Revival, as reported to the missionary writer Frank Bartleman, claimed that a multitude "have come here from all parts, have humbled themselves and got down, not 'in the straw,' but 'on' the straw matting, and have thrown away their notions, and have wept in conscious emptiness before God and begged to be 'endued with power from on high.'" Another claimed that "Suddenly the Spirit would fall upon the congregation. God himself would give the altar call. Men would fall all over the house like the slain in battle, or rush for the altar en masse, to see God. The scene often resembled a forest of fallen trees," for here in this old church in Los Angeles, "All was spontaneous, ordered of the Spirit." This worshiper conveys the terrifying aspect of theophany, using metaphors of militarism and felled forests.

All that was lost on the beat journalist and headline writers for *The Los Angeles Times,* for whom this integrated crowd was "Breathing strange utterances and mouthing a creed which no sane mortal could understand." Describing the church as a "tumble-down shack on Azusa Street," the penitents were "devotees of the weird doctrine" who were practicing "fanatical rites," and preaching "the wildest theories," having worked themselves "into a state of mad excitement in their peculiar zeal." The author, racial dog-whistle firmly in mouth, compares this mixture of "Colored people and a sprinkling of whites" to a primitive bacchanal. He writes of the "howlings of worshipers who spend hours swaying forth and back in a nerve-racking attitude of prayer and supplication." Just so nobody could accuse the editors of subtlety, the headline read "WEIRD BABLE OF TONGUES: New Sect of Fanatics is Breaking Loose."

Despite, or perhaps because of the disdain in which the reporter held the Azusa Street gathering, Seymour's revival provides the template for subsequent movements of the Holy Spirit in North American religious history, from the Toronto Blessing, which occurred at a Vineyard Church in 1994, to the Brownsville Revival a year later and the Lakeland Revival in 2008. Since Seymour's gathering, Pentecostalism has gained almost half-a-billion adherents, across the global south of Christendom—only slightly fewer in number than all other Protestant sects combined. It is by far the fastest-growing denomination in the world. Even Roman Catholics have gotten filled with the Spirit, when in 1966 a group of Duquesne University students on retreat experienced the supposed gifts of the spirit, inaugurating the movement known as Catholic Charismatic Renewal, a development which has been warily eyed by the Vatican as a potential means to stave off conversions to Pentecostalism in both Latin America and Africa.

There are reasons for the popular and disdainful caricature of Pentecostalism: that it is irrational, superstitious, dangerous. The prosperity gospel, which many contemporary Pentecostal churches encourage, is as pernicious a bit of market idolatry as has ever been promoted, a consummately heretical doctrine. And the monarchical model of church governance can cede so much sovereignty to the individual pastor that a racially egalitarian-minded minister like Seymour can dangerously alter into a cult leader like Jim Jones. And, of course, in the modern political context, charismatic churches, like others, can embrace any number of retrograde and condemnable positions from institutionalized homophobia to misogyny. In a word, Pentecostalism's politics can be dubious.

But we would do well not to forget the utopian impulse of Seymour's initial revival, the spiritual genius that fully enacted Paul's teaching that "There is neither Jew nor Greek, there is neither bond nor free, there is neither male nor female." As historian Randall J. Stephens explains, "The Holy Ghost seemed to be available to all worshipers, regardless of age, color, or sex." For Seymour there was neither black nor white; there was neither poor nor rich, and indeed there was neither male nor female, for he recognized the complete religious authority of women, both a religiously and politically radical position.

Besides, a Dionysian creed like Pentecostalism, whatever its conscious overtures to conservatism might be, will have unconscious attractions to antinomianism. Pentecostalism claims to be a religion of Sunday morning, but in its ecstatic heart it knows that it belongs to Saturday night. Scholar Peter W. Williams in his *Popular Religion in America* explains that while "practices [such] as drinking, gambling and non-marital sexuality fall under taboo in daily life, structurally similar practices become positively sacred when performed in a sacred context." For a more personal confirmation of that observation, consider J. Rodman Williams, professor at Austin Presbyterian Theological Seminary, who described his own conversion in the spirit, one day in 1965, by explaining that he "began to ejaculate sounds of any kind, praying that somehow the Lord would use them.... Wave after wave, torrent after torrent, poured out. It was utterly fantastic I was doing it and yet I was not… Tears began to stream down my face – joy unutterable, amazement incredible." Interpreting this doesn't require much complex Freudian psychoanalysis, does it?

We must not obscure the sheer radicalism of Azusa, even if we can keep the conservatism of its descendants at arm's length, for Seymour embraced a fundamental truth at that Second Pentecost – that in religious ecstasy there is an erasure of borders. It's not for nothing that a Chicago newspaper writing about Parham's Kansas church in 1900 ran with the headline "occupants of Topeka mansion talk in many queer jargons." Essayist Anthony Heilbut in a February 2017 *Harper*'s article elaborates that "For generations, poor gay boys have flocked to Pentecostalism — the denomination of the working class…because worship therein allowed an intensely expressive devotion that would be frowned on anywhere else." Pentecostal academic and writer H. Vinson Synan reflects on glossolalia at the moment of his conversion by explaining that, "Here was an experience that truly cast aside the constraints of human convention and gave free rein to the Spirit. In ecstatic speech the action of human agency was completely denied, and the basic structure of language was itself set aside." If so much of institutional religion is precisely about defining who is elect and not, what is allowed in and who is left behind, that which is pure and that which is unclean, then Seymour understood that there is liberation from those systems in bliss, that speaking in tongues allows us to briefly translate our emotion into the very language of heaven. That novel tradition sees emancipation from language itself as the abolishment of those very systems which serve to enslave us. Not for nothing, but it was Pentecostalism's rhythms that inspired rock and roll; Jerry Lee Lewis and Jimmy Swaggart were first cousins, after all. Saturday night and Sunday morning, all in one.

If glossolalia operates as a kind of obscured *idée fixe* upon the Christian consciousness, then I'll go a step further and say that it's at the very core of human communication itself. Again, this is not a singular practice, but a universal one. That is to say that to build meaning out of sounds unrelated to an objective world is not just a question of semiotics, but at the very core of Being, which theology makes its provenance. A veritable golden thread of similarity connects speaking in tongues not just to that first Pentecost from the New Testament's Book of Acts, but back deep into ancient human history, and possibly to even the beginnings of language itself. Despite our own preconceptions as to who it is that speaks in tongues, it is a shockingly common activity. For though we may individually speak English, French, Italian, German, Japanese, Arabic, Latin, or Hebrew, from what charged field of comprehensible nonsense did such tongues arise? From what primordial soup of untethered sounds, phonemes like amino acids organized out of chaotic disarray, did meaning first evolve? For whatever exegete can offer her correct interpretation of the following paragraph shall have fully anatomized the tongues of fire:

U aei eis aei ei o ei ei os ei.[1] Ah pe-am t-as le t-am te ;pp/O ne vas ke than sa-na was-ke/lon ah ve shan too/Te wan-se ark e ta-ne voo te/lan se o-ne voo/Te on-e-wan tase va ne woo te was-se o-ne van/Me-le wan se o oar ke-le van te/shom-ber on vas sa la too lar var sa/re voo an don der on v-tar loo-cum an la voo/O be me-sum ton ton ton tol a wav – er tol-a wac-er/ton ton te s-er pane love ten poo.[2] Terema Suremi ki si janda o t, tra o te tre o te ras√u r lidZi, Si kajanda, rIpiti rQili bUu Sak t´ sala ma ra, ka l´ba Z´p´resi ji ana so, tu l´bijando, bŒm ma hu t√u kera ba lQndo rÅdZ´ di ki biabi ba tru sil lil j, i o prQi ba, bo ri si ri Ql Ini Qi In Si di ma h√mb√u Åstraja.[3] A.a.o. – o.o.o. – i.i.i. – ee. E. – u.u.u. – ye. Ye. Ye./Aa, la ssob, li li l ulu ssob./ Scjumschan/Wichoda, kssara, gujatun, gujatun./io,ia, – o – io, ia, zok, io, ia, pazzo! Io, la, pipazzo! Sookatjema, soosuoma, nikam, nissam, scholda./Paz, paz, paz, paz, paz, paz, paz, paz!/Pinzo, pinzo, pinzo, dynsa./Schono, tschikodam, wik-

gasa,mejda./Boupo, chondyryama, boupo, galpi./Euachado, rassado, ryssado, azlyemo./io, ia, o. io, ia, zok. Io nye zolk, io ia zolk.[4] gadji beri bimba glandridi laula lonni cadori /gadjama gramma berida bimbala glandri galassassa laulitalomini / gadji beri bin blassa glassala laula lonni cadorsu sassala bim /gadjama tuffm i zimzalla binban gligla wowolimai bin beri ban /o katalominai rhinozerossola hopsamen laulitalomini hoooo /gadjama rhinozerossola hopsamen /bluku terullala blaulala loooo.[5] Boo bi yoo bi, Bi yu di di ooh dun, dabba oohbee, Boo di yoo di, Di yu di dee dee doohdun, di di oohnbee, Bu di yu dan dan dan, Dee boognbee, Aheedee doo doo abbi woo do ee, Woah ba bee ba bap beya oh, Ein bap bap dein.[6]

Well, that pretty much says it all, doesn't it?

As a sound-poem it ranges across centuries and thousands of miles, including a bit of transcribed glossolalia from an apocryphal Coptic Egyptian gospel, presumably a record of the actual utterances of some ecstatic worshipper in the earliest days of Christianity, a transcription of a Shaker named Jack who was slayed by the spirit on a cool fall day, October 6th 1847, as surely as Parham or Seymour or Jerry Lee Lewis would be a century hence; a linguist's transcription of Pentecostal glossolalia; the 1836 transcription by a man named I. Sakharov of Russian shamans' tongue-speaking, which was latter refashioned into a modernist sound poem by the avant-garde Futurist Velimir Khlebnikov; his contemporary, the Dadaist writer Hugo Ball's classic bit of nonsense verse "Gadji beri bimba," which was later set to music by the Talking Heads; and of course, the incomparably sweet scat singing of Ella Fitzgerald.

The genre of comprehensible nonsense is a wide one, and its practitioners similarly so. One could certainly hypothesize literal connections of influence between ritualized glossolalia and some of these examples of cultural production – it is not a stretch to conjecture that scat singing draws directly from tongue-speaking in the black church; that Khlebnikov was directly inspired by the strange utterances of the Russian shamans recorded a century beforehand is a fact. And yet the wide breadth of the phenomenon testifies to the impossibility of direct influence in all cases. The Zurich cafes where Ball shaped his aural sound sculpture are far from the steppes where Sakharov communed with central Asian animists, which are far from the recording studio in New York where Fitzgerald recorded "How High the Moon."

If any plucky linguist would care to analyze the admixture of phonemes in each of those seven individual samples they would no doubt find that the Siberian nonsense sounds a bit Turkic, Ball's a bit German, Fitzgerald's a bit English. But what unites all these worshipers is a faith in aural abstraction, in the production of language reduced to sound, and thus elevated to truth. Glossolalia is to speech what abstract expressionism is to art, representation stripped to its bare essence. Speaking in tongues is thus the purest poetry. Bloom writes that for the Pentecostal slain in the Spirit everything "falls away...for where the Spirit is, there can be nothing else." Bloom describes a type of kenosis, as does the Sufi nun who wished she could burn down heaven and let the cool waters of paradise quench the flames of hell, so that people would worship God only for Himself. Similarly, in severing meaning from language we can indulge in those pure qualities of sound itself. For those quoted in my nonsense paragraph, meaning has been replaced by sound, and in that interpolation there is, paradoxically, all the more sense.

Like those portions of Ezekiel forbidden to the exegetes of Midrash, the parsing of tongues is an impossibility. Meaningful nonsense has no sentences to diagram, no New Critical close readings that are possible. The gifts of spirit are as Ludwig Wittgenstein's fabled and impossible "private language," an idiom known only to God and the speaker (and maybe not even the speaker). Each one of the disciples had achieved that purest of literary abstractions, their own language only comprehensible to a readership of one, a solipsistic private language shared only by the poet and his audience of the Lord. What, I wonder, is the connection between the earliest of language and this phenomenon? Was it from similarly meaningful nonsense that actual language itself evolved on some Tanzanian field?

We take it as a given that religion is born out of language, but perhaps we have it backward. Maybe all tongues were originally sacred, maybe all tongues were that mystical nonsense, and meaning only froze out of them as the ecstatic temperature dropped. Maybe baboon-faced Thoth's first words were simply divine nonsense; perhaps in the beginning the Word was unpronounceable. The spiritual acumen of the tongue-speaker is that they enact that primordial idiom; and the wisdom of the tongue-speaker is that who the tongue belongs to is irrelevant. They are but a vessel through which glorious nonsense pours through, for the medium is most emphatically not the message. In fact, what the message is at all becomes complicated. That is the deep, primal, truth about glossolalia: that theological truth can't ever be expressed in literal language, but rather only through imperfect metaphor and limited vocabulary. However, some truths can be expressed in language, provided that that tongue is beyond both the literal and the metaphorical, in some other accent. Philip and Carol Zaleski write that the charismatic traditions have given "birth to something never before witnessed, except by the apostles: a tongue co-created by God and human to offer praise on high, to drench the heart in joy, and, it may be, to confound the nonbelievers." Though I am a nonbeliever, I too can paradoxically find joy in my confounding.

The wisdom of glossolalia is that it knows God is not a noun, but a verb. The Spirit is a great emergence of divine truth that bursts forth from entrails and surges up out of the stomach through the throat and out the mouth. Speaking in tongues is an overabundance of this Spirit, a spontaneous overflow of pure feeling that, like logorrhea or love, is an untamable energy that can't be circumscribed in simple formulas or sentences. In speaking in tongues we liberate ourselves, we embrace a foolish wisdom, we utter the very syllables of the divine.

[1] From the Holy Book of the Great Invisible Spirit, also informally known as the Coptic Gospel of the Egyptians. Discovered at the Nag Hamadi site in Egypt, 1945.

[2] The Shaker "Jack" at Holy Ground, October 6th 1847, recorded in Jerome Rothenberg's ethnopoetic anthology Poems for the Millennium: The University of California Book of Romantic and Post-Romantic Poetry.

[3] Transcribed Pentecostal "gifts of the spirit," as gathered by the linguist Heather Kavan.

[4] "Northern Russian incantations from an 1836 gathering recorded by I. Sakharov and brought to later attention by Russian futurist poet Velimir Khlebnikov," as quoted in Rothenberg's anthology.

[5] Hugo Ball's Dadaist poem "Gadji beri bimba."

[6] "How High the Moon," performed by Ella Fitzgerald.

The American Apocalyptic Sublime and the Twilight of Empire

"Thus every one before the Throne/of Christ the Judge is brought, / Both righteous and impious, / that good or ill had wrought."
Michael Wigglesworth, *The Day of Doom* (1662)

"Are you ready/For the great atomic power? /Will you rise and meet your Savior in the air? /Will you shout or will you cry/When the fire rains from on high?/Are you ready for the great atomic power?"
Ira and Charlie Louvin, "Great Atomic Power" (1952)

"It's coming to America first/the cradle of the best and of the worst."
Leonard Cohen, "Democracy" (1992)

"Hear the trumpets, hear the pipers. /One hundred million angels singin'. /Multitudes are marching to the big kettle drum. /Voices callin', voices cryin'. /Some are born an' some are dyin'. /It's Alpha's and Omega's Kingdom come."
Johnny Cash, "The Man Comes Around" (2002)

Michael Wigglesworth would have heard the sobbing winds off the coast of New England; here where the very landscape seemed to conspire in rejecting his people. The minister would have laid in a creaking wooden bed, under rough wool blankets, and at the midnight hour listened to the battering of storms and nor'easters, much more violent than anything in his placid birthplace of Yorkshire. He would have heard the imagined (or sometimes real) war cries of the Wampanoag, the Abenaki, and the Narraganset who seemed to dwell as ghosts but a few miles from the rocky coast to which the settlers huddled here on their errand into the wilderness. In the panicked mind of the minister, the country itself seemed to always be chilled through with a shivering fever dream. For the Reverend Doctor Wigglesworth, pathetic fallacy was no aesthetic deficiency, but rather a necessary interpretative aspect of the world itself, one with crucial personal implications. Clouds and shoals and weather and seasons were all equally open to being read as clearly as scripture was – and sometimes what was interpreted were terrifying aspects of a terrifying world, especially for a man naturally predisposed to nervousness. God's providence still existed in this godless place, even here in the country of Satan's Throne. God's divine countenance still dwelled among every pine cone and smooth black beach rock, and it was the job of Puritan divines like Wigglesworth to read the landscape as clearly as they would parse the significance of a particular Hebrew conjugation in Daniel, or Greek declension in Revelation. And like those old books, the landscape of this New World signaled that the revealing was upon them; indeed the discovery of this fourth part of the world at the moment the true Christian remnant blasted her horn against the trumperies of the false Romish Whore of Babylon and signaled that the final seals in heaven would shortly be broken, for these were miraculous days of miraculous wonders, especially at the ends of the world where he awaited the end of the world.

And so, he wrote. As nature was but a language, he could enter into her conversations through quill and paper of his own, and as a contribution to that dialogue Rev. Wigglesworth produced the most popular book in colonial America; indeed, arguably one of the per capita most read works ever written by an American (and no doubt one which very few of you have ever heard of, much less read) – the epic apocalyptic poem *The Day of Doom*. So popular was *The Day of Doom* that virtually no complete copies of that first printing survive in their entirety, the pages worn away by the feverish repeated consultations of those who owned the books, the ink smudged off by the entropic readerly enthusiasm that is really a form of love. In colo-

nial New England the only book held closer to the bosom would
have been the Bible itself, and no other work of contemporary
literature would have occupied their imaginations as fully as
Wigglesworth's apocalyptic epic. If his book were as similarly
popular in the contemporary United States, adjusted for per capita population difference, then more than 17 million Americans
would own a copy of *The Day of Doom.* And in colonial New
England, libraries were not large; Harvard University's library
was founded in 1638 only a few decades before Wigglesworth
penned his epic, with an initial gift of only 400 books, less than
the collection in a contemporary Harvard professor's personal
collection. Remember too, individual copies would have been
shared; when the size of colonial New England families is considered, it is not unlikely that half of all homes owned a copy.
The Day of Doom went through ten printings, and even in the
early-nineteenth century it's reported that New Englanders
grew up hearing the jingle-jangle rhythms of Wigglesworth's
verse. From the crooked cow paths of muddy Boston to the frozen shoals of the cape and the red brick environs of Cambridge
and throughout all of New England, what thundered forth from
pulpits and was quoted in conversation and reflected upon in
private was the deceptively simplistic rhyming doggerel of one
Michael Wigglesworth. "Thus one and all, thus great and small,/
the rich as well as poor,/And those of place, as the most base,/do
stand their Judge before:/They are arraign'd, and there detain'd/
before Christ's judgement seat/With trembling fear their Doom
to hear,/and feel his angers heat."

There is sometimes a certain cringe among those of us who
study early American colonial poetry, a sense that the literature
of the time is deficient when compared to the richness of what
would come in the nineteenth and twentieth centuries. Anthologies will include the immaculate verse of Anne Bradstreet,
thicker collections will often see fit to include the metaphysical
speculations of Edward Taylor, but Wigglesworth, when he en-

dures, is mainly seen as a subject for specialists. And while the best of colonial American poetry can stand next to the canonical usual suspects of seventeenth-century English verse, it would take a special type of critical sophist to argue that Wigglesworth can compare to the triumphs of the decade in which he wrote, remembering that John Milton published *Paradise Lost* only five years after *The Day of Doom* was written. Part of me sometimes likes to defend Wigglesworth; and though no doubt he wouldn't consent with this particular reading of his work, I detect a gothic sensibility in his Puritan plain style, the proto-Augustan rhyming couplets giving the overall tenor of the poem not just a sort of wry and ironical singsong quality, but also a feeling of supreme unease, as if we're reading a particularly long, uncanny, and creepy nursery rhyme. His broad ballad meter makes his verse simple, but in that simplicity there is terror. Imagine a choir monotonously repeating, "For day and night, in their despight, /their torments smoak ascendeth:/Their pain and grief have no relief, /their anguish never endeth. /There must they lye, and never dye; /though dying every day; /There must they dying ever lye; and not consume away." *The Day of Doom* was unequivocally the first contemporary bestseller in American history, and though you have never heard of it, its legacy is profound for the moment it both initiated and also embodied. What *The Day of Doom* announced as clearly as the trumpets that heralded the breaking of the seals in Patmos' Revelation is that American civilization would not just be an apocalyptically obsessed one, but perhaps the most eschatologically inclined culture ever, and that this desire for a collective Thanatos would define what it means to be an American, for sometimes better and oftentimes for worse, across religion, ideology, and culture.

So, the aesthetic qualities of his poetry are less important than the sort of unseen, and uncommented on, fiery thread of what could be called *eschatomania*, which link his moment to ours. Here in the United States of Apocalypse we've always been obsessed with a particular aesthetic that might as well be termed the "American apocalyptic sublime," and though Wigglesworth inherited his chiliasm from older sources he made it distinctly American and traces of it are everywhere in our culture, both religious and secular. Many colonial Puritans thought that the New World held a certain eschatological promise, and that belief still defines our civil religion.

That the United States is a particularly apocalyptic-minded culture should not be a controversial claim. We have always perversely taken our own destruction as our own birthright. In the centuries since Wigglesworth, apocalypticism, and specifically a type of premillennial dispensationalism (which can often enough be secularized), has thrilled Americans across religious and ideological lines. We take an eroticized thrill in considering our own demise. How many times have we seen the skyline of Manhattan or the great monuments of Washington DC destroyed by invading armies, terrorists, natural disaster, asteroids, or space aliens? The actual destruction of some of those buildings, which people commonly remarked "looked like it was from a movie," could scarcely quench our insatiable thirst for tales of our own destruction.

In language eerily prescient of a nuclear attack, Wigglesworth wrote, "For at midnight broke forth a light, /which turn'd the night to day:/And speedily an hideous cry/did all the world dismay." Which puts me in mind of the passage from Cormac McCarthy's 2006 masterpiece of post-apocalyptic literary genre fiction *The Road,* where speaking of the unspecified calamity which ends civilization the nameless narrator explains that, "The clocks stopped at 1:17. A long shear of light and then a series of low concussions." Paul Boyar, a scholar of millenarian movements, writes that Wigglesworth "memorably pictured the Second Coming and Last Judgement as lightning-bolt eschatological events, with no reassuring hint of gradual betterment or an intervening Millennium." There has always been this tension in American culture between millennium and apocalypse, or perhaps more accurately between pre-millennialism and post-millennialism.

On the one hand there is the utopian allure of progress, think of John Winthrop's contention aboard the Arbela in 1630 that we shall be as a "city on a hill," or Martin Luther King's oft-quoted contention that "The arc of the moral universe is long, but it tends towards justice." But there are also our ever-present apocalyptic nightmares, which pulse like an ominous metronome implicitly and sometimes explicitly in our politics and culture. Wigglesworth writes, "God began to pour/Destruction the world upon, /in a tempestuous shower." The colonial Puritans were not just fearful but excited, just as we are when we read and consume our apocalyptic literature, television, and film. This is neither a liberal nor a conservative predilection, but rather an American one. This should not be read as condemnation, nor God forbid celebration, but rather simply as observation.

The American apocalyptic sublime is evident in all the usual places, from the jeremiads of the seventeenth century to your A.M. radio dial. And of course it has long been a vestige of popular culture, a common theme in genre fiction and film. From Stephen Vincent Benet's 1937 pre-nuclear era post-apocalyptic fable "By the Waters of Babylon" through the entire oeuvre of director Roland Emmerich, Americans have been enmeshed in a type of secular eschatology, the aforementioned *eschatomania*. The last decade and a half has seen the American apocalyptic sublime move from the genre ghettos of science fiction and horror to the esteemed shelves of literary fiction. In part a reaction to the apocalyptic traumas of 9/11, the Great Recession, and ecological collapse, and perhaps a manifestation of the writer's ever prescient ability to pick up on those historic frequencies that can only be heard with one's creative ear to the ground, literary fiction has seen a flowering of the American apocalyptic sublime. Critically acclaimed and often award winning, we've entered the renaissance of literary manifestations of the apocalyptic, of works that embody the unveiling inherent in Wigglesworth's moment when "Skies are rent asunder, /With mighty voice and hideous noise, /more terrible then Thunder." As exemplified by Cormac McCarthy's relentlessly dark post-apocalyptic travelogue *The Road*, a reading list of this moment in contemporary literary history could include Jim Crace's *The Pesthouse* (2008), Kevin Brockmeir's *The Illumination* (2012), Ben Marcus' *The Flame Alphabet* (2012), Lauren Groff's *Arcadia* (2012), Peter Heller's *The Dog Stars* (2013), Karen Thompson Walker's *The Age of Miracles* (2013), Tom Perrotta's *The Leftovers* (2014), Greg Hrbek's *Not on Fire, But Burning* (2015), Emily St. John Mandel's *Station Eleven* (2015), Edan Lepucki's *California* (2015), and Alexis M. Smith's *Marrow Island* (2016).

The works are divergent – from Lepucki's frighteningly realistic description of an incredibly divided nation with a rapidly fraying social contract to Marcus' depiction of language itself turning into a type of virus, or Groff's long-sweep Great American Novel beginning in a 1960's intentional community and ending in pandemic in our own near future to Crace's rewriting and reversing of the perennial American myth of westward expansion transposed onto a far primitive future where Americans await the arrival of a god named Abraham whom they find evidence for on copper medallions dispersed across the ruined North American landscape. But for all their variety, they share literary fiction's tone, style, and rhetoric. In language, narrative, pacing, and characterization they owe more to *The New Yorker* than *Amazing Tales*. The emergence of this movement, or collection, or trend, or whatever you want to call it is important for several reasons. As I mentioned earlier, these works are in part a direct reaction to the disastrous events of the twenty first century: the wars in Iraq and Afghanistan, the economic collapse, impending environmental cataclysm, and so on. With their descriptions of how the world can change irrevocably in one moment, they reenact the traumas of epoch-altering historical events. And they are all consummately American, especially in their evocation of capitalism's relation to Armageddon. Consider the passage in *The Road* where McCarthy's characters, a nameless boy and his father traipsing across a scarred wasteland, find that "On the outskirts of the city they came to a supermarket... By the door were two soft drink machines that had been tilted over into the floor and opened with a pry bar. Coins everywhere in the ash. He sat and ran his hand around the works of the gutted machines and in the second one it closed over a cold metal cylinder. He withdrew it slowly and sat looking at a Coca-Cola." What could be more American than that? Everyone is dead, the world is extinguished, but somehow that most American of products still endures. Even after the blasting of the trumpets you can still buy the world a Coke. Philosopher Frederic Jameson anticipated scenes just like this, writing that "Someone once said that it is easier to imagine the end of the world than to imagine the end of capitalism."

And the thing is, no matter how shackled or oppressed our monotonous lives may feel, we would still love a Coke. Who wouldn't? We simultaneously yearn to be liberated by the systems which constrain us as we still nestle into their comforts, and paradoxically apocalypse provides us a means to do both. In Mandel's achingly beautiful *Station Eleven,* which follows the almost medieval and carnivalesque Great Lakes meanderings of a group of Shakespearean actors in the decades after an extinction level epidemic has decimated the world, she pauses to reflect on all of the daily assumptions of life in late capitalism that have disappeared from her new world. Listing chlorinated swimming pools, baseball games, and airplanes, she finally ends with a description of something we all often claim to hate (or at least to have extreme annoyance with) while thrilling over its addictive hold on us: the internet and social media. She writes that after the end there shall be:

No more internet. No more social media, no more scrolling through litanies of dreams and nervous hopes and photographs of lunches, cries for help and expressions of contentment and relationship-status updates with heart icons whole or broken, plans to meet up later, please, complaints, desires, pictures of babies dressed as bears or peppers for Halloween. No more reading and commenting on the lives of others, and in so doing, feeling slightly less alone in the room. No more avatars.

Part of what is so striking about the new *eschatomania,* this new manifestation of the American apocalyptic sublime, is how eerily familiar it seems. As Wigglesworth wrote in the language of his dominant faith, so to do our new authors write in the vocabulary of our totalizing religion. And as his readers' simultaneously feared and desired apocalypse, so do ours.

Wigglesworth's audiences got a thrill out of Christ appearing in the sky to inaugurate the millennium as surely as modern audiences derived a strange pleasure from McCarthy's similarly world-ending nocturnal luminescence in his novel. In the promised land of America, apocalypse is not something just for Holy Roller sermons and Hal Lindsey screeds, for evangelicals clutching *Left Behind* books or viewers of *The 700 Club.* We're all Wigglesworth's children, and the secular can match Tim La-Haye with *The Stand,* or *The Hunger Games,* or wondering who Negan is going to club to death this Sunday night on AMC. We get off on this stuff, always have, always will (that is at least until the apocalypse actually comes, and worrying prophecies always have had a way of being self-fulfilling). While we're certainly not the first civilization to view ourselves as an apocalyptic "redeemer nation," to borrow the historian Ernest Tuveson's memorable phrase, we're certainly the only one to achieve the status of superpower, and furthermore the first to invent the mechanism by which apocalypse could actually be literally and materially made manifest though human hands in the form of nuclear weapons. British philosopher John Gray wrote in his book *Black Mass: Apocalyptic Religion and the Death of Utopia* (the one indispensable book on political theology in the last decade) that American culture is defined by "a current of the millenarian ferment that passed from medieval chiliasm through the English Revolution. The sense of universal mission that is such a prominent feature of American politics is an outflow from this ancient stream." And central to this sense of mission is that apocalypse must itself mean the dissolution of America, that the two possibilities are intimately intertwined. Americans find it impossible to envision a world without us, so it is easier to simply envision there not being a world at all. The fear that we must all have is what happens when a nation that sees itself as the one indispensable empire in world history, against all evidence, perceives itself to be minimized? How dangerous is a snake in its death throes? And how terrifying is the country that invented the means of destruction which Patmos could only hallucinate? We've never been the land of the free and the home of the brave so much as the land of utopian and millennial dreams and apocalyptic nightmares, a complementary if paradoxical pair. What finally may draw us to the American apocalyptic sublime are not just the vagaries of aesthetics, but the anxious sour stomach of prophecy. What the new apocalyptic authors of the twenty-first century offer us are not just reflections of what has already happened, but horrifyingly they may also offer us transcriptions of that which they heard when they placed their ear to the ground; the increasingly loud frequencies of those four sets of horse hooves galloping towards us from those arid deserts in the direction of dusk.

I Dreamed I saw Bob Dylan: On an American Prophet

There is no living American poet who deserves the characterization of being a prophet more than Bob Dylan. Both a product of his land and his land a product of him, Dylan the prophet has been Jeremiah by the rivers of Babylon, blind Milton dictating his verse, and William Blake opening the doors of perception. As a poet and prophet he has no ultimate muse or Lord, save for the collective American vernacular, which he gladly appropriated or stole from, in that process of cultural hybridization which is necessary to produce anything new or true. Robert Zimmerman, the good Jewish boy from Minnesota, was anointed by Woody Guthrie while on the road to the Village, where he borrowed the name of a Celtic bard and became Dylan. Along the way he filched from the blues, Scots-Irish folk music, country and western, rag-time, rock and roll, T.S. Eliot, Ezra Pound, Uncle Walt, and the rest of what Greil Marcus astutely calls "that old, weird America." That Dylan is a mercurial character is an observation made so often that it has become trite – yet it is also true.

And in that stations of the cross by which those in the sect of Dylan mark their devotion – from the Gaslight on MacDougal, to plugging in at Newport, going electric at the Royal Albert Hall, crashing his motorcycle at Woodstock, finding Jesus and then losing him again – there is now a new station on that *Via Crucis*. There was shock in 2016 when it was announced that Dylan had won the Nobel Prize in Literature, an unprecedented award for a pop musician. That shock has continued into this week, when in true Dylan fashion, calling forth nothing so much as the (faux?) belligerent press conferences as recorded in D.A. Pennebaker's classic *Dont Look Back*, Mr Zimmerman has yet to return the Swedish Academy's phone calls. So far, the only comment that Dylan seems to have had (other than one obligatory social media announcement put out by his publicist no doubt) is the addition of an obscure Sinatra tune entitled "Why Try To Change Me Now?" into his concert rotation.

Confusion and cynicism were certainly on ample display, as was genuine and legitimate criticism. Stephen Metcalf at *Slate* writes that "Bob Dylan is a musician and not a poet...You don't go to the hardware store for oranges, as they say, and if you want poetry, you don't go to Bob Dylan," to which I would reply that psalms have always been songs, and that even Orpheus carried a lyre. Anna North at *The New York Times* fairly and humanely writes that "Mr. Dylan's writing is inseparable from his music. He is great because he is a great musician, and when the Nobel committee gives the literature prize to a musician, it misses the opportunity to honor a writer." I do not agree with her assessment.

While acknowledging that the Nobel Prize is always contingent, politicized, subjective, and influenced by forces far beyond objective aesthetic criteria (whatever those are), the committee accomplished one important thing in awarding Dylan the prize. They've somehow gotten seemingly everyone in the press and on social media talking about what literature is, and what deserves to have laurels bestowed. But you don't need Cultural Studies with its democratization of the text, or high modernism with its fragments shored against our ruins, to see poetry in music. After all, David sung his compositions in the Temple, he had no need of the white page or the printing press. Whether Dylan is "literature" or not (and I think the word "literature" can be as mercurial as Mr. Zimmerman's identity), the question alone has always been one of the driving issues of culture, and that a committee of ossified old Swedes has us talking about it on Facebook is notable enough. There are certainly legitimate issues to ask about questions of genre and influence, the definition of poetry, and the passing over of important marginalized voices. That those conversations are happening on internet threads and on

editorial pages and not just in graduate seminar rooms is an unmitigated good.

But what was I saying again? Oh, right, that Dylan is not just
a poet, but a prophet (see, I can one up even the Nobel committee!). Certainly, few pop stars, and probably none still living, though Leonard Cohen was still alive when Dylan won the
prize, and he certainly also would have been worthy for the hon-
or approach that prophetic mode which Milton, Whitman, Blake,
and Ginsberg composed in. Listen to a few verses of "A Hard
Rain's a-Gonna Fall," especially during this season, and tell me
that you don't hear a voice in the wilderness foretelling Jerusalem's destruction. Taking a seventeenth-century ballad from
the English border country, and marrying it to American nuclear
paranoia, Dylan sang of a "black branch with blood that kept
dripping," and "guns and sharp swords in the hands of young
children," all prophetic visions from "the depths of the deepest
black forest." Or on "Desolation Row," one of his unmitigated
masterpieces, when in the first sentence he alludes to Moloch's
inferno where both slavery and the Shoah originated, singing
"They're selling postcards of the hanging/They're painting the
passports brown."

Langston Hughes, himself the author of immaculate lyrics
firmly based in the oral and musical tradition of the African
American twelve-bar blues, wrote, "I, too, sing America," for
America has always been a thing to sing, "essentially the greatest poem" as Uncle Walt said, and perhaps the greatest of songs,
too. Whitman declared that, "I hear America singing, the varied carols I hear," and Dylan supplied a few hundred verses to
that song. In Dylan, with his varied, quicksilver reinventions, we
have the Whitmanesque reconciling of contradictions. Dylan is a
trickster god, just like the country that was his father, and in his
lyrics and music there is the marriage of dynamic east coast with
stolid Midwest, agrarian South with urban North, reactionary
conservative and transgressive radical, Judaism and Christian-

ity, white and black. Despite his dalliances with the Judaism of his youth when he was "Talkin' Hava Negeilah Blues," the New Left of the '60s, or the born again evangelical Christianity of the '70s, at the end, the source of all of Dylan's poetry is his God, and the name of that God is America, even if he dreamt that he saw St. Augustine along the way.

Because when I say that Dylan is an American prophet, that's precisely what I mean, and I argue that the Nobel committee's awarding of the prize to such an unconventional nominee is an acknowledgment of a particularly American genius for religion. Harold Bloom, always hewing close to the (not inaccurate) principle that it is better to be interesting than it is to be right, claimed in his 1991 *The American Religion* that over the course of two centuries the United States developed an idiosyncratic, heterodox, heretical, Gnostic faith which long ago replaced Protestant Christianity as the authentic religion of the nation. He writes that, "We are a very religiously mad culture, furiously searching for the spirit, but each of us is subject and object of one quest, which must be for the original self, a spark or breath in us that we are convinced goes back to before the creation."

What does that describe more than the cycles of continual creation and destruction which Dylan creatively engages, the constant self-invention, the sin and the redemption? If we're rugged individualists in anything, it's in forging our own religions, lest we be enslaved by those of another man's. Dylan simply bootstrapped his way into a new scripture. Bloom explains that the "American self is not the Adam of Genesis but is a more primordial Adam, a man before there were men or women. Higher and earlier than the angels, this true Adam is as old as God, older than the Bible, and is free of time, unstained by mortality. Whatever the social or political consequences of this vision, its imaginative strength is extraordinary." Extraordinary indeed! Or, as the titular character from the Coen Brothers Dylanesque homage *Inside Llewellyn Davis* put it, "If it was never new, and it never gets old, then it's a folk song."

Finally, there is the poetry itself. The strangely melancholic amphetamine jitters, awe, and reverence of "Ain't it just like the night to play tricks when you're tryin' to be so quiet?" The broadsheet, fairy-tale imagery of "She can take the dark out of the nighttime/ And paint the daytime black." The intimations of mortality and apocalypse in "Shadows are falling and I've been here all day...Behind every beautiful thing there's been some kind of pain." The psychotic intensity and honesty of "Don't know if I saw you, if I would kiss you or kill you/It probably wouldn't matter to you anyhow." The prophetic injunction to justice in "But you who philosophize disgrace and criticize all fears/Take the rag away from your face/Now ain't the time for your tears." The understated, ironic pain in "Most of the time/ I'm clear focused all around... I don't even notice she's gone/ Most of the time." And yes, the bulk of the pathos in that last line, or any of a dozen of his, or a hundred of them, is in the performance, the way he uncertainly pauses after what seems a definitive declaration only to mitigate it by wryly telling us that the previous statement is true only "most of the time." The collected lyrics of Bob Dylan are magnificent, but it's true that organized on the page they do not match the technical acumen in prosody one sees in an Auden, Stevens, or Eliot. But, if rhythm, rhyme, enjambment, end-stopping and so on are aspects of the poet's trade, there is no reason why performance can't be either, for poetry was always sung before it was ever read (indeed as drama is meant to be acted). Caedmon's hymn reached the ears of his fellow monks before it was ever scratched into goat skin.

No less a tweedy old critic than the Miltonist Christopher Ricks (controversially) claimed that, "The case for denying Dylan the title of poet could not summarily, if at all, be made good by any open-minded close attention to the words and his ways with them," and the Nobel committee agreed with that (even if maybe Dylan himself didn't). What they acknowledged was that in the body of Dylan's poetic work is a reservoir of the beautiful American vernacular, Whitman's "tongues of nations," an expansive, large, democratic vocabulary capable of expressing those axioms of faith which were delivered among the nations of this land. In recognizing the corpus of his songs as not just literature, but great literature, it took an institution of foreign ears and foreign eyes to demonstrate to Americans, in this, our season of ugly nativism, that there are alternative and expansive ways of conceiving our nationality. For that, Dylan is a prophet and a poet, whether you see fit to grant him an arbitrary award or not.

Remember that the Devil is Quite a Gentleman

The Cathars of thirteenth-century Languedoc, ensconced on their hilltop cathedral at Montségur where they made their last stand, cut an unmistakably romantic figure. Like the Zealots at Masada, the Albigensians of Provence held on to the last man, after decades of military engagement with both the French crown and the Church. Eventually the Crusaders would break through the fortifications on a sunny Lenten day in 1244, after the Cathars had nearly held on for a year, the last of their kind. The survivors, all of them "Perfects," as their faith called them, were immolated at the base of their castle, in a place that has come to be called the *prat dels cremats*.

One should note that among these Perfects were numerous women, attracted to a feminine gospel where Mary Magdalene was more important than St. Peter and human souls were sexless. For the crusaders who murdered the Cathars of Languedoc, the belief that there was no distinction in the gender of a soul was among a set of heresies that were devilish enough to warrant the slaughter of those believers without regard to their gender.

Only fifty years before that, St. Dominic had held his famous disputation with these heretics, consigning both orthodox and Cathar holy texts to the flames as a test of their divine validity. When the orthodox books supposedly levitated, unscathed, out of the inferno, Dominic claimed a spectacular victory over his adversaries. And yet, in the smoke and fog of Inquisition, might it not be hard to tell which books were which? Something so profoundly true that it borders on cliché (which are really only the truths that have withstood the longest) is Heine's observation that, "Where they burn books, so too will they in the end burn human beings." There is, of course, a direct line from Dominic's burning of books to the eventual burning of bodies, and half a century isn't even that long of an interim. What then were the teachings of these pacifistic, vegetarian, celibate Cathars that the Church found so disturbing, that they felt the urgency to so effectively erase the entire denomination (for who among us has ever met an Albigensian)?

The Cathars pushed to its logical conclusion that old truth, held by many groups before, that maintains that Lucifer is the prince of our world. They understood that if Satan is our potentate, than he is our creator too, and that his acts are enumerated upon in the Holy Books of the very Church that now persecuted the Cathars. The *Rex Mundi* is not God, but Satan. That much was orthodox enough. But the Cathars said that the two were really the same thing, that the Dark One was the demiurge of our creation and that a greater, purer, truer God dwelled beyond the realms of our profane cosmos. Of course claiming that God is really Satan was, to that same Church, an unmistakably diabolical assertion. And so the Cathars, who loved their true God and feared their true Satan, were killed by Catholics, who loved their true God and feared their true Satan as well. All of it was a minor question of correctly identifying the connection between names and identity.

One of the tragedies of the demonic is its ambiguity. It's never clear who the Devil really is, and one man's Devil can be another's God. The accusation that one is an agent of Satan can itself be a powerful tool for Satan. The innocent are often eliminated because they are accused of being diabolical, but the very act that eliminates them is also authentically diabolical. One of the other tragedies is that indiscriminate accusations of being demonic in some sense nullify the very power of accusing someone of being demonic – especially when the accuser himself is the one who is diabolical.

That the Albigensians saw their persecutors as demonic, and that their persecutors saw the Albigensians as such, should not be read as an endorsement of unthinking false equivalence, or victim-blaming. In the sieges across southern France that marked the dreary calendar of the late twelfth and early thirteenth centuries, there is only one side which was Satanic, and it was not those burnt at the foot of Montségur. Indeed the orthodox, aka the mainstream, aka the normative, aka the majority, achieved self-definition through exclusion, and as such the Cathar were among several "devilish types," marginalized groups that those in power could project and punish anxieties about their own fallenness onto. Cathars were of a devilish type known as heretics, but they were not the only group upon which the orthodox saw nightmares, and so enacted those nightmares upon the oppressed. The prince of this world is very adept at seeing devils everywhere but in his own mirror.

If heretics were one such group, then certainly Jews are perennial members of that confraternity of the excluded. In 1543 the learned but bawdy, pious but exuberant, devoted yet sometimes obscene former monk named Martin Luther put all of his scholastic skills into penning 65,000 words of unmitigated dreck. Luther's *On the Jews and Their Lies* may reflect the author's religious anxieties and frustrations over the unequal enthusiasm for Reformation in Europe, but it's also hateful, scurrilous, and dangerous propaganda, which makes ample use of accusing the dejected, marginalized, and powerless of somehow being devils. Luther looked at the relatives of Christ, and loudly declared them to be cousins of the Devil. The theologian claimed that synagogues needed to be razed; rabbis harassed, exiled, and murdered, Torah scrolls and the Talmud burned, and all their possessions confiscated. Progenitor of the Reformation that he was, Luther wrote that as concerns the Jews, "we are at fault in not slaying them."

Writing of the synagogue, the center of Jewish life since the destruction of the Temple, Luther says that it is a "defiled bride, yes, an incorrigible whore and an evil slut." Note that as regards the status of women, the reformer is in agreement with his old nemesis the Catholic Church, who, at Montségur three hundred years before, enthusiastically put to the blaze and blade women Perfects of the Cathar church. Luther's horror and anxiety at religious difference and the Other in his midst is manifested by transposing what he finds shocking about the female body onto the Jewish one. As if a matter of self-evident, axiomatic truth, Luther simply states that the Jews are "surely possessed by all devils." His call to expel all the Jews from Germany, and to murder those left behind, was not attempted by authorities during his lifetime, but note that Luther's 455th birthday was commemorated with the atrocity we've come to call Kristallnacht. Dehumanization and demonization are a tandem pair. The Jews suffered, and still suffer, by being conflated with the devilish.

As is often the case with those who are marginalized through conflation with the demonic, anti-Jewish rhetoric of the medieval, early modern, and modern world often focuses on perceived physical difference. Examine the Netherlandish painter Hieronymus Bosch's work *Christ Carrying the Cross,* which was finished in 1516, a year before Luther would nail his complaint to the cathedral door in Wittenberg, and now hangs in the museum at Ghent. At the center of the tableaux is a pale, goyish man of sorrows, who is surrounded by a legion of Jewish faces depicted as swarthy and leering, all wide hell-mouth sneers and thick lips, bestial features and hooked noses. Medieval art often depicted Jews as indistinguishable from their gentile neighbors, with markers of difference defined by clothing, such as the distinctive and legally obligatory conical *Judenhut,* rather than by physiognomy. Only fourteen years before *Christ Carrying the Cross,* the Italian painter Lucca Signorelli produced his massive fresco *Sermons and Deeds of the Antichrist.* Here we have a depiction of that who is most fully human, as well as fully devil, in the infernal hypostatic union of the Antichrist. Signorelli depicts a red, reptilian Satan with horns curved above his smooth, hairless head, whispering into the ear of his son, who looks out at his audience with cool, cunning eyes. As if to acknowledge the central tension of centuries of Christian anti-Semitism, Signorelli's Antichrist looks unnervingly like Christ, save for a few features meant to represent as characteristically Jewish: the curl of *payot* hanging from the side of his head, his beard rabbinical.

This is true, of course, for any group which the dominant culture defines itself in opposition to. In terms of anti-Semitic libel, many of these markers of supposed physical differentiation are well-known, and, disturbingly, endure into modern depictions. But there are more obscure slurs from Luther, Bosch, and Signorelli's era which rightly strike a modern audience as strange. For Bosch and Signorelli the Jewish body could be twisted, obscene, demonic, but it was marked by another quality as well, one which was viewed as complementary and equivalent to those previously listed properties, and that was that the Jewish body was often explicitly feminized. After all, it was in the *De secretis mulierum,* a 1493 French gynecological text falsely attributed to Albertus Magnus, that the anonymous author claimed that Jewish men menstruate. The anti-Semitism and misogyny of the author was such that he frequently conflates the word *"menstrum"* for the Latin word "monstrum." And so, the imagined monstrous body of the Devil was not just Jewish, but also that of a woman.

This category of the perennial demonic Other may be the most enduring. For if there is a commonality in the fear and oppression of heretics and Jews, then the devil has just as often been depicted as a woman. The inborn misogyny of the western mind is such that, like the Devil himself, its machinations and influences can seem invisible to those not personally affected by it. If the eras I have recounted were ones of crusade and pogrom, then they were inevitably also periods of profound misogynist violence, all the more so because gender violence through those centuries into today is so often rationalized, reduced, or relegated to a subset of some other injustice. From the late fifteenth to the early eighteenth century, at least 60,000 men and women would be executed as witches, as consorts and collaborators with the Devil.

Some revisionist historians have estimated that a more accurate number is close to a half a million; still others place the full accounting of deaths at over a million. Certainly many men found themselves upon the gallows, the scaffold, and the pyre, but the uncomfortable fact remains that the bulk of the deaths were of women, and that the witch-hunts of the early modern period enacted a profound violence towards women who were identified as devils. Arthur Miller may have made John Proctor the hero of *The Crucible,* but he was only one of six men to be martyred in Massachusetts; the other fourteen were all women. Salem was an uncharacteristically late example of a witch-trial; the divisions are even starker if the phenomena is viewed in its entirety. Of the murdered in Europe and America, many demographers estimate that fully 85% were women.

Radical scholars have written of the witch-trials as a holocaust of women, a veritable gendered genocide, and even if most historians don't concur with that particular interpretation of the events, the essentially misogynist nature of the phenomenon remains undeniable. That women suffered the brunt of the persecutions, and that this violence was justified by affectively calling collective womanhood the Devil is apparent in reading the historical record. The German Dominicans Heinrich Kramer and Jacob Sprenger's 1487 *Malleus Maleficarum* was the classic witch-hunting guide, utilized centuries later by both Catholics like Nicholas Rémy and Protestants such as Matthew Hopkins. In it, Kramer writes that women have a "temperament towards flux," and like the mythical menstruating male Jews, it is this mercurial tendency towards change which makes women suspect.

Witch-trials were a shockingly contemporary phenomenon; like so many aspects of barbarity associated with the medieval past they were more a product of a modernizing present. There are arguments about what exactly the events signified (such as interpreting them as the final depaganization of Europe), and of who the worse perpetrators were, Catholics or Protestants (this in part depends on the sectarian allegiance of the scholar answering the question). But that witches were understood as a particular feminine category is not doubted; as Kramar and Sprenger write, "woman, therefore, is evil as a result of nature because she doubts more quickly in the faith."

Rémy, the French magistrate charged with witch persecutions, wrote that it was not "unreasonable that this scum of humanity, should be drawn chiefly from the feminine sex." Even if the Devil is a man, then his consort is Lilith, and it is the succubae who threatens to emasculate, castrate, and denigrate the fragile masculinity of those who define their identity through the domination of women. Wounded patriarchal pride has a particular fear of the perceived sexual vivacity of women, Rémy concurred, writing that "The Devil uses them so, because he knows that women love carnal pleasures, and he means to bind them to his allegiance by such agreeable provocations." Consider a print in the Italian priest Francesco Maria Guazzo's *Compendium Maleficarum* of 1608. Entitled "The Obscene Kiss," the picture depicts the supposed satanic sacrament of Osculum infame, that is, the group performance of analingus upon the sphincter of the Devil. Here, Guazzo (or rather, his illustrator) presents several respectable women, distinguished by the stiff and starched collars and the long velvet dress ruffles of seventeenth-century fashion, all patiently waiting in line to kiss the asshole of a caprine and winged demon. Note that it was a medieval text, *Errores Haereticorum*, which provided a dubious etymology for the name of our old friends the Cathars, claiming that it was derived "from the term cat, whose posterior they kiss, in whose form Satan appears to them." Close to two hundred years later, and in 1798, the great Spanish artist Francisco Goya finished his painting *The Witches' Sabbath*, which improves in technical acumen the themes of Guazzo while sacrificing none of the misogyny. For here is a democratic assembly of women; and only women, young, old, rich, poor, offering up the sacrifice of an infant to a massive Baphomet sitting upon his hind legs, green garlands wrapped about his horns.

Of course the hatred of women has never only been of an occult or superstitious nature. Patriarchy has often been fine with using "devil" as a mere metaphorical adornment in expressing the fear of women. Nowhere is this more clear than in the rage which surrounds the possibility of a woman sovereign; it is not only fear of women's sexuality and reproductive capabilities that motivates misogyny across politics and religion, it is also the specter of female leadership. Even with the biblical precedents of Judith, Ruth, Esther, Deborah, and Mary, women's collective agency was strongly resisted. As an example of arch-misogyny, regard the somber and dour founder of Presbyterianism, the Scottish divine John Knox. While exiled in theocratic Geneva, and with a head full of total depravity, unconditional election, limited atonement, and double predestination, Knox penned a nasty little pamphlet entitled *The First Blast of the Trumpet Against the Monstrous Regiment of Women*. Perhaps a misogynistic artifact of a misogynistic age, but the fact remains that Knox's words were so incendiary that he kept his authorship anonymous, so that not even John Calvin (not exactly a proponent of women's rights) would know who wrote that to "promote a woman to bear rule, superiority, dominion, or empire above any realm, nation, or city, is repugnant to nature."

No doubt Knox hoped that the word "trumpet" in the title would connote Gabriel's horn, and the breaking of Revelation's seals. Yet even in the sixteenth century the word "trumpet," appropriately enough considering the language of Knox's pamphlet, had another meaning. Knox's fellow Scotsman Gavin Douglas, in his 1513 translation of *The Aeneid*, wrote of the "fals man, by dissait and wordis fair/With wanhope trumpit the lele luwair." Thus, Knox's audience could read the "first blast of the trumpet" as also signifying a first blast of flatulent nonsense, one of those moments when synchronicity alerts us to the true meaning of things, hidden in her literal words.

Knox, he of a cold heart and a cold gospel, was a victim of the Marian persecutions when he lived in England, and that horrific experience, representatively described in works like John Foxe's *Acts and Monuments,* perhaps inculcated him into a particularly virulent chauvinism. With Mary on her throne in Westminster, and his fellow countryman, that other Mary, Queen of Scots, in Edinburgh, Knox polemicized against the dread Virago he associated with Catholic women monarchs, writing that they were "repugneth to nature" and that "al women" were "foolishe, madde and phrenetike" when compared to men. In Knox's estimation the Devil was the princess of the world, and the Catholic Church with its veneration of Mary and the Saints was only so much effeminacy. For Knox, the sitting of a Queen on a King's throne was a vile abomination and affront to God himself.

Forever looking westward to his British home, he awaited news that the Babylonian captivity was over and that he could return upon the installation of a Protestant monarch. His wish was fulfilled a year after his diatribe was written, and that harlot Queen Mary died. But, let it not be said that the Lord does not have a sense of humor, for Knox's prayed-for, crowned, Protestant savior would be named Elizabeth. And his return to Edinburgh would be stalled, as he had not been issued the proper documents to travel unhampered through the Kingdom of England. It turns out that the new monarch had read his *The First Blast of the Trumpet Against the Monstrous Regiment of Women.* Not surprisingly, she did not agree with Knox's argument.

One need not have too much guilt at feeling a bit of *Schadenfreude* concerning Reverend Knox's predicament, but the Devil of marginalization, of prejudice, of bigotry, of hatred, of oppression sadly does not give up so easily. Of course the perseveration on binary oppositions, and the identification of a convenient Other as demonized scapegoat is intrinsic to the oppressive system we've always lived under; we are always prisoners in that dungeon. Heretics, Jews, women, and other Others were the perennial outsiders of the past, but let us not commit to the chronocentrism that embraces the fallacy of positivist progress. In some cases, the aesthetics haven't even changed that much. Today screeds are composed on smart phones and computers instead of on vellum and parchment, and the details of who exactly are the dejected and spurned may have altered, but that there are the dejected and spurned is a constant. There is a direct genealogy between the marginalization of groups then and now; between the accusations of Luther and Bosch, and the black legends which impugn the immigrant; between the libels of Kramer and Sprenger and the diminishment of sexual violence and the legislation against women's reproductive freedom. We are not so far from the electric potency and that corrupt trick which sees the Devil everywhere but in our own reflections. Projecting that accusation of devilry onto your enemy, so as to acquire a bit of that profane power offered to Christ in the desert, remains a venerable tradition among those that seek that supremacy that is the domain of the prince of this world. For, what else could embolden someone to stand in public, say, in Missouri (that most wholesome and middle-American of places), and with an accusatory and unironic point of the short finger declare, yet once again, that a woman is "the Devil?"

With apologies to Baudelaire, the greatest trick the Devil ever pulled isn't convincing the world that he doesn't exist; it was convincing the world that those whom he persecutes are actually the demonic ones. Of course it is in the Devil's best interest that we can't identify him, and what better way to achieve that than to confuse whom the Devil actually is, and all the more evil an accomplishment if he diverts that attention to the very people whom he wrongs? Simply because the wrong people are often labeled as devils does not mean that no man is ever a devil. The Other is often charged with being Satanic; the ultimate irony is that the dispossessed are always the children of God. It is the one who impugns them with being demonic that must himself be the actual Devil. But by embracing such relativism, in questioning the validity of the entire enterprise, the demonic calls into question the very words we can use to identify him, and thus, perhaps, eliminates the utility of a potent vocabulary. If one looks for the Devil in our modern world, then it is best to find he who most exuberantly claims that title for others.

American Jezebels: Let Us Now Praise Anne Hutchinson and Mary Dyer

In 1637, Mary Dyer of Boston gave a monstrous birth and its midwife was Anne Hutchinson.

Both were Puritans of-a-kind: Hutchinson the notorious advocate of the so-called "covenant of free grace," she of the antinomian controversy. Her patient, Dyer, would ultimately reject the scriptural inerrancy of her Puritan brethren in favor of the inner light of the Quakers. Both endure as symbols of American theological individualism, the logical culmination of Luther's call for a "priest-hood of all believers." In their example they anticipated Emersonian self-reliance, following Whitman's call to "dismiss whatever insults your own soul." In 1634, Hutchinson and her husband devotedly followed their minister John Cotton from Boston, England to Boston, New England after he'd been dismissed by Archbishop William Laud due to the minister's Puritan enthusiasms. When she boarded the *Griffin* for America, at the age of 43, she had just given birth to her fourteenth child. She would give birth one more time before she died. And two years after emigration, she would find herself accused of having "troubled the peace of the commonwealth and churches" – all by leading what a modern might assume to be innocuous women's bible studies. A year after Dyer's hideous progeny, and Hutchinson's heterodox religious stance would come to embroil all of Massachusetts in its first major internal crisis, a theological debate which seemingly pitched faith against works, grace against the law, and women against men. It would become the first full-blown domestic emergency of this godly City on a Hill, one with profound implications not just for the Puritans who were citizens of that imaginary community, but indeed for the country that claimed to be born from their precepts. Ultimately both women would die for the sins of these godly men who led that failed experiment on the frontier.

Twenty years Hutchinson's junior, Dyer exhibited similar resolve when she faced persecution. And as she was born two decades before Hutchinson, so would Dyer come to die some two decades after her mentor, under differing circumstances but in an equally violent manner. Theologically they would differ as well; though there are arguably similarities between the antinomian gospel taught by Hutchinson to the women of Boston (and eventually the men, as those initial groups proved so popular that the male population clambered for their own homebound bible studies as well) and Dyer's ultimate Quakerism, but they are certainly not reducible to one another. Perhaps Hutchinson would have gravitated to the Society of Friends had her life not ended when it did, perhaps she wouldn't have. But what both were united in was an absolute commitment to the individual's freedom of conscience. In that sense, what the inner light and the covenant of free grace shared was precisely that – freedom. While still in Britain, Hutchinson's family were of the middling classes, her father a Church of England priest with Puritan sensibilities who used to delight young Anne and her siblings with mocking imitations of the Bishop of London; Mary's childhood circumstances were modest enough that we don't even know her maiden name.

These two different women, united in that commitment to spiritual freedom, were allies during the antinomian controversy which threatened to upend the growing community, and they were forever conflated in the fevered brains of the men who were their prosecutors, who saw not just an ideological affinity between the two, but indeed a conspiracy of monstrosity as well, based on the delivery of Dyer's unfortunate miscarriage. Both of them were theological renegades, of the type that Americans celebrate, having long since rejected our Puritan errand into the wilderness, embracing the anarchic possibilities of heresy. We think of colonial New England as a dour place of dour men with dour wives and dour children preaching a cold gospel in church services of half a day, but that exact same time and place produced visionary heretical prophets like Roger Williams, Thomas Morton, and for good-measure the witch John Proctor. And of course Mary Dyer and Anne Hutchinson.

To a non-specialist the kerfuffle which has come to be designated as the antinomian or free grace controversy seems to largely be an exercise in what Freud called the "narcissism of small differences." Indeed in as consummately a post-theological age as our own, words like "soteriology" move few, even those who profess to be Christians. In one ironic sense the ultimate victory of Hutchinson's revolution has been the embrace of a certain *sola Affectio*, where questions of belief are settled neither by tradition nor by scripture, but rather by feeling. Obviously these differences were anything but small to those involved in the controversy. Initially the conflict emerged between the respective partisans of two different ministers, Reverend John Wilson who was the more traditionally minded, and Hutchinson's favored authority, Cotton. Departing perhaps more rhetorically than theologically from the Puritan consensus, Cotton argued that all members of the elect are as if a "mystic participant in the transcendent power of the Almighty," and that salvation is attained entirely through the free impartation of grace. As far as Protestant orthodoxy goes there is nothing overly unconventional about any of this, and yet Cotton's disparagement of works drew the accusation (as it would towards his most famous parishioner) of antinomianism, that is of being "against the law."

In Wilson's preaching, Hutchinson detected advocacy for the position that salvation is granted through works, which to her pious Protestant nose had the stench of popery about it. Wilson of course was as committed a Calvinist as the rest of the assembled godly, but Hutchinson saw in him a lack of enthusiasm, which more damningly evidenced a lack of "sanctification." Wilson, it must be said if the contemporary testimonies are to be believed, was a right son-of-a-bitch whose chief pleasure in life when not condemning heretics was annoyingly making anagrams out of his friends' names. Ultimately he'd be able to claim Mary and Anne's lives, as well as that of the "witch" Ann Hibbins. Hutchinson contrasted Wilson to Cotton, for she felt that the latter deeply, intuitively, and fully understood salvation not to be a matter of man's individual striving towards good but entirely the freely given and undeserved imparted gift of God. If she had kept her negative opinions of Wilson to herself than perhaps all could have been avoided, but Hutchinson did not suffer a fool gladly, and in the increasingly popular discussions of scripture which she led, she did not hesitate to tell all assembled – whether man or woman – her feelings. And not just about Wilson, but indeed on the rest of the divines of Boston who she felt had departed from true doctrine. Committed readers of Augustine and Calvin both, the differences between Cotton and Wilson would scarcely register to us today, but despite the prosecution's protestations, what was most galling about Hutchinson's critique was not the critique itself but Hutchinson. Her example, of women's teaching and preaching, threatened the political order and the social cohesion of Boston more than scholastic pronouncements or scriptural exegesis ever could. That is because the greatest argument which she had was herself, which of course made that argument all the more dangerous.

So this stiff-necked and obstinate woman was put on trial. She was not tried by her peers – for she had none. Nor was she tried by "Elders," for she said she did not recognize the assembled men as such. The accusations were helpfully summarized by her accuser and judge, the sometimes-governor John Winthrop, who on October 1st, 1636 wrote of "her two dangerous errors: 1. That the person of the Holy Ghost dwells in a justified person. 2. That no sanctification can help to evidence to us our justification." Her charges were antinomianism and familalism. The first had those libertine implications of standing against the

170

law, the second referred to the strange and beautiful doctrine whose believers advocated for the possibility of a type of utopian perfectionism on this Earth, and which had been associated with the heretics of Munster known as the Family of Man who emerged from the communist theocracy of that German city immolated by a combined Catholic and Lutheran army in the sixteenth century. This "Mrs. Hutchinson, a member of the church at Boston," as described by Winthrop, was "a woman of ready wit and a bold spirit," and as such was not without her defenders, including Henry Vane, who was a former governor of aristocratic forbearance and old world manners, the minister John Wheelwright, and John Cotton of course. But the list of powerful detractors was longer, including not just Winthrop and Wilson, but Zachariah Symmes, Thomas Dudley, Simon Bradstreet, John Endecott and so on, all in their smart black smocks with their rounded Puritan haircuts, staring down at the defiant woman who refused to recant her belief in the person of the Holy Ghost dwelling in the heart of a justified person. And she knew who the justified people were. And they were not these men. And of course whether defender or detractor what they all were was men. And in that fact Hutchinson did not have a choice.

She of course had plenty of allies in the community, not least of whom was the unfortunate girl that she had tended to with such compassion during that difficult birth a year before. Ultimately Winthrop would have his way. Vane had returned to an England on fire with revolution, the power of other sympathizers waned, and Hutchinson would be convicted, excommunicated, and exiled from the community. Hutchinson walked out of the magistrate's chambers with unblinking forward gaze and head aloft, holding the hand of Dyer as she progressed down the aisle. An observer records that a man in the crowd asked Hutchinson if she would recant, to which she replied, "Better to be cast out of the Church than to deny Christ." Winthrop inquired as to the identity of the young woman consoling Hutchinson, which is how he discovered the alleged monstrous birth. Kept secret and known only to the women who had witnessed it, and to Reverend Cotton who had counseled its burial lest Boston's ecclesiastical authorities use the unfortunate as still more evidence of Hutchinson's heresy, the former governor ordered the fetus' exhumation. He writes that the assembled "went to the place of buryall & commanded to digg it up to [behold] it, & they sawe it, a most hideous creature, a woman, a fish, a bird, & a beast all woven together."

Before Hutchinson would be portrayed by men like Governor John Winthrop as the single biggest threat to religious orthodoxy in the English New World, she was the accomplished midwife with all of the matronly wisdom that early modern English cunning-women supposedly had as regarding issues of pregnancy and birth. A birth such as Dyer's couldn't help but impugn the purity of the woman tasked with delivering that infant. Intoxicated with his dislike of the woman, Winthrop sputtered without any evidence that Hutchinson had "brought forth not one, but thirty monstrous births or thereabouts." Her defender Wheelwright snarked that the judge's outlandish accusation was more "a monstrous conception of his brain, a spurious issue of his intellect" than it was of reality. Still, Puritans couldn't help but read nature as a book, a type of scriptural allegory written on every stone and leaf and tree here in his cold demon-haunted wilderness, and Winthrop's claims only added to the sense that something apocalyptic had been averted in casting Hutchinson out of Boston as God had caste Eve out of Eden. Nature's language was hermeneutics, not ecology. That being the case, the signs based on the baby delivered by Mistress Hutchinson were not good. Winthrop's formulation was simple: "as she had vented misshapen opinions, so she must bring forth deformed monsters." And so he believed that the court of Boston, here in the land where the bestial cries of pagan Abenaki and Pequod were heard but a few miles from the shoals of the Atlantic, had discovered in this middle-aged nurse the "Master-piece of the old Serpent." If Winthrop could have guarded Boston with mile-high Seraphim brandishing swords of flame so as to keep Hutchinson from ever returning, he would have. Luckily for him she would willingly just go to Rhode Island.

Governor Winthrop, following the desecration of the child's grave, recorded in his diary that delivery had been half a year before, on a cold autumnal October 11th. In attendance were the mother, Hutchinson, and one other woman named Jane Hawkins, and a nameless female observer. Winthrop wrote that the fetus was described as having a "face, but no head" for "the ears stood upon the shoulders and were like an ape's." The unnamed, unbaptized child "had no forehead, but over the eyes four horns, hard and sharp....All over the breast and back full of sharp prics and scales." The unfortunate child was "A strange fish!" as Trinculo said of Caliban in Shakespeare's *The Tempest,* for this similarly New World denizen was equivalently bestial, having "two mouths, and in each of them a piece of red flesh sticking out," and "instead of toes on each foot three claws, like a young fowl, with sharp talons."

Now, for a second, consider the circumstances of this birth. Envision Dyer, bereft of analgesic, in a candle-lit, drafty room with warped and creaky wooden floorboards and metal-paned window looking out on the stormy harbor. In labor, for how many hours? Surrounded by Hutchinson, Hawkins, and some other woman whose name isn't recorded. And after all of that struggle, her baby is born dead. She and her husband – who in her own coming time of political and religious persecution would always remain a steadfast ally – must have considered the child's sex, must have thought up names for her. And now, in the comfortable privacy of his study in his manse, Winthrop, a man who was perfectly capable of his own exulted and compassionate contemplations as evidenced in his celebrated sermon "A Model of Christian Charity," with pen of feigned dispassion writes with barely contained cackle about the misfortune which has befallen her family. Winthrop's gaze reduced Dyer's tragedy to cold analysis, moral judgment, typological evidence, and sideshow curio all in one. Winthrop, who for all of those grand sentiments delivered in that sermon upon the *Arbela* was also a man, a religious man, which is to say chiefly one for whom however beautiful his other sentiments, might be still concerned himself with how women reproduce, the circumstances of their reproduction, and the results of that reproduction, with little concern for the integrity, safety, or emotions of said woman. Winthrop and the other judges were similarly edified when word reached Boston that Hutchinson's last pregnancy had ended similarly to Dyer's, as her doctor John Clarke had recorded that the midwife gave birth to some slippery "transparent grapes" somewhere in the New England wilderness.

In the reasoning of modern medicine such an infant – if it were to be delivered at all – would be conceived of in the language of pathology and etiology, but for Winthrop and the assembled men of the court such a bestial progeny delivered to a blasphemous woman by a heretical one could only be read of as a sign that God did not dwell in the bosom of such a creature as Anne Hutchinson. The stillbirth was not the only justification for Hutchinson's exile – but it surely didn't help. She spent a short period in Williams' religiously free Rhode Island, until the threat of that colony's invasion by her former persecutors (an incursion which never happened) forced the Hutchinsons to set out even further south to New Netherland. One day in 1643 she would be massacred by a marauding group of Siwanoy Indians, scalped with the rest of her family save for her one nine-year old daughter, who was held captive by the braves and renamed "Autumn Leaf" on account of her red hair. According to Hutchinson's biographer Eve LaPlante, the Narraganset drew a less fortunate daughter "back again by the hair of the head to the stump of a tree, and there cut off her head with a hatchet" in those secluded woods which would one day be more widely known by their Dutch name of the Bronx. If Winthrop was callous at the stillbirth of Mary Dyer, than the Reverend Peter Bulkley of Concord was positively cruel when preaching about Hutchinson's murder, telling the assembled, "Let her damned heresies, and the just vengeance of God, by which she perished, terrify all her seduced followers from having any more to do with her." For good measure the minister added that Hutchinson was as if an "American Jezebel."

Hutchinson's patient didn't fare much better, for a little under two decades later in 1660 (that year of Restoration in Britain) Hutchinson would find herself upon the scaffold at Boston Common, hanging with three other Quakers from the end of a noose. Winthrop wrote of Dyer that she was "of a very proud spirit, and much addicted to revelations," and indeed it was that prophetic sense which eventually led to her prophet's fate. Dyer had followed Hutchinson to Rhode Island, but had returned to England for the period of five years following her mentor's death. Converted to the Society of Friends by its founder, George Fox, Dyer would in many ways embrace a far more radical faith than even Hutchinson had. In their belief that the inner light of God is the guiding conscience of truth in both men and women they had fully embraced that charge that the "Holy Ghost dwells in a justified person." Quakers reject all sacraments, reject all tradition, reject all authority. Taking their hats off to nothing and no one. For this Dyer would serve prison time in England, and upon her return to America where she would evangelize in the name of the new faith she would be expelled multiple times from both Connecticut and New Haven, and from Massachusetts. She even found herself upon the gallows before her last expulsion, before her sentence was commuted and she was permanently exiled from Boston with the rest of her Quaker brothers and sisters. That was May of 1660. She was back on that scaffold less than a month later. For Mary Dyer was warned. She was given an ex-

planation. Nevertheless, she persisted. While awaiting her hanging she was asked to repent, by none other than Anne Hutchinson's old nemesis, a now elderly Reverend John Wilson – who
had once been shepherd to the flock that Dyer herself belonged
to. Dyer's response at his request: "Nay, man, I am not now to
repent." And so she joyfully hung. Shortly thereafter one of her
executioners converted to the Society of Friends.

Forgive my gothic elaborations, for it is a gothic tale. Nathaniel Hawthorne, who was proud of his ancestors and even more
thankful to not be one of them, was haunted by those past generations for a reason. Early American history was composed of
"barbarous years" as the poet John Donne preached in a sermon
to the Virginia Company safely back in London. If audiences in
the capital thrilled to Senecan revenge tragedy than New Englanders had no need for such Jacobean theatrical affectations
– here history was being written in executions and scalping and
monstrous births upon the frosty frontier. Those earliest days
saw the nation so deep in a type of original sin that blood should
pluck as upon blood. Hutchinson and Dyer were the condemned
but they were not the condemnable, and like those other women
martyrs of Massachusetts in Salem of 1692 their example would
indelibly mark the nation which claimed to be descended from
them. Conflicted genealogies, haunted burial grounds, hidden
secrets, deformed progeny. Gothic? Of course America is gothic.
But don't let my lurid purple prose obscure the meaning of both
Hutchinson and Dyer.

Faith, transcendence, and God unmediated can offer profound liberation, but as concerns the mind forg'd manacles of institutionalized religion, it is undeniable that deep and profound
misogyny lay at the center of every human spiritual tradition at
its worst. The regulation of women and their bodies is the trade
of the temple. What Hutchinson preached is secondary to the fact
that she preached, for in her example she challenged the monopoly of those divines who privilege their connection to that idol of

god they had constructed in their cold hearts. Lord knows that the world doesn't need another essay by a faux-sensitive guy about the trials and tribulations about womanhood; that essay is not mine to write. But the world could always use more essays about Anne Hutchinson and Mary Dyer. They are not our American Jezebels, they are our American Esthers, and they reflect the uncomfortable truth that in God's tongue the word for the Holy Spirit is grammatically feminine, whatever Wilson or Winthrop or Bradstreet may have believed. Religion (heretical or otherwise) is the only means of resistance in a world where the only things worth resisting are also religious. For theirs was a gospel of free conscience, a quality which necessitates a free body. As Hutchinson told her accusers at her sentencing, "You have no power over my body, neither can you do me any harm—for I am in the hands of the eternal Jehovah, my Saviour." Theirs, and ours, is a world of policing both free consciences and free bodies, but as Hutchinson knew, and as Dyer knew, the glow of that inner light is brighter than those "godly" restrictions, the hum of the Holy Ghost in the sanctified soul is louder than man-made rules.

Utmost Malice of Their Stars

And two dire Comets, which have scourg'd the Town
In their own Plague and Fire have breath'd their last,
Or, dimly, in their sinking sockets frown.
John Dryden, *Annus Mirabilis: The Year of Wonders, 1666*

I saw both these stars, and, I must confess, had so much of the com-
mon notion of such things in my head, that I was apt to look upon
them as the forerunners and warnings of God's judgements.
Daniel Defoe, *A Journal of the Plague Year*

The summer of 1666 had been exceptionally dry and hot. These
were dangerous conditions for London, which despite its increasingly massive population was still basically a medieval
walled city, composed of thousands of rickety, half-timbered
wooden buildings shadowed underneath St. Paul's (which itself
would not survive the autumn). Sources seem to agree to where
it started – at the bakery of a one Thomas Farriner on a Sunday
night, September 2nd of that *annus Mirabilis, annus, Horribilis,*
annus Apocalypsis. The baker and his family survived, but the
maid did not, as she became the first victim of what came to
be called the Great Fire of London. What started as a kitchen
fire in a shop on the appropriately named Pudding Lane quickly
spread to adjacent buildings. Sir Thomas Bloodworth, the Lord
Mayor, was called to the scene and encouraged to demolish the
closest shops and homes so as to abort the quickly spreading fire
which had begun to consume this neighborhood just north of
the Thames. Yet Bloodworth refused, unable to find the owners
of the buildings (as these were rented hovels) and dismissing
concerns that the conflagration could consume the whole city,
notoriously saying that, "A woman could piss it out" if firefight-
ers were so worried about the situation becoming more dire. Ac-

cording to historian Roy Porter, by September 5th there would be 13,500 destroyed residences, 87 churches immolated, 44 company homes burned, as well as the Royal Exchange, the Custom House, Bridewell Palace, three gates to the city, and St. Paul's Cathedral, whose steeple had collapsed in another fire a century before, and with almost a quarter of a million Londoners homeless. In language almost biblical, John Evelyn wrote that, "there was nothing heard or seen but crying out and lamentation." The official death toll was absurdly low – supposedly only six people. Yet with parts of the center of the city as hot as a crematorium – the iron locks on the gates were melted – some historians think that communities of the unrecorded poor were decimated, and that the actual toll was of many thousands of deaths. It was recorded that as survivors sifted through the debris, finding bits of broken ceramic and tile, that fractured human bones were common, having been reduced to sizes so infinitesimal that it was impossible to tell what part of the body they came from.

Samuel Pepys rather predictably sought shelter in an alehouse south of the river, and watched as the flames consumed London as surely as they had Sodom and Gomorrah. Observing as it crept across London Bridge like some sort of insatiable living beast, Pepys recorded that the burning of the structure appeared as if "a bow with God's arrow in it with a shining point." Pepys was a navy man, a drinker and a lecher, and so apt not to have listened to the stern denunciations of the religious radicals who had crowded the streets of the capital (even if he had once been a supporter of Cromwell) in the days before Restoration. But some of those prophets of Interregnum had predicted this year of all years to be one when a cleansing fire would obliterate the works of man, and they had spoken in these tongues of fire, ranting from Fleet Street to the Court of St. Paul's years before the travesty of Oak Apple Day.

This inferno enacted God's vengeance on that Whore of Babylon, Charles II, with his drinking and his dalliances and his pageantry and his popery. For the religious non-conformists it was as if a biblical judgment was being visited upon this English Pharaoh. For groups like the millenarian Fifth Monarchy Men, who were awaiting the Kingdom of Christ upon the end of the world, 1666 approached as an apocalyptic year, with the numerological significance of its last three numbers all but obvious. Daniel Defoe, writing some fifty six years after the events of 1666, remembered that the subjects of London were "addicted to prophecies, and astrological conjurations, dreams, and old wives' tales." These were years of vision – the English having found themselves baptized through the traumas of civil war and Puritan theocracy were predisposed to read the apocalypse in signs. Defoe described the steady business occultists and cunning men and women had in reading dreams, he writes of those who saw "a flaming sword held in a hand, coming out of a cloud, with a point hanging directly over the city," and more presciently of "heaps of dead bodies lying unburied."

These images seemingly predicted something even more terrifying than the purging inferno, as that was not the worst thing to happen to the city of London in 1666. It was May the year before that the characteristic bubo of the plague were first observed among people living in the crowded environs of St. Giles in the Field. Dockworkers had spent days unloading cargo from Dutch ships which had brought *Rattus rattus* to England's shores, the rats in turn smuggling *Yersinia Pestis* into the largest city in Europe (not that the authorities would have understood the epidemiological reality of the plague bacterium). Over the next year that city would be alleviated of 100,000 suffering souls, the most massive loss of humans to the bubonic plague in London since the almost mythic Black Death of the fourteenth century. For if fire was one of the Egyptian plagues God sent to the Stuart king, then pestilence was the first. Defoe described the burning as "sudden, swift, and fiery," whereas the earlier plague was "slow but severe, terrible, and frightful."

The record keepers may have fudged the deaths caused by the flames, but they couldn't obscure the fact of the bodies heaped into mass graves, more than a quarter of London escaping to the countryside to survive, where they wondered zombie-like among the woods, starving to death. Pepys exclaims, "But, Lord! how sad a sight it is to see the streets empty of people, and very few upon the 'Change. Jealous of every door that one sees shut up, lest it should be the plague." With Charles and his court abandoning the capital as surely as they had been forced to during the years of revolution two decades before, London was left over for the terrified, convulsing, toxic crowd, even as the writer Edward Cotes prayed that, "Neither the Physicians of our Souls or Bodies may hereafter in such great numbers forsake us." One of the doctors who did not forsake the city was Nathaniel Hodges, who surveyed the destruction which ravaged London, writing:

> Although the Soldiery retreated from the Field of Death, and encamped out of the City, the Contagion followed, and vanquish'd them; many in their Old Age, and others in their Prime, sunk under its cruelties; of the Female Sex most died; and hardly any children escaped; and it was not uncommon to see an Inheritance pass successively to three or four Heirs in as many Days; the Number of Sextons were not sufficient to bury the Dead.

Defoe, who fictionalized his childhood memories of the plague a half-century hence in his novel *A Journal of the Plague Year*, wandered the same stricken streets as Dr. Hodges. At one point he recollects seeing a cart with sixteen or seventeen naked bodies heaped together, though "the matter was not much to them, or the indecency much to anyone else." In London during the summer of 1665 and into the fall and then the winter of 1666, the dead were democratically "huddled together into the common grave of mankind...for here was no difference made, but poor and rich went together." Note that though demographers still debate what the exact death toll was, at the height of the epidemic there was a pit in Aldgate where more than a thousand bodies would be dumped from carts like the one Defoe saw.

The year 1666 was supposed to be when the world ended, and in some ways that world did end, and another one came to replace it. From the ashes of the Great Fire a new, grand, modern city would rise; Christopher Wren would punctuate the skyline with the triumphant gilded dome of St. Paul's, the medieval crowding of London's past would be replaced with a glowing capital worthy of their new empire, a shockingly modern place of commerce and science, newspapers and coffee-shops, a London which shares more with the modern city than it did with the London of even a few decades before the plague and the fire. It would be an egregious historiographical error and a rhetorical fallacy to claim that the plague and fire birthed this new world – they emphatically did not. Social, cultural, economic, ideological conditions allowed for the emergence of a modern and liberal consensus; I am not practicing a type of Whig history where plague rats and a clumsy baker are the progenitors of modernity. The modern world had already been conceived, it was going to be born in one way or another. But, in the 350th anniversary of *annus Apocalypsis* it does behoove us to reflect on the ways in which history can crest towards particular years like breakers off the shoals of a beach, the past and future on either side looking placid by comparison.

The year 1666 could perhaps be nothing other than an *annus Apocalypsis*. Some years have a built in numerological import, 1666 could perhaps be nothing different from what it was, no matter what happened during it, due to the infernal association built into its very numbers. Millennial years are similarly endowed with a meaning set like clockwork from when our calendar system was first conceived, with those who believe in that calendar marching towards those years with predetermined significance regardless of how history chooses to behave itself. Then there are years which have come to be a type of *annus Apocalypsis* not because of anything intrinsic in their distance from the first year, but rather because of the merits of their own historical importance; often revolutionary years, they are embedded in the cultural memory in such a way that to varying degrees they can function as almost single names in and of themselves: 70, 135, 325, 476, 1054, 1066, 1381, 1453, 1517, 1588, 1618, 1649, 1776, 1789, 1848, 1860, 1914, 1918, 1939, 1945, 1968, 1989, 2001, and maybe 2016?

Three and a half centuries ago apocalyptic prophets and poets alike, as well as doctors and kings, feared harbingers of destruction in that "Year of Wonders." Today we similarly scan the news and wonder if this might not be a similar year that crests as those waves upon the shore do. And, as 1666 (perhaps arbitrarily) marks a certain transition of one world shifting into a different one, many of us fear that this year may mark the beginning of the end of that very world of modernity that began roughly 350 years ago.

The populace noted and feared the emergence of two comets in the skies over Europe that many ultimately believed had foretold plague and fire. What are our comets today, how do we identify the malice of our stars? We no longer put much stock in astrological inanities and divinatory sophistries, now we comb through *Foreign Policy* and *The Economist* hoping to get a sense of what history awaits us, of what rough beast slouches towards Brussels or Washington to be born. The millenarian delusions of nationalism and fascism once again seem to be roaring forward in elections across the West. The mercury in the thermometer is inching higher and higher, year after year. If 1666 gives us any lesson it's that the world always seems to be dying and being born anew, the question, as always, is if the world will be a better or worse one? And the answer, as always, is "awaiting further evidence." And 1666 presents another lesson, that even after plague and fire, morning still breaks, and some of us at least are still here – a cursory type of hope, but a hope none the less. It's possible, if not likely, that 2016 may prove to be a type of *annus Apocalypsis* more significant than that apocalyptic year centuries ago, but as our future history has yet to be written it remains impossible to say whether 2016 is the year that sees a new birth of illiberalism, or the year when the forces of reaction and totalitarianism are pushed back to the holes where they belong. The waves continually break on the shore, but it's hard to read the storm clouds with any certainty until they rain, or until they move back to sea.

The Remembrance of Amalek

"The essential American soul is hard, isolate, stoic, and a killer. It has never yet melted."

D.H. Lawrence, *Studies in Classic American Literature* (1923)

"No ink, but blood and tears now serve the turn/To draw the figure of New England's urn."

Benjamin Tompson, *New-England's Crisis* (1676)

Bloody Brook, Massachusetts – forty killed. South Kingstown, Rhode Island – seventy English killed, ninety-seven Narraganset warriors, maybe a thousand Indian women and children. Springfield, Massachusetts – forty-five of sixty homes burnt to the ground. Sudbury Massachusetts – thirty killed. Turner's Fall, Massachusetts – thirty-nine English killed, close to two-hundred Nipmuc, mostly women and children. 1675-1676, around one thousand English and their Pequot and Mohegan allies killed, around three thousand Narraganset, Nipmuc, and Wampanoag, as well as other Indian allies killed.

Cotton Mather wrote that "we have now seen the Sun Rising in the West," and he meant it in a millennial sense. But it is not just a millennial image, it is an apocalyptic image as well. In America dusk and dawn are as conflated as Genesis and Revelation. In the newest world, that is also the land primeval; our creation myth began with a conclusion. This moment signified the end of the world for the natives who lived here, but also in a sense for the New England colonists whose survival was no foregone conclusion.

When Mather was still a child, the colonists were almost pushed back from their nascent frontier into the Atlantic waves by a Wampanoag chief named Metacomet, better known as "King Philip." This was an ending that was, at the same time, a type of new creation, for what emerged from the event were not Englishmen and women but an entirely different kind of person. The national mythology of our civil religion perhaps half-remembers the baptism of blood that inaugurated our sense of American exceptionalism, but we often locate that moment in Gettysburg, or Valley Forge. But really, it's those villages clinging to the coast of New England where this new person, this millennial creature, this American was made.

In terms of percentages King Philip's War is the most violent in our national history, and ignoring the per capita numbers, it was in its ferocity and almost gothic horror perhaps the most genuinely violent event in the whole American narrative. As historian Jill Lepore wrote in her masterful account of the event, King Philip's War was a period when New England was "a landscape of ashes, of farms laid waste, of corpses without heads." We have never really recovered from the trauma.

America became a land and a polity defined not by ethnicity, or even religion, but by new, sometimes even darker, criteria. In America you conceptualized yourself not by the blood flowing in your own veins, but by the blood of others that you spilled. The history of French and Spanish colonization in the New World is no less violent, but something different happened in New England. The charter colonists felt abandoned by the English Crown, who had little interest in defending these schismatic congregants who had sided with Cromwell during revolution and Interregnum. And so where the French colonists saw themselves as French, and the Spanish as Spanish, and even the Southern colonists as English, the men and women of New England began to self-apply a designation that heretofore had only been applied to the natives, their ostensible belligerents in this mutually genocidal war for existential survival. The English of New England began to call themselves "Americans," which was unheard of in the New World.

Like Jacob wrestling with the angel and acquiring a new

name that would designate a nation; the English would battle not just real opponents, but also their own fantastic phantom projections of what they assumed the Indian represented. And as Jacob at least in part acquired some of the attributes of that angel (who was God himself) the New English became versions of their invented Indian, christening themselves "Americans." They assumed the imaginary mantel of citizens of Eden, as inheritors of no history; they were New Adams. That the actual Indian was foreign and Other to the English was of no accounting in the English construction of the Indian. Lepore writes that "the principal cultural anxiety behind King Philip's War was confusion of identity," and in many ways the solution to that confusion was the invention of a new identity. Certain attributes were applied to the Indian – that is the American – and in becoming Americans themselves the English took on these definitions, whether they were accurate to the indigenous or not. And what were these attributes? They were of the Indian as a primal man, a rugged individualist, willing to resort to unspeakable violence, of nature but also controlling nature, a person of the most base physical humanity but seemingly paradoxically also participant in an elevated spiritual state. Literary critic Richard Slotkin writes that the colonists wished, "to create a world of divine law pure and simple" and that both in order to defeat, but also to "convert the Indian, they had themselves to become more like the Indian." And of course if the English were to become Americans, they had to destroy the contradictory evidence that they were really not Americans, and so they had to murder the Indians. And so they did.

It's this legacy more than anything, more than Plymouth Rock, or Jamestown, or Winthrop's "City on a Hill" which characterizes and defines America, our sacramental nationhood. We are a nation, as it were, built on a literal graveyard, a haunted one at that. Literary critic Renée Bergland writes that, "For more than three hundred years, American literature has been haunted by ghostly Indians." In her study she charts the central place that the Indian ghost, as well as the Indian graveyard, has played in American literature. She explains that "the Indian" is a spectral presence in writers like "Charles Brockden Brown, Washington Irving, James Fenimore Cooper, Lydia Maria Child, Edgar Allan Poe, Nathaniel Hawthorne, and Herman Melville," not to mention more contemporary writers like Stephen King. She explains that "When European Americans speak of Native Americans, they always use the language of ghostliness. They call Indians demons, apparitions, shapes, specters, phantoms, or ghosts." This is a process of both guilt and rationalization, and it permeates American culture. Consider the name of military hardware like the Apache helicopter, the *USS Geronimo,* or team names like the Atlanta Braves or Washington Redskins where fans insist on clinging to titles that are unambiguously racial slurs. This is the logic of not just love and theft, but a type of hatred and theft as well, an internalized appropriation of our understanding of America's native inhabitants. A covenantal ambivalence, for while the jeremiad may claim that our nobler aspirations define us, it is a fallacy to embrace the amnesia which excludes the details of how we got here. This is a nation for whom our god is a bridegroom of blood, and while King Philip's War is forgotten by most, it is not really forgotten at all, for its new battles are named every night on the news and listed every day online. Writing about the chain that connects these events primeval to American traditions of racism and violence, Slotkin says that, "myths reach out of the past to cripple, incapacitate, or strike down the living." The reformers reduced seven sacraments to two, and in the new religion of America there is one, the sacred ritual of violence. Domination, aggression, hatred, murder are the ur-texts of American identity. As D.H. Lawrence once astutely observed, "The essential American soul is hard, isolate, stoic, and a killer. It has never yet melted."

This King Philip's War, which made us, is now close to three-

and-a-half centuries into the past. Yet what remains, and has not ended? The exorcist cannot caste out demons until he knows their names, so now, in our continuing American season of violence, it is required of us to identify these creatures so that we may balm the traumas they have inflicted. As Slotkin wrote, "A people unaware of its myths is likely to continue living by them." Bearing witness to these half-forgotten atrocities is paramount if we are to root out the psychic disturbances that always draft the next massacre.

Here is what we know: the war ostensibly begins with the possible murder of John Sassamon, a so-called "praying Indian," a convert to Protestantism who was involved in John Elliot's massive translation of the Bible into Wampanoag. Found in a frozen creek bed only days after warning the Plymouth colonists of an impending rebellion from the sachem Metacomet. There were bruises on his purpled neck but no water in his lungs, which indicated that he had not drowned but was rather discarded there after being killed. From this first death, there would ultimately be 4,000 more. The numbers seem comparatively small to us today, but in terms of per capita death it was twice as bloody as the Civil War, and seven times that of the Revolutionary. More than half of New England's villages were confronted with Indian attack, and the colonists responded with equal brutality, and ultimately answered with genocide. One must not assume that English triumph was a foregone conclusion at the time, though. Crucially we must not condescend to them, it is a disservice to the Indians themselves to assume that in the seventeenth century there was any certainty to their losing the war. As historians like Daniel Richter have pointed out, the "inevitability" of colonial victory in North America was not something that was obvious until well into the nineteenth century, and indeed with half of New England settlements destroyed Metacomet had pushed the English back unto almost the very shoals of the coast. The Anglo-American psyche would not still be troubled by the traumas of this event had it not actually been traumatic.

Perhaps what was most horrifying to the English was that they were confronted with a type of warfare they were inexperienced at; this was not the regimented, orchestrated, and choreographed dance of phalanxes approaching each other on the theatrical set of a battlefield. Rather, King Philip's War involved the unpredictable, chaotic, terrifying, and brutal murder of men, women, and children on all sides, seemingly indiscriminately. The Puritan saw the Indian as part of the very land that the English occupied, and as such it was as if the very land was rejecting their presence. For the English, "the Indian" was seemingly a vestige of the wilderness, and so the English made themselves a vestige of it as well. Robert Frost famously wrote that "The land was ours before we were the lands," as oracular a bit of New England exegesis if ever there was one.

Sassamon's murder and the subsequent trial ultimately resulted in 4,000 dead. But the assumption was that the Praying Indian was murdered because he was to betray Metacomet's plans for attack, but what was the sachem's justification? What were the causes of the war? Historians are split as to the immediate reasons that Metacomet embarked on a campaign of extermination against the newcomers; the English themselves who were so eager to deny interiority or even consciousness to the Indians depicted them not as rational actors exhibiting military and political agency, but rather as demonic aspects of apocalypse scourging the second-generation of Puritans who had fallen away from their covenant to the God of this New World. And again, that it was ultimately a type of apocalypse for both native and immigrant is clear. Edward Wharton, a witness to the war, wrote to a correspondent in London:

"This may informe thee…that a most bitter Spirit is entered the English, and Indians; in which they greatly endeavor the utter destruction one of another." This was certainly not the first Indian war, the Pequod War of a generation earlier had been similarly violent, though it lacked the sheer scope and breadth of King Philip's War, and it didn't have the existential urgency of required victory. And it would certainly not be the last Indian war, as Lepore reminds us "it has been the fate of the American frontier to endlessly repeat itself." Whether Metacomet was a short-sighted and vicious ruler, an emancipatory figure that was fighting for the survival of his people, or something in between, remains ambiguous.

For that reason, a few words need to be spent reflecting on he who gave his name to the war. Metacomet stands as one of the unknowable figures of the event. He took the European name "Philip" in supposed emulation of that Macedonian king who sired Alexander the Great, but for the Puritans it seemed more apt a comparison to that most sovereign and Catholic regent of Spain who had once barred down on their own great-great-grand-parents when the Armada threatened the coasts of England. This historical rhyme simply reiterated in the Puritan imagination that history was typological, and that our own lives are in some sense scriptural in their repetitions; indeed as King Philip's War itself would be forevermore repeated in the American propensity towards violence. In many ways, this particular sachem (whether called King Philip or Metacomet) can stand in as an ambiguous cipher, in the way that Indians often have in the American imagination. Feared and hated, he exemplified the supposed characteristics of the Narragansett braves that the Puritans wished to emulate. In New England there are dozens of place-names in his honor, including several streets, a mountain ridge, a pond, a middle school in Connecticut, and perhaps most unlikely, a golf club in Rhode Island.

Metacomet was celebrated in John Augustine Stone's early nineteenth-century play *Metamora; or, The Last of the Wampano-ags*, where he was depicted by the great Shakespearean stage actor Edwin Forest, whose working class fans were so fervent that they nearly burnt down New York's Bowery in protest of a

rival English actor's stage performance. For both Stone and Forest the sachem was a symbol of American independence, it was
after all the English (of a type) whom he rebelled against, just as
the revolutionary generation of the late eighteenth century had.
For playwright and actor, declaring their independence from
English literary tradition, Metacomet was a consummate American. In the fireside poet John Greenleaf Whittier's "Metacom,"
printed in 1831, he presents the king as a tragic victim of progress, who in his death warns of a future, despoiled continent, declaring that "from this awful hour/The dying curse of Metacom/
Shall linger with abiding power/Upon the spoilers of my home."
A century later and Stephen Vincent Benet would place King
Philip in the satanic Jury of the Damned in "The Devil and Daniel Webster." As Stone, Forrest, and Whittier can attest to, Philip
has not always been demonized. Strangely enough it was that
old Knickerbocker himself, the New York author Washington Irving who reflected a century and a half later after Philip's death,
that he "was a true born prince, gallantly fighting at the head of
his subjects to avenge the wrongs of his family; to retrieve the
tottering power of his line; and to deliver his native land from
the oppression of usurping strangers."

Metacomet's name became metonymous for the new American identity which was being created, for as surely as the English were beginning to pretend to be natives, the Indians had
been influenced by the Europeans for two centuries as well.
The hybridization of these identities was so complete that when
combined with the Europeans' demonization of the Indian there
was a tendency to project English brutality onto a native origin.
This process of rhetorical rationalization is what the historian
Peter Silver has called the "anti-Indian sublime." Perhaps there
is something to be learned about the nature of national myth that
it was Metacomet's father, the sachem Massasoit, who was the
guest of honor at that legendary first Thanksgiving in Plymouth.
Half a century later his son's head would be placed on a pike

overlooking that same town, decaying in the elements for two years as his rotted eyes watched the arrival and birth of new colonists. If King Philip's War did anything to the English, it made them question the simple dichotomy of "civilized" and "barbarous" which had structured their perspective from the earliest days of colonization. After all, remember that the first historical reference to scalping appears in Herodotus. The practice was not solely an Indian invention.

One thing that seems clear is that miscommunications and assumptions throughout the war led to an increasing escalation in violence. In this war, both sides found that they were so far in blood that sin would pluck on sin. We have a litany of horrors across the later months of 1675 into 1676 that can be examined. Read George Ingersol's account, dated September 9, 1675:

> When I came to the place, i found an house burnt downe, and six persons killed, and three of the same family could not be found. An old Man and Woman were halfe in, and halfe out of the house neer halfe burnt. Their owne Son was shot through the body, and also his head dashed in pieces. This young mans Wife was dead, her head skinned.... [she] was bigg with Child..... [and her other two children] haveing their heads dashed in pieces...laid by one another with their bellys to the ground, and an Oake planke laid upon their backs (sic).

Or consider Nathaniel Salstonstall's report, where he writes of the victims that, "if they were Women, they first forced them to satisfie their filthy Lusts and then murdered them; either cutting off the Head, ripping open the Belly, or skulping the Head of Skin and Hair, and hanging them up as Trophies; wearing Men's Fingers as Bracelets about their Necks, and Stripes of their Skins which they dress for Belts." I have argued elsewhere that the most proper and American of literary modes is that of the apocalyptic, and this is due in no small part to our innovation of the first American-born genre, that of the captivity narrative. In these accounts, most frequently written by women, we see first-hand the traumas penned by people held in bondage throughout the course of the war. By far the most popular of these narratives was by Mary Rowlandson, whose account was one of the first bestsellers in American publishing history (appropriately enough alongside Michael Wigglesworth's apocalyptic-themed epic doggerel *The Day of Doom*). Rowlandson writes that "Thus were we butcherd by those merciless heathen, standing amazed, with the blood running down to our heels." Good Puritan woman that she was, she echoes Job when she writes "Come, behold the works of the Lord, what desolations he has made in the earth" telling us of "twelve killed, some shot, some stabbed with their spears, some knocked down with their hatchets." Rowlandson focuses on the image of one colonist "who was chopped into the head with a hatchet, and stript naked, and yet was crawling up and down."

These atrocities are certainly not to be doubted, but as it was the literal (and literate) victors of the war who crafted its histories, one can forget the reciprocity of hatred that marked both sets of combatants. Irving later complained that Puritan accounts of the war dwelled "with horror and indignation on every hostile act of the Indians, however justifiable," while there are "mentions with applause [of] the most sanguinary atrocities of the whites." No account of the war written by a native survives, if indeed there ever were any. Yet the English themselves sometimes recorded their own atrocities, or betrayed evidence of their own barbarity that is sometimes subtly (and not so subtly) cast like a dark shadow from their celebrations of their eventual military victories. This is demonstrated by Benjamin Tompson's remarkable epic poem, first published as *New-England's Crisis* in Boston in 1676, with the fires scarcely quenched and the metallic tinge of blood still in his nostrils. In London it was printed a year later as *New-England's Tears*. The later title would be particularly evocative to an audience in the home-country, as it seems to mimic the English title of the Dominican friar Bartolomeo de las Casas' sixteenth-century classic *The Tears of the Indians*. This text, which recounted Spanish brutality in the conquering of the Aztecs, was foundational in the English construction of *La Leynda Negra*, or "The Black Legend," which purposefully contrasted peaceful English relations with the natives to the savagery of Catholic colonizers. One can envision Tompson's dispatch from the colonies taking up space at book stalls on Fleet and Grub Street, or being hawked in the courtyard of St. Paul's alongside de las Casas' century old book (recently translated into English by none-other than John Milton's nephew). But where the "tears" in that older text were of the Indians, Tompson writes of "New-England's tears." Paradoxically while the race and religion of the oppressed had altered, their identity as "Americans" remained constant.

This, as I mentioned earlier, is the period that sees the New English's self-identity transform into American. The relative lack of assistance during the trials of the war, and the suspicion the Puritans held the Restoration monarchy in ("suspicion" may be too gracious a word) further exacerbated this mental split from England. As Tompson wrote, "Poor New Englands dismal tragedy...../But in its funeral ashes write thy Name/So fair all nations may expound the same:/Out of her ashes let a Phoenix rise/That may outshine the first and be more wise." This was, for Tompson, the veritable birth of a nation. Concerning the original occupants of this land, he encourages "Limn them besmeared with Christian blood & oiled/With fat out of white human bodies boiled./Draw them with clubs like mauls & full of stains,/Like Vulcans anvilling New England's brains." And in what is surely the most unsettling of poetic verses from the epic (where one would do well to remember the previous atrocities), he writes concerning the English destruction of an Indian village, describing "The flames like lightning in their narrow streets/Dart in the

face of everyone it meets,/Here might be heard an hideous indian cry/Of wounded ones who in the Wigwams fry." As if that final verb, with its culinary associations, isn't disturbing enough,
Tompson makes that word's connotations literally and visceral-
ly clear, writing "Had we been Canibals here might we feast/On
brave Westphalian gammons ready drest."

It's hard not to think that the poet doth protest too much. I
do not mean to claim that the colonists engaged in literal cannibalism (though archeological evidence has demonstrated it did
occur during some lean times), but the dodge of "Had we been"
strikes the reader as supremely disquieting. The couplet has a
sense of demonic power about it, for while it emphasizes that
cannibalism was not engaged, that there was at least still the
possibility that it could be entertained. Tompson, in his almost
gleeful recounting (think of how disturbing the word "fry" is in
that earlier line) seems delighted by the fact that the English had
the possibility, or the choice, to violate this taboo. Transgression need not be performed, the possibility of it is enough. To
paraphrase Matthew, he who considers cannibalism has already
committed it in his heart. This interpretation is not a stretch, for
Tompson conjures the image of a "feast," and most disgustingly
of all compares the scorched bodies of fellow human beings to
the smoked pinkness of expensive Westphalian ham, of "gammons ready drest." From Montaigne's ironic *Of Cannibals*, to
Shakespeare's anagrammatic Caliban, natives had often been
impugned with this particularly heinous sin. While cannibalism's ritualistic import has been noted among all peoples of the
Earth (including Europeans, of course), it was a particular blood
libel that early moderns associated with the Indians, and yet
Tompson proudly takes on the potential mantel of cannibal in
an orgiastic, Dionysian celebration of the ultimate victory of the
white settlers in New England. A Phoenix did arise, out of the
burnt ashes of human remains, from a barbecue's fire pit.

But as it was in the biblical era, so too shall it be in this millennial third age (after that of the Father and the Son) in the fourth part of the world (separate from Europe, Asia, and Africa). The nature of Holy War itself is that transcendence necessitates transgression, and as the Godly Republic had collapsed in their native England it was the task of the colonists to assemble the Book of Daniel's Fifth Monarchy of God here in the howling wilderness of the New American continent. Scholars from Perry Miller to Sacvan Bercovitch have noted how the American Puritans lived in a stunningly typological world, where their own experience was to be read by the rules of hermeneutics, and where our personal narratives can take on the import of scripture. The dangerous process of canonizing King Philip's War as a chapter in this new American scripture began while the spring rains scarcely had time to wipe away the red tinged snow of 1676's winter of discontent. Read the Puritan divine Increase Mather's post-war sermon in which he questions God's purpose in bringing the scourge of Philip upon the settlers. Puritan sermons, modernizing the four-fold exegetical structure of medieval bible commentary, would focus on a scriptural verse, then supply the theological doctrine, followed by the logic which justifies this teaching, and ending with the climax of what the application of the verse should be. For this particular sermon, Mather chose to focus his attentions on Exodus 17:14. Of course even if the rhetoric of Puritan preaching didn't make Mather's meaning abundantly clear, his choice of scriptural verse certainly would. The Lord Jehovah says, "I will utterly put out the remembrance of Amalek from under heaven." So as the Israelites had escaped bondage in Egypt only to find Canaan filled with the pagan Amalekites, so too had the Puritans escaped their Stuart Pharaoh to find American Israel filled with the barbarous Indians. And Mather's meaning was clear, as the Israelites had to strike the very fact of the Amalekite's existence from the face of the Earth, so to be it the task of the English to eliminate the Indians from this continent. As if Mather were to say "Who, after all, speaks today of the annihilation of the Amalekites?"

Mather preaches that for the "Heathen People amongst whom
we live, and whose Land the Lord God of our Fathers hath giv-
en to us for a rightful Possession" that a "Sword, a Sword is
sharpened... to make a sore slaughter." In Mather's sermon we
see the nascent origins of what Slotkin has coined "regeneration through violence;" that is the mechanism by which one of
the central American myths operates, a ritual of sacred violence
whereby the millennial nation makes itself worthy of the Kingdom of God through the almost Eucharistic spilling of blood.
This is important to remember in our own era, when we almost
daily read of meaningless massacres, and watch the painful ritualized mourning that is inaugurated upon the contemporary
slaughter of innocent Americans. Slotkin writes that "the myth of
regeneration through violence became the structuring metaphor
of the American experience," and it is imperative to remember
this when we ask why the murder rate in the United States is so
disproportionately high. Lepore writes that it could be argued
that the war never really ended since "in a figurative sense, it
was the archetype" of wars which followed; but in its anarchic
randomness New England's most brutal war reminds one not so
much of the battles planed by generals in the Pentagon than it
does to the sword of Damocles which hangs over every citizen's
head – where we are all held hostage by the enthusiasms and
idolatries of those for whom the firearm is a sacred tool. Indeed
in the very rhetoric of those for whom the Second Amendment is
an inerrant textual idol, we see traces of Slotkin's claim that "The
archetypal enemy of the American hero is the red Indian, and
to some degree all groups or nations which threaten us are seen
in terms derived from our earlier myths." In both our paranoid
fear of the Other, which in our history has included the Indian,
the slave in potential revolt, the bomb-throwing anarchist, the
Papist of nativist fantasy, and now the Islamic jihadist, we've
been playing out the sacred ritual of reenacting King Philip's

War over, and over. The terrible irony of course is that none of these groups has ever exerted a fraction of the damage on us that our own fear coupled with our own destructive capabilities has.

If we are to name these demons, again so that we may exorcise them, there is perhaps no more pressing time to do so than the current. History may not repeat itself, as it is said, but it certainly echoes. These dark elements of the American civil religion – the sacred violence, the purification of blood through blood, the stark definition of who exactly is the Other – all of this reoccurs like an idée fixe in a symphony written in the minor key. We see it in the rhetoric of the Know Nothing, the Klansman, the John Bircher, and we of course see it today. What seemed politically impossible prior to 2016 became commonplace; the leading candidate for the presidential nomination of one of our political parties talking glowingly about the possibility of the largest ethnic cleansing in human history. He talked about databases categorizing people by ethnicity and religion. He talked about targeting for assassination the innocent family members of suspected terrorists, and he was as indiscriminate and gore-happy as the marauders who killed women and children in Indian villages, once, long ago. His rallies are characterized by bullying, by demagoguery, and increasingly by actual violence as dissenting voices are shoved, kicked, and threatened. As what had seemed impossible came to pass, one fears that that which seems impossible now will be commonplace six months into the future. Much of the rhetoric that bolsters not just this politician, but this movement which he represents, focuses on those venerable American archetypes of the pioneer, a rugged individualist defending the land on an ever western frontier which burns across the continent to fulfill our eschatological destiny. Lepore is indeed right that King Philip's War has never ended.

That great explicator of sacred violence, the philosopher Rene Girard, writes of the scapegoat mechanism, where the innocent may die, but it is paradoxically their very sacrifice which is meant to prevent the death of other innocents. As Gary Wills put it in a column written after one of the countless, endless, perennial massacres which mark daily life in the modern United States (as surely as if we lived in colonial New England), "It was the sacrifice we as a culture made, and continually make, to our demonic god. We guarantee that crazed man after crazed man will have a flood of killing power readily supplied him. We have to make that offering, out of devotion to our Moloch, our god. The gun is our Moloch." King Philip's War has more than a whiff of the allegorical about it, it is a typological example of a recurring event in American history, a chapter in the dubious sacred scripture of our civil religion, and we witness its continuing battles every day. Logic and reason alone will not bring armistice, as it is the language of myth that binds us, it must be the language of myth which ultimately liberates – but I know not what that language sounds like. What I do know, and what I fear, is that in our mythic America, which is perennially sustained by legends of being made "great again," that what for many seems to look like a golden dawn is really the dusk.

Wheresoever They Come They Be at Home

For its name literally meaning "No Place," echoes of Utopia seem to be everywhere. Early autumn and a week before the pope's visit and I am at the corner of 53rd and 5th, halfway between St. Patrick's Cathedral and one of Auden's "dives," when a truck rumbles slowly past, and on its side: "Utopia Trucking Company – Flushing Queens."

"Utopia" – a term more of political abuse than descriptive reality – a word that in 2016 was a half millennium old. Thomas More, lawyer, author, theorist, radical, martyr, saint, gave us this word in 1516 with the publication of *Utopia*, but in many ways he merely described the contours of a country which had in some sense always existed, from the coasts of Plato's Republic to the hills of medieval Cockaigne. Yet in explicating the rules of that fictional nation to which some of us feel we must ever strive, he created one of the most potent and useful critical concepts that a radical can have in their vocabulary. It is true that the term is often used disparagingly – we must resist this. It is true that the word is used so frequently that it seems to lose its significance – we must parse this. And it is true that considering its origins, the term is unmistakably theological – we must embrace this.

My encounter with the delivery truck demonstrates just how universal "Utopia" has become – again seemingly everywhere for being nowhere, demonstrably real and yet completely fictional. The delivery company takes its name from a neighborhood in Queens, which in turn took its name from the parkway running through it. In addition to that Utopia, the United States also boasts towns by that name in Kansas, Ohio, and Texas. Remains of places that didn't carry the literal name, but are in some sense "utopian" (for that term is used to describe so-called "intentional communities") line the back roads of the "Burnt Over Country" of the American Second Great Awakening, with exotic names like Ephrata and Oneida. This was not just a religious impulse, or not explicitly always one, for nineteenth-century socialists founded communities such as Brooke Farm, or the various Phalanxes organized by economic and social precepts that could in some sense be called utopian.

The potential of utopia as both impetus and ghost has inspired and haunted Americans while the creator of that word was still alive. In 1535, the Franciscan friar Vasco de Quiroga translated Thomas More's *Utopia* into Spanish while working as a missionary in Mexico. The now-lost text was sent to the English lawyer, though he was beheaded before he could read the translation, executed for opposing the king's divorce (among other reasons). De Quiroga was undaunted, the year of More's death he began to organize the Indians into planned communities based on the political principles from his hero's book, the first intentional communities in the New World or anywhere else which explicitly and consciously took the name "utopian."

In many ways de Quiroga's example highlights the profound ambivalence in the very word itself, for while his program of emancipation, economic self-sufficiency, equality, and social services was undeniably progressive (if not radical) it was also clearly tainted by the sins of colonialism. These sorts of ambiguities are noted in almost every community that has ever strived towards a utopianism. The very word has always had a conflicted history, at best it is used as a synonym for a type of social quixotism; at worst it's taken as a given that a utopia must always devolve into a dystopia. This is when we can even agree on how to define the term, for while unmistakably left-wing systems are often called "utopian" (whether in an affirmative or derogatory sense) the word has also been applied to everything from free-market absolutism to counter-revolutionary fascism.

One-and-a-half miles north of where I watched the Utopia Company's delivery truck drive by, and a portrait of More hangs on the dark chestnut walls of Henry Clay Frick's mansion. The

Carnegie Steel executive had to decamp to Millionaire's Row in New York after he unleashed the Pinkertons on striking steel workers in Homestead, Pennsylvania in 1892. He ultimately absconded permanently from Pittsburgh and began to amass an art collection to impress New York City aristocracy. Here, the backwoods inheritor of the Old Overholt Rye fortune acquired the 1527 portrait of Sir Thomas More by Hans Holbein the Younger. Perhaps as evidence of either a boorish sense of humor, or a lack of awareness, Frick displayed a portrait of Thomas Cromwell (the primary agent in the orchestration of the Chancellor's execution) on the other side of the fireplace. Or maybe the capitalist's interior design was really a warning to any would-be utopians, like Alexander Berkman, the anarchist who unsuccessfully tried to assassinate Frick.

It is the most iconic depiction of More, his lush velvet sleeves jut out from underneath a somber yet still rich silken black, ermine-trimmed cloak, the heavy chancellor's chain weighed heavy around his neck, a curtain of forest green behind him. The portrait was painted twelve years after More had written his most famous work, the book which gave us not just such an important critical term, but a means of categorizing and directing our political aspirations as well. But the years between penning *Utopia* and sitting for Holbein's portrait had been long. Only a year after *Utopia* first ran off of the English presses and a rude monk would nail a German pamphlet to the cathedral door in Wittenberg. The reformations would be as violent as any ideological struggle before or after, and a horrified More decamped zealously to the Catholic side. When his employer Henry was still a "Defender of the Faith" More penned pamphlets attacking Luther and his English allies such as William Tyndale. The latter was the man who would put the language of the English working classes into Christ's mouth, who was later to be burnt at the stake in Belgium, under the orders of the English king. In all More was responsible for six executions (seven if you include Tyndale due to the Chancellor's campaign, though he was ultimately killed after More himself), and there have long been accusations that the philosopher may have personally tortured these Protestant agitators. Upon the discovery of copies of *Utopia* following the siege at the German city of Munster where a brief communist theocracy was established before being violently subdued by a duel Catholic and Protestant military campaign (Europe's first moment of eccumenicism....) and More wished he could consign all copies of his most important book to the flames alongside the people who he had helped to burn at Lollard's Pit and elsewhere. As has been written before, the first great utopian was also the first anti-utopian. Holbein had the fortuitous luck to paint the elder More staring intently towards the right.

It is this later More rather than the idealistic author of *Utopia* who unfortunately often comes down to us today. Witness the Thomas More Society, a kind of ersatz right-wing version of the American Civil Liberties Union. They embrace the later version of More rather than the youthful one, a group for whom the rallying cry of "Religious Liberty!" is associated with the man who burnt heretics and not for the author of the communist blueprint which envisioned true freedom of conscience as a basic principle of societal organization. For another example envision the reactionary Supreme Court justice Antonin Scalia who wore an exact replica of the hat depicted in the Holbein painting to the second presidential inauguration of Barack Obama, a gift from the aforementioned society, and widely interpreted as a political statement against the healthcare mandate. More's fictional Utopia envisioned a state where medical care was an assumed human right, but the More who Justice Scalia emulated was the supposed defender of religious "liberty" manning the greenwood of the *auto de fe* where Scalia and others like him define "conscience of faith" as the right to deny others theirs. Viewed from this vantage point, perhaps the Gilded Age industrialist Frick enshrining More in his mansion is not so inappropriate if a modern anti-labor, anti-woman, anti-gay, anti-Muslim justice can similarly tether his identity to the founder of Utopia.

But as with all things related to More, and by extension his conceptual invention of utopia, there are ambiguities and contradictions; for some 4,668 miles from Henry Clay Frick's mansion in New York City there once stood a monument to More and others called the Alexander Garden Obelisk, and which is described as a memorial to the "Prominent Thinkers and Leaders of the Struggle for the Liberation of the Working People." Here, in the Kremlin, More is listed alongside Saint-Simon, Fourier, Proudhon, Bakunin, Engels, and Marx as an intellectual partisan in the cause of workers' liberation, the collection personally approved by Lenin in 1918 during the Russian Revolution. Some 1,447 miles south west of Moscow, and seventeen years later More would receive a very different recommendation when Pope Pius XI canonized him as a saint in the Roman Catholic Church in St. Peter's Square. For those of us on the left, what is to be done with Thomas More, the knighted communist, the canonized radical? To what More, and to what version of utopia, do we orient ourselves? With the indefinite nature of More the radical, More the capitalist, More the communist, More the saint, to whom do we turn? Or has "utopia" become at best an empty signifier, at worst a pejorative for misplaced idealism that can border into fanaticism? Does the left have anything left to learn from utopia, and can she still be a universal homeland to which we sail?

As radicals we abandon *Utopia* at our own peril. As critics it is our task to not just rehabilitate the word, but to reinvigorate it as well. For humanists this is done through the critical sentiment and approach to analysis that Marxist critic Frederic Jameson explains as a process where the critic must "Always historicize." It is true that *Utopia* has accumulated attendant cultural connotations, both during More's lifetime and the long half millennium after; and it is also true that the genius of the text (as well as the attendant literary mode which it inaugurated) is complex, nuanced, and in many ways hard to separate from satire. Yet in analyzing that text there are certain conclusions that can be made. That is that when we are confronted with More the capitalist, the communist, or the saint we can categorically eliminate the first (and thus recapture him at his best from the right) and we can reconcile the last two. In understanding what precisely is radical in Utopia, and thus what is still ideologically pertinent, we must (perhaps uncomfortably for some Marxists) not just understand but embrace the religious and theological category, which undeniably structures both the original text and the subsequent utopian mode.

Utopia is a text more often mentioned than actually read, but it is only in going back to the book itself, and considering the early sixteenth-century context in which it was composed, that its radicalism becomes so evident. To begin with, the short text is really divided into two books; the first recounts a conversation between, a roman a clef version of More himself (prefiguring so-called "post-modern" literature and skirting the line between reality and fiction) and a sailor named Raphael Hytholday, who More meets while on a diplomatic trade mission in the Low Countries. Hytholday (who critics have noted has a name that basically means "Nonsense speaker") has sailed with Amerigo Vespucci to the New World, where he visited Utopia, the exact location of which he cheekily informs us that he does not remember. The second book is composed of Hytholday's recounting in detail what he encountered in Utopia that is their approach to economic, social, political, cultural and religious structures. It is the later book that has become the more heavily quoted and popular of the two, and in many ways it is more in keeping with the proto-science fiction feel of the overall text (it's not for nothing that More included both maps and an alphabet for his fictional country, inaugurating the intense world-building of later fantasy texts). While the first book is admittedly drier, it is also the section of Utopia that helps to place the book in a historical context that demonstrates its full radicalism.

More's own biography demonstrates that he was complex and contradictory, and that in many ways his life followed an all too familiar and all too depressing right-ward trajectory which is often seen in disillusioned radical intellectuals. But these inconsistencies do not imply that *Utopia* is itself not a revolutionary text. It is true that the work is multivocal, that the competing discussions between More's fictional surrogate and Hytholday (among others) generate a sort of Keatsian negative capability that makes a definitive point of view difficult to ascertain (or which implies there is not one perspective being endorsed). As a result critics, particularly conservative ones, have argued that the work is purely satire, an ironic portrait of an impossible society (whose name, once again, does mean "No Place") rather than a critique of early modern power structures, or certainly any kind of recommended concrete platform for reform. As literary critic Susan Bruce writes, "for critics of the right it is irksome that one of the most canonical texts in English literature appears to express so profound and explicit a critique of the economic system underlying all Western societies" with the implication being that this circle is squared by arguing that More didn't really believe what he wrote. While it may seem unlikely that More ever meant book two to be a genuine political proposal, there is no reason to think that the sentiment which held that "the whole island is as it were one family or household" was one that he didn't hold to as an ideal.

The multivocal aspect of the text, or its "heteroglossia" as Mikhail Bahktin called it, is not necessarily evidence of disingenuousness, nor do they prove that Utopia is a straightforward satire (even if it shares some aspects of that mode). Rather these qualities merely categorize the text as a precursor of the novel, and speak to its narrative complexity. It's true, Utopia is not didactic agitprop nor is it simple manifesto, but rather it is as a complex narrative work prefiguring the precise heteroglosic virtues which we celebrate in the novel as a form. Yet in this particular example the politics remain radical. This is nowhere more obvious than in the first book of *Utopia*, which establishes the work as a radical critique of increasingly unequal economic power in England and the consolidation of state power in London (which he would soon be a part of). *Utopia* comments on the hegemonic structures then emerging in rapidly changing and urbanizing England. In many ways Utopia is a carnival mirror image of England, and like all great speculative fiction it serves as a comment on injustices within the society it reflects back. As a nation Utopia has 54 subdivisions, the same as England. Bruce again writes that "Utopia and England, for example, ostensibly invoked in the text as each other's opposite, are in many ways very similar: like the British Isles, Utopia is an island; its main town and river resemble London and the Thames, as contemporary commentators were quick to note." Yet for this mirror similarity in some respects, More evokes the lyrics of the radical song "The World Turn'd Upside Down" from the civil wars of a century and a half later – for that which is last in England is first in Utopia.

More's text can be characterized as a conservative satire only when totally disentangled from the specific historical context in which the work was written. Late fifteenth- and early sixteenth-century England was undergoing massive shifts in power dynamics, and changes in the actual landscape of the country. A close reading of the time period from roughly the Tudor ascension in the late fifteenth-century through their stewardship of the nation throughout the following century reveals changes that were often profoundly detrimental to the common-people of the era. It is a convenient lie of Whig historiography that sets the early modern period as "Renaissance" away from the medieval that is stereotyped as the "Dark Ages." An honest appraisal of the actual quality of life between the late middle ages and the earliest years of the English Renaissance would not recommend the latter to most people. Shifts in the economic policies of land-

ed aristocracy and the central monarchy led to disruptive changes to the livelihood of the working classes who had maintained
a particular way of life for centuries. Chief among these alterations to the medieval economic system was the introduction
of enclosure, whereby the common lands which the medieval
proletariat had shared freely for agriculture, lodging, livelihood,
and recreation for half a millennium were rapidly privatized for
the purpose of sheep grazing, so that the nobility would generate capital in the increasingly productive and lucrative wool and
textile exportation trade. It is thus crucial that More and Hytholday's meeting is directly related to the wool industry (which, as
some critics have not unfairly pointed out, the historical More
did invest in, despite his criticisms). As Hytholday says of England: "these noblemen and gentlemen...not contenting themselves with the yearly revenues and profits...leave no ground for
tillage; they enclose all into pastures; they throw down houses;
they pluck down towns, and leave nothing standing but only the
church to be made a sheep house." This was a nascent form of
market capitalism, and despite the damage it did (and does) to
the English working class it makes sense that conservative critics would act as handmaiden to reactionary justifications of the
capitalist order by denying the journalistic integrity of More's
criticism and claiming Utopia as merely satire.

The enclosure movement, which continued throughout the
early modern period (with privatization it arguably continues
today) had a catastrophic effect on the working classes. With
an inability to adequately support themselves in the manner
of their ancestors, a massive vagrant class was created which
flooded into a London whose population was exploding. With
their traditional means of support eradicated many of this class
were forced into petty crime to merely survive, which led to
draconian punishments by a rapidly centralizing police state.
Prisons like Newgate which were packed full and were colonies
for plague could be virtually death sentences, and the criminal

code was revised in the strictest manner, making the slur "medieval" much more accurate to apply to the Renaissance. Hytholday discusses this anarchic lawlessness in England and the
emergence of a criminal class generated by necessity, birthed
by economic conditions. He speaks of "this wretched beggary
and miserable poverty" which generates "riot." Yet what is
more horrific are the methods of state punishment to corral the
hungry masses, and the sailor from among the Utopians speaks
of how he thinks that it is "not right nor justice that the loss of
money should cause the loss of man's life. For mine opinion is
that all the goods in the world are not able to countervail man's
life" and that "God commandeth us that we shall not kill. And
be we then so hasty to kill a man for taking a little money?"
Execution for theft was an innovation of the so-called modern
world, and it was one whose existence was justified by this rapidly changing economic order.

Hytholday (or More) contrasts this with the, well, utopian example of the Utopians. On that upside down mirror image island
the Utopians "never lack work, and besides the gaining of their
meat and drink, every one of them bringeth daily something into
the common treasury." It is a firm political and economic belief
of the Utopians that the "only way to wealth is of a commonality" where "equality of all things" must be maintained. Of the
54 polities which constitute the area of the nation, "None of the
cities desire to enlarge the bounds and limits of their shires, for
they count themselves rather the good husbands than the owners of their lands" and that within the homes of Utopia "there
is nothing with the houses that is private or any man's own."
The author anticipated the common critique of utopia and indeed socialism itself, that it would create a boring, colorless,
utilitarian society. He explains how the Utopians work only a
nine-hour day (a number in keeping with the sorts of working
conditions labor fought for in the twentieth century) and where
during time not used for "work, sleep, and meat" that time is

spent as "every man as he liketh best himself." He prefigures the nineteenth-century radical motto "Eight hours for work, eight hours for rest, eight hours for what we will!" Indeed More intuitively understood that far from erasing distinctions or creating a monochromatic world, the life of man under socialism was one in which every individual would have full ability to self-fashion themselves. The Utopians are given the right to play, a right which More would have associated with a rapidly disappearing "Merry Old England" which was vanishing as hedges were planted to cordon off private property from the common treasury of the English people, and where enclosure abolished the shire which was the property of all men. But it is only when people are liberated from the deprivations of economic survival that we become truly at liberty to be human, and that far from being a dreary or boring place, Utopia is a land where no "supper is passed without music." In Utopia one has bread, but one also has roses.

It was a common sentiment in radical English literature that had it that "Merry Old England" was a type of pastoral Eden, an Anglo-Saxon Arcadia, and that their ancient liberties were violated during the Norman Conquest. It's a thread which runs throughout working-class English discourse from the mystical anarchists of the Middle Ages explicated by historian Norman Cohn, to the radical religious non-conformists of the seventeenth-century who inspired Marxist historian Christopher Hill, to the Fabian socialists of the nineteenth century. For all of its myth (not to speak of a sometimes troubling ethnocentrism) a convincing case can be made that the introduction of privatization and a market economy greatly reduced both the security, comfort, and freedoms of the common English. This detriment to quality of life has been explained away as a necessary difficulty, or erased with the teleological constructions surrounding language of "progress." The English proletariat saw land that had rightfully belonged to them taken away, from the fields now enclosed, to the monasteries that would shortly be dissolved and have their altars stripped during the Henrician Reformation. Read in this context and More's *Utopia* can be seen as a condemnation of particular injustices at a particular time, and in this way the general sense of utopianism, which is so often dismissed, can be regrounded and thus resuscitated as a potent symbol against different injustices at different times.

Sometimes the term "utopian" is used as a slur against free-market absolutists, anarchic libertarians, neo-conservative Straussians, fascists, and other reactionary ideologies. This is a duel mistake – to begin with none of those are utopian belief-systems – and secondly there is nothing wrong with ideologies that actually are utopian. As intellectual historian Russell Jacoby writes in his excellent *Picture Imperfect: Utopian Thought for an Anti-Utopian Age* "the utopian vision has flagged; it sparks little interest. At best, 'utopian' is tossed around as a term of abuse; it suggests that someone is not simply unrealistic but prone to violence." Jacoby explains that liberal anti-utopianism has become the de facto logic of late capitalism, and this use of the word "utopian" as a mere synonym for what is totalitarian (actual meaning of the word be damned) has made such a position the conventional, common sensical approach of contemporary political theory; but, Jacoby continues, referring to this liberal consensus, that "To the extent that their critique blackens all of utopian thought, I object." As must we, for the vagaries of More's biography are one thing, but More as a symbol of Utopia can be separated from More the conservative, More the capitalist, and More the reactionary.

But while we can separate out More the radical from that previous unholy trinity, we cannot separate him from More the saint. Utopia is an unmistakably theological concept; a humanist steeped in both orthodox as well as reformist Catholicism, and privy to the rich traditions of religiously motivated medieval political radicalism, from the Brethren of the Free Spirit to the Beguines, created it. Marxist historians such as Hill and E.P. Thompson, for as invaluable as their work has been, have sometimes minimized the theological language in which radical politics was written from the Middle Ages through the seventeenth century (and indeed often later as well). There is sometimes an implication that biblical typology, theological concepts, and the vocabulary of the sacred, the divine, and the transcendent were simply a religious veneer over secular concepts, a tool for convincing the pious proletariat to a radical cause. This is a profound category error, for religion was not a code to conceal a secret language of radicalism, but rather it was the language itself. Theological language was not always motivated by material conditions, but indeed shaped those conditions, both in the examples of hegemonic oppression and radical resistance to those powers. That is to say that religious language was not mere artifice to adorn secular conception, nor was it sugar to make socialistic medicine more palatable, but rather because "secularism" itself is such a problematic concept, political and religious radicalism were often simply identical. It calls to mind Walter Benjamin's parable from "Theses on the Philosophy of History" where he compares the operations of history to an infamous eighteenth-century chess-playing "robot" dressed like a Turk, and whom a dwarfish prodigy secretly operated. In this anecdote Benjamin compared the chess-playing robot to "historical materialism," who he said can only work if he "employs the services of theology," the sentient human chess-player who "is small and ugly and must be kept out of sight."

Furthermore, utopianism as philosophical approach as well as literary mode in large part relied on the fertile creativity of working class apocalypticism and millennialism. I have heard it said that millennialism is a type of working class utopianism, stripped of the refinement of classical learning as exhibited in texts like More's but also Thomas Campanella's *City of the Sun*, Francis Bacon's *The New Atlantis*, and *The Commonwealth of Ocea-*

na by James Harrington among dozens of other early modern examples. The implication is that the rhetoric of millennium is the
result of a type of trickle-down learning, but the opposite is actually true. Millennialism as an approach to critique and action
has a genealogy going back to Daniel, utopianism only emerges
in light of this earlier, religious discourse. It owes it everything.

Many Marxist critics have long rejected this claim that Marxism in particular or utopianism more generally is a form of secularized theological concept. A former professor of mine who is
a prominent and brilliant Marxist scholar of Shakespeare positively bristled at the suggestion that Marx's divisions of history, the assumed teleology, or the seemingly millennial-goals
were any way indebted to a type of secularized religious vision.
Indeed the association of medieval and early modern religious
movements with radical left-wing politics has often been made
as a presumed condemnation of the latter. Though *Pursuit of the
Millennium* remains the best historical overview of religious and
political radicalism from the middle ages to the English civil
wars, Cohn in part chose the description "anarchists" to make an
unfavorable comparison to campus radicals at the time he was
writing. Philosopher John Grey writes that "It has often been
noted that for its followers communism had many of the functions of a religion," and many on the left have reacted negatively
as surely as my professor did at this suggestion. However, I do
not dispute Grey's analysis, I merely contend that it is time for
us to get religion.

We must lose the cringe at the specter of the theological, or
at a genealogy that places radicalism and utopianism within a
theological tradition. There are two reasons why it is imperative
that we give the devil – or rather "God" – his due in this regard.
The first is that to divorce religion from a proper analytical consideration of how power structures operate is to try and do radical critique with one arm tied behind our backs. The second is
that in denying radicalism's theological origins we sell out our

birthright for a mess of pottage. The philosopher Grey, who is no friend to the utopian impulse, nevertheless remains a crucial thinker for those of us on the left to engage with, for though he stands in opposition to what he sees as the dangerous idolatry of progress in utopianism, his other lesson that utopianism is a species of the theological is an important one to incorporate into our understanding. He writes that "Modern politics is a chapter in the history of religion," and indeed this interpretive rubric must be engaged with if we're to properly chart where we've been and where we're going. Many theorists of left resistance of course already acknowledge this. Slavoj Žižek, Giorgio Agamben, and Simon Critchley are only a very short list of politically radical philosophers who are perfectly willing to engage the theological as a category in which left discourses can and need to operate. Again we do not need to choose between More the radical and More the saint, because in all the ways that matter they are identical.

Oscar Wilde in *The Soul of Man Under Socialism* wrote:

A map of the world that does not include Utopia is not worth even glancing at, for it leaves out the one country at which Humanity is always landing. And when Humanity lands there, it looks out, and, seeing a better country, sets sail. Progress is the realization of Utopias.

It is a type of *via negativa* approach to utopianism, a means of holding in our mind's eye the possibility of utopia and charting an ever and ever closer course towards her shore, even if the strand must always in some sense be inaccessible. But the fact that Utopia itself can never be reached is not to advocate for an abandonment of utopianism. No, the opposite is true. We must still hold true to these maps, and we must understand who those cartographers were, which is true wherever we find ourselves, be it the Kremlin, St. Peter's Square, or the corner of 53rd and 5th.

Debts Owed to Death

"We are all debts owed to death."
Simonides of Ceos

"I don't want to achieve immortality through my work; I want to achieve immortality through not dying."
Woody Allen

Chidiock Tichborne, of unlikely name but aristocratic birth, spent the evening of September 19, 1586, in the Tower of London awaiting his execution the following morning, and he contemplated not just the dawn that would bring his impending extinction, but indeed struggled to fit words into rhythm, feet into line, and lines into rhyme as he composed an elegy to his own death. Heretofore he was a poet of no particular distinction, and after his composition of what has been called "Tichborne's Elegy," or more romantically "My prime of life is but a frost of cares," a poet of no other accomplishments (for obvious reasons, as his head had been cut off, so subsequent accomplishments would be hard to come by). Embroiled in the Babington Plot to assassinate Elizabeth and place her cousin Mary Queen of Scots on the throne, Tichborne was but one of hundreds of recusants executed by the monarch in her tenure, which rivaled her sister Bloody Mary's in said bloodiness. Dr. Johnson claimed that nothing quite focuses the mind like a hanging, and if that is the case then the gallows must prove the ultimate deadline for an aspiring writer, for Tichborne's mind was very focused indeed. In the golden age of English verse, poor Tichborne only has three short lyrics to his name, and this elegy of eighteen lines divided into three stanzas of six lines each. Written in a steady metronome of monosyllabic iambic pentameter (which mimics a heartbeat until it stops), "Tichborne's Elegy" is his only poem even to be anthologized, or even remotely well-known (and the threshold is low for this kind of thing).

But though it be but one poem, what a poem it is! For his elegy must count as one of the most haunting evocations of our ultimate fate written in that melancholy, death-obsessed era. Using that favored Renaissance trope of antithesis, he movingly writes (being somewhere between the age of 23 and 28) that, "My youth is gone, and yet I am but young." New Critical orthodoxy (which nobody really believes anymore) would have us separate the circumstances of the elegy's composition from the poem itself, and yet it would be dishonest to say that some of the sublimity of Tichborne's lyric isn't in the fact that we envision him in a cold, unforgiving stone cell of the Tower desperately pressing pen to parchment as he attempts to get all of the words left within him out onto paper. Nobody would claim Tichborne to be the equivalent of a John Donne or George Herbert. And yet, is there not an incredible frankness that moves one equally when you remember that the poem, which ends with "and now my life is done," was completed with the author's full knowledge that indeed within hours his life would end? Tichborne, along with his fellow Elizabethan, the Jesuit martyr Robert Southwell, offers a Western example of the Japanese poetic genre of the jinsei, writers composing a poem knowing that they are shortly approaching death. It is the genre that is best able to encapsulate what it means to hear a fly buzzing, to remind us that death may be abstract but that it is also always particular. As a result, despite death's universality, it isn't really an abstraction to any of us. But, Jesus, Tichborne knew that score more than most.

I've been thinking about Tichborne recently, not because I am an expert on him (is anyone an expert on Chidiock Tichborne?) but because I couldn't help but contrast his approach to death with that of the transhumanist tech denizens profiled in Tad Friend's excellent *New Yorker* article of April 3rd 2017, "The God Pill: Silicon Valley's Quest for Eternal Life." Friend

interviews investors, scientists, and advocates for both the (obviously admirable) cause of life extension and the (delusional)
one of technological immortality. He discusses both biological
life-extension with the (appropriately named) English gerontol-
ogist Aubrey de Grey, and the technological Singularity with the
seemingly brilliant but huckstery inventor Ray Kurzweil, who,
I should mention before appearing too snarky, did manifestly
improve the lives of millions with his invention of the Kurzweil
Reading Machine. What emerges in Friend's piece is a collective
portrait of tanned, toned, supplement-swallowing, vitamin-ob-
sessed, emotionally-stunted Silicon Valley technocrats who, not
content to have altered everything about how we communicate
and interact with human beings over the past generation, now
have the arrogance to assume that they can easily "hack" death
as well. Journalist and advocate for death with dignity, Ann
Neumann, said in an interview with *America Magazine* that ours
is a society "where death is hidden inside institutions." Among
the most privileged of our citizens, that invisibility of death in
our culture is taken to its logical conclusion by erasing the understanding that death even needs to exist. In my last piece for
Marginalia I wrote that in our current moment "awareness of
death is as repressed [as] sex was to the Victorian," and what
better example of repressing this awareness than the sanitized
fantasy of dotcom millionaires and billionaires pretending that
technological immortality is not just possible but likely?

Mythically it's a profoundly old story, the assumption that
there is an easy material cure for death, traceable as far back as
Gilgamesh confronting the immortal Utnapishtim and learning
that death is indeed the mother of beauty. Figures in Friend's
essay, like Peter Thiel and Jeff Bezos (neither of whom he interviews), come across with all the hubris of characters from Greek
myth, as if inventing PayPal and writing checks to de Grey's
Strategies for Engineered Negligible Senescence ensure that they
can still that bell which tolls for all, or halt the wheels on time's

winged chariot. Friend quotes Arram Sabeti, founder of something called ZeroCater, who says, "The proposition that we can live forever is obvious. It doesn't violate the laws of physics, so we will achieve it," to which I respond with: "Ask not for whom the heat death of the universe ultimately cools, it cools for thee." Sabeti's proclamation is a stunning bit of positivist hubris, not least of which because it's literally incorrect, for in the end nobody and nothing, not even the universe, can escape the most poetic law of physics, the Second Law of Thermodynamics. But what does Tichborne have to do with Sabeti, or Google co-founder Sergey Brin, who sunnily tells an assembled party in Mandeville Canyon, Los Angeles, that "I'm not actually planning to die?" What does Tichborne, who perhaps melodramatically, but still honestly, wrote that he "sought my death and found it in my womb, / I looked for life and saw it was a shade, / I trod the earth and knew it was my tomb, / And now I die" — what does he have to do with Brin, who thinks that if he writes a big enough check he can bribe the Grim Reaper?

The difference between the assembled technological utopians and Tichborne is that despite his melodramatic posturing, his romantic pose, and his at times overwrought verse, Tichborne's approach to mortality was fundamentally more mature, and in his maturity he conveyed a deep wisdom that de Grey, Kurzweil, and the rest of them lack. This maturity isn't because the techno-utopians believe in immortality and Tichborne didn't – far from it. Despite the fact that at no point in the elegy did Tichborne ever hint at anything concerning an afterlife, I have no doubt that as a staunch Catholic willing to be martyred, he firmly believed in a heavenly reward. Five years before his execution, Tichborne and his father narrowly escaped punishment for smuggling Catholic relics from the continent into Britain. A man willing to risk decapitation for some bits of bone, rag, and wood is not wishy-washy, milquetoast, or agnostic when it comes to questions of the afterlife. No, what made Tichborne more mature was his despairing honesty. What made Tichborne more mature is that he understood that he was going to die, he knew that whatever came next that the process itself wasn't an option or a choice. And he knew that fact, though he was on an abbreviated schedule; he knew that it's a fundamental truth for all of us – maybe the only universal and fundamental truth. What also made Tichborne more mature is the presumed basis for his trust in an afterlife, for in embracing religious justification for such a belief, he was, I would argue, on much more legitimate epistemological ground.

Do not mistake what I'm arguing; I am not claiming that a supernatural life-after-death is "real" or not. I of course have absolutely no certainty about that. Like most people aspiring to honesty I'll admit that at some moments, I'm sure that we're nothing but meat for vermiculation, and in the next, I'm certain that there is a transcendence that we're all destined to enjoy, a world of light unto which we shall all ascend. Sometimes I have those contradictory feelings in the space of a few minutes. Except for those people that know neither the score nor the definitions, there are no atheists or theists, only an admixture of both. This isn't a claim for some personal superiority, merely an observation on the contingency of doubt since the dawn of modernity. But what I do know with certainty is that if there is to be true, genuine, eternal life, then there is no materialist explanation for such a possibility. That is not a dictate of theology; it is one of science, which the transhumanists abuse and make an idol out of so as to balm their fear of death. Since Karl Popper's useful "falsification principle" it has been a philosophical matter of course to evaluate whether a proposition is scientific or not based on whether there is the possibility for said claim to be empirically falsified. That is to say, can one envision an experimental or observational method by which a claim can be proven false? Note that the falsification principle can't verify the accuracy of a claim, only its status as a scientific one. So, as the famous example goes, the claim that "All swans are white" is a scientific claim, because whether correct or not it's possible to envision a situation in which the statement can be falsified, namely the discovery of a black swan. Now a theological proposition such as the Filioque clause is one that can't be empirically falsified: it is epistemologically beyond measurement. No cyclotron can falsify either the Latin or Greek Church's positions on the issue of whether the Holy Spirit proceeds from the Father alone or also from the Son.

Some philosophers, historically the logical positivists of the first few decades of the twentieth century, against whom Popper was reacting, would argue that such theological claims (and indeed the claims of aesthetics, metaphysics, myth and so on) are logically meaningless. That may or may not be the case; of course the great objection to such a "verification principle" (associated with the analytical philosopher Rudolf Carnap) is that the principle that the only legitimate statements are those that can be confirmed empirically is itself self-contradictory. But I digress, my task is not necessarily to denigrate logical positivism as an epistemic system, but rather to point out that religious claims about immortality, as they lay beyond the realm of Popperian falsification, are beliefs that belong epistemologically to a different category than do claims that could be empirically proven false. But of the whole litany of transhumanist snake-oil chicanery—from the Robot Jesus of Kurzweil's Singularity, a human consciousness downloaded to a computer hard-drive, to cryogenic chambers and visions of electronic immortality dancing in our heads—what of those? Well, those are claims about the material world, privy to potential falsification. And, unless I'm missing something, there is no physical process or law which can ensure the immortality of an individual human consciousness—none. Certainly life-extension is a possibility, and even if de Grey is correct that scientists will soon be able to extend human life-spans to a minimum of a millennium (though I'm dubious), that's just a more extreme version of good ol' fashioned life-extension facilitated by throwing out your cigarettes, pouring your tumbler of Scotch down the drain, eating your spinach, looking both ways before crossing the street, and being the beneficiary of pure good luck. No, for eternity-eternity, as in forever-eternity, there can be no physical guarantee, only supernatural hope, for once again we come upon that most poetic law of physics, one which enshrines mortality in the dictum that all things must eventually tend towards entropy.

In Friend's article, Martine Rothblatt, the CEO of a biotech firm with the distressingly ambiguous name United Therapeutics, matter-of-factly claims, "Clearly, it is possible, through technology, to make death optional." Clearly. Or not. I can't even keep the computer that I am writing this on from crashing. Clearly it is possible through technology to extend life, and one would hope also to improve it. We know that that's true because that's the history of modern medicine. Ideally one would hope it's possible to extend and improve the lives of the largest number of people possible, and not just the millionaire anarcho-capitalists of Silicon Valley, but that's a political question for later. But Rothblatt isn't talking about modern medicine; she's talking about modern magic masquerading as medicine, for this isn't life extension but the making of death itself "optional." For some techno-utopians this is the ultimate validation of a certain libertarian-minded fetishizing of their god the Invisible Hand, which becomes so powerful it can still Death itself. For the techno-utopian libertarian, late capitalism is late not because of the impending collapse of the market under its own excess, but because eschatologically what lies beyond is immortality purchased through check (or PayPal). In the fevered brain-in-a-vat imaginations of such transhumanists, death can be an option, like a choice of appetizers in a Palo Alto bistro or between different shades of paint you might pick for your glass-walled living room overlooking Big Sur. For Rothblatt is like Max von

Sydow's knight in *The Seventh Seal*, except she is naïve enough to believe that she can pay Death to throw the game. But the techno-utopian forgets that the house always, always wins. Peter Thiel, despite his worst intentions to enshrine inequality into the very nature of metaphysical reality, is thankfully, like all of us, mortal.

Death always has a way of coming to the programmer, no matter how plucky or optimistic. Because again, whether in flood or fire, in Big Freeze or Big Crunch, the universe must die and so shall you. That is the dishonesty of the transhumanist promise – it has already failed the falsification test. By seeking a materialist explanation for an afterlife it lost the race before the starter fired. Now, none of this means that religious versions of the afterlife are necessarily true (or what "true" might even mean in that context). But what it does mean is that theological explanations for immortality, in that they are epistemologically not under Popper's jurisdiction, are ones that can't be disproven empirically. A less complicated way of putting this is that heaven and hell may or may not be bullshit, it's impossible to know either way; but we know that totalizing transhumanist claims must ultimately be bullshit, for they come up against the very laws of physics that they claim undergird their plans. And in that sense I see far more maturity in the religiously faithful, even (or maybe especially) those of an orthodox bent, because taking that leap of faith into the unknown is a more authentic and more honest approach to the universal tragedy of death than pretending that immortality lies in injections, Elizabeth Bathory-style, with the blood of healthy young people (seriously, in the article...) or having a digitized version of your brain merge with the infinite interconnected Cloud, which Kurzweil prophesizes will independently emerge by the year 2045.

For that matter, an engaged and serious atheism, which rejects the possibility of the perseverance of identity after death, is also a more authentic and honest approach to extinction. My argument concerns not whether one should believe or disbelieve metaphysical claims about an afterlife, only that believing in an afterlife for metaphysical reasons is more legitimate, and as a result more mature in its honesty, than believing in a heaven programed into a computer or a resurrection facilitated by liquid nitrogen. The chimeric mirage of physically finding an elixir for everlasting life is as old as Tithonus and as recent as Thiel. The motivation lay behind Gilgamesh searching for the boxthorn at the bottom of the sea and Ponce de Leon looking for the Fountain of Youth in Florida. A very old potion in new test tubes, for transhumanism offers nothing novel, just a positivist religion written in the metaphysics of materialism, ironically a philosophy that disproves the precepts of the cybernetic and cryogenic faith. What's telling is that from the Wandering Jew to Sir Galahad immortality is never seen as a prize, but a curse. Tichborne may have bemoaned his early departure, but he didn't want to wander the Earth forever either, for again his was a mature relationship to death. Lest I be too hard on the men and women interviewed in *The New Yorker* article, I should state that I clearly and deeply understand their desire – but I think the leap of faith into belief in religious immortality has the benefit of not being so easily disprovable as transhumanism.

But what do I know? Who am I to talk about transhumanism as easily "disprovable?" It's true, I am a lowly literary scholar, no more well-versed in cybernetics, cryogenics, artificial intelligence, or uploading consciousness to a computer than any other educated reader perusing articles like Friend's – but can you begrudge me my skepticism? As a humanist, who has spent his adult life enmeshed in texts both canonical and not, texts from *Ecclesiastes* to Julian Barnes' brilliant *Nothing to Be Frightened Of*, works penned within the valley of the shadow of death, I know that no traveler has ever returned from that undiscovered country. When Austrian roboticist Hans Moravec, a prominent transhumanist not mentioned in Friend's article and a professor at my alma mater Carnegie Mellon University (we've never met), says innocently that he has "already mentioned the possibility of [digitally] making copies of oneself, with each copy undergoing its own adventures," and that as a result "Concepts of life, death and identity will lose their present meaning," can one fault me for feeling that we've left the domain of science and entered that of a secularized religion, a positivist theology which enshrines technology as the engine of teleology? Moravec is a committed atheist (whose wife, fascinatingly enough, is an evangelical Christian), and yet despite his atheism he seems unable to shed the traditional comforts of religion at its most basic level. Since I do not know Moravec, I have no insights into his psychology, and no desire to play the armchair psychoanalyst for him. But I wonder if in general, those techno-utopians, those transhumanists, are not largely composed of men (and to a lesser extent women) who have intuited that because of the insights of the scientific revolution, the supernatural promises of faith must be incorrect, but who have not yet personally dealt with the implications of that supposed fact, and so they immaturely use the tools of positivist materialism to construct a new promise of immortality. Thiel, for his part, was raised as an evangelical Christian during his youth in Germany, and he still claims to be a religious Christian (even appearing on a dais with the Anglican theologian N.T. Wright).

Barnes writes, "I don't believe in God, but I miss Him." Kurzweil once said, "Does God exist? I would say 'Not yet.'" Parse the difference, for the transhumanists push their religious anxiety to the point of deigning themselves gods and then patenting the afterlife. The difference, however, between a Christian, or Jewish, or Islamic, or any other view of the afterlife and Moravec's is that the former are not constrained by physical limitation, the metaphysical rules which define them are different from transhumanism's. Note that that doesn't mean that they are correct or not, merely that they can't be dismissed in the same manner, because to critique them within the schema of materialism is to perform a category mistake. Transhumanism on the other hand is defined by materialism, a materialism that by the very nature of physical law means that ultimately the transhumanist promise itself must fail. British philosopher John Gray, one of the wittiest and most cognizant critics of the new immortality, writes, "transhumanism is not as rational as it seems....Deriving from mystical philosophies such as Platonism and gnosticism, it is an idea at odds with scientific materialism." But Platonism and Gnosticism both have the dignity to understand what they are, and not to masquerade as provable sciences. The promises of Christian resurrection may or may not be true, but they are promises that by their very definition are not of this world, and thus whether we believe them or not, we must judge them by a different criterion than that of Popper's falsification principle. But transhumanism? Well, I know for a fact that you can always unplug a computer. Or debug it of the ghost in the machine.

Not just as a humanist but also as a human I am fully aware of that most precious wisdom which explains that *"Sic transit gloria mundi."* In our ever-continuing season of disciplinary mortality, humanists churn out copy concerning the utility of the humanities, with arguments normally running within the relatively narrow spectrum of appeals towards pragmatic utility (critical thinking!) to mealy-mouthed, rapturous canonicity (the Great Books!). Here is what I think is a novel argument to inject into that discussion: the humanities provide the wisdom that reminds you that you too shall die. If all of culture, all of art, all of literature, indeed all of religion is one great reaction against that most fundamental of truths, then the transhumanist promise is just one more bit of denialism that pretends that mortality is a problem to be simply solved by human ingenuity. Montaigne said that "to study philosophy is to learn to die." Peter Thiel doesn't like academics or college much; no doubt he rejects most philosophy as only so much navel-gazing (in spite of, or perhaps because of, a B.A. in philosophy from Stanford). Far more practical to envision Randian utopias floating as constructed islands on the Pacific or eternity as organized on the circuit boards of an artificially intelligent super computer. He would do well to put a statue of himself amongst the sands of Silicon Valley with the admonition that we should "Look on my works, ye Mighty, and despair!" But might I humbly suggest that the immature rejection of such a basic fact as one's own death robs one of life before it has even ended? For in rejecting the very idea of death, we by necessity reject the idea of the good death, of the Ars moriendi.

This is a dangerous road to travel, and ironically the fantasies of Silicon Valley and the tremendous accumulation of capital, which they represent, indicate a deeper malignancy in our body politic. While Peter Thiel's friends dream of electronic immortality, the president, whom he advises, oversees the dismantling of our healthcare system and the condemnation of twenty-four million Americans who will lose their insurance. Transhumanists attend TED talks about how death for them is "optional," while advocating for a system that denies the poor based on "pre-existing conditions," and so we witness the new eugenicist doublethink logic of a type of genocide. Death is inevitable to all, but the myopia and narcissism that allows the über-rich to pretend that they alone can escape it while denying others the medical care that we know we are capable of as a society has very real implications. Death might be inevitable, but a good death is not. The first is the purview of God and nothing can be done about it, the latter is the purview of humans, and we should offer to as many as possible the dignity of the Ars moriendi. While Peter Thiel and Jeff Bezos pretend that they will live forever, others suffer and die. It's an obvious obscenity. Transhumanism, far from being a regenerative or imaginative world-view, is one that is moribund to the core; it suffers from a profound lack of creativity in terms of restructuring social organization, preferring instead to masturbate to thoughts of a mythic lifeboat, one reserved for the very rich, which will preserve them from our common end. Again, if humanism has any wisdom to impart against the machinations and mirages of theologized techno-utopianism it's that old adage that "This too shall pass." Perhaps, as with the Roman generals of old, men like Thiel (or the president Thiel endorsed) would do well to have an assistant at their side, periodically whispering in their ear *Respice post te. Hominem te memento.* "Look after yourself. Remember that you're human," whether you've taken your ninety vitamin supplements or put your head on ice or not.

Kurzweil says, "It's a common philosophical position that death gives meaning to life, but death is a great robber of meaning....It robs us of love. It is a complete loss of ourselves. It is a tragedy." Kurzweil is wrong, but for understandable reasons. Death is most certainly a tragedy; to paraphrase Donne the loss of any human diminishes us all. And the fact that death is intrinsic to life, well, that's by definition one of the most unfair things conceivable. Where Kurzweil errs is in thinking that death's tragic nature makes it a "robber of meaning," for nothing about the nature of tragedy necessarily implies meaninglessness. Again, don't mistake what I'm saying. Nothing is more insulting in its triteness than consoling those left behind with the cheap adage that God must have his reasons. Rather I am arguing that death in and of itself neither implies meaning nor meaninglessness, but rather it is the job of the living to endow life with meaning. Our Editor-in-Chief Samuel Loncar recently wrote in *Marginalia,* "We can believe death ends this poetry of bodies making meaning in the world, or merely interrupts it, but in either case we can find in death not just an ending but a beginning of wisdom." The sentiment is less a rebuke to a worldview like Kurzweil's and more of a promise, or even a consolation, to one who fears that death is the end of meaning – which is all of us sometimes. And meaning is what defines a numinous experience, for religion has always had meaning at its core and not just the opiate comforts of immortality. Religion seeks to endow the profane with the charged electricity of the sacred, whether we survive individually or not. What faith at its fullest expression promises, whether through *"Carpe Diem"* or *"Memento Mori,"* is not necessarily the existence of life after death but rather the capacity to live your life with such beauty, justice, truth, and love that it doesn't matter whether life continues after death or not.

I do not wish to be callous, but as death is our common fate (whether the party in the article acknowledges that or not) I feel like I have a stake in such questions and can render my judgment. I understand the fear which motivates the transhumanist perspective, for I am human and let nothing which is post-human be alien to me – but what is more human than to fear death? And not just the process, but also the possibility of nothingness itself. Our old friend Tichborne, in a different poem, this one to his old friend Anthony Babington who got him into that whole mess in the first place, sweetly writes that God "shall remove our grounded ship far from this dangerous place... And keep ourselves on land secure... Sweet friend, till then content thy self." Who doesn't pray for some secure destination away from this dangerous place of life, some field on the other side of true and false where we may once again see those we have loved, and love still? Kurzweil explains how he lost his father at a relatively young age, as indeed many of the transhumanists have, indeed as I did as well. Friend writes that Kurzweil "hopes to someday create a virtual avatar of his father and then populate the doppelgänger's mind with all this information, as well as with his own memories of and dreams about his father, exhuming a Fredric Kurzweil 2.0." His hope is understandable, even poignant, but it is also unspeakably sad, for it appears to be much more of a delusion than those dusty desert promises of religious faith that have been roundly rejected. I do not suggest that faith comes easily, or that we want to have a cheap faith; no, a faith worth anything must be very expensive. I ask not to trade the delusions of technocratic fundamentalism for those of a primitive religious faith, but I do believe that, however uncomfortably, we can dwell in contradiction, for in that ambiguity there is always hope. Perhaps we all shall meet again, but I both doubt and hope that it will not be in a hard drive.

I contrast Kurzweil's hologram with something said by the children's book author Maurice Sendak, who discussed the death of his beloved brother Jack with the NPR interviewer Terry Gross. Like Kurzweil, and de Grey, and Moravec, and the others, Sendak couldn't reconcile himself to traditional religious faith. He told Gross that "When [people] die they're out of my life, they're gone forever," but he continued, "I still fully expect to see my brother again." There is a beauty in that view of mortality, having shuffled off certainty with our bodily coil, finding more hope in a paradoxical promise than in that old myth that eternal life can be found just around the corner, or in some exotic land, or in some alchemist's elixir. Such a perspective is beautiful not in spite of the doubt at its center, but because of it. Such a perspective has a particular kind of truth precisely because of that doubt. Such a perspective is the very essence of genuine faith.

An Almost Chosen People

*"Power always thinks that it has a great soul and vast views....
And that it is doing God's service when it is violating all His laws."*
John Adams.

"The point is that you can't be too greedy."
Donald J. Trump

*"Shall you reign because you enclose yourself in cedar? ... Yet your
eyes and your heart are for nothing but your covetousness, for shed-
ding innocent blood, and practicing oppression and violence."*
Jeremiah, 22:15-17

What ten sentences have been more scriptural than the ones
delivered by Abraham Lincoln in that southern Pennsylvanian
killing field? Not just scriptural in rhetoric, with the president
imitating the simple Anglo-Saxon vocabulary and the Hebraic
parallelism of the King James Version of the Bible, but indeed
quasi-scriptural in import to the American project. Lincoln's
words, chiseled on Union war monuments and memorized by
generations of school children, should be more central in the
American canon than either the Declaration of Independence or
the Constitution, both penned a bit more than a hundred miles
to the east of where Lincoln would ultimately deliver his oration.
That's because whereas the Declaration contains the utopian
promise of an America never realized, and the Constitution is a
profoundly flawed, problematic, and anti-democratic document,
the Gettysburg Address achieves a subtle union of the two, by
interpreting the imperfect reality of the Constitution through the
paradisiacal millennialism of the Declaration. In such a reading
Lincoln's address is as if Midrash for the scripture that is the
Constitution and the Declaration, a type of secular exegesis that

created fresh interpretations of canonical texts so as to create new, equitable political arrangements. This particular hermeneutic of Lincoln's owed much to his conversations with Frederick Douglass, as sociologist Philip Gorski makes clear in his incomplete, yet illuminating, new book *American Covenant: A History of Civil Religion from the Puritans to the Present.* In Gorski's formulation, Douglass's reading of the "preamble of the Declaration, with its promise of equality, overrode the articles of the Constitution with their tacit recognition of chattel slavery," and this was indeed the interpretation that Lincoln would express across some three odd minutes, and in only 272 words.

Garry Wills' account of the event is strikingly theological, writing that "Lincoln was here to clear the infected atmosphere of American history itself, tainted with official sins and inherited guilt. He would cleanse the Constitution...He altered the document from within, by appeal from its letter to the spirit." Wills, prophetic-minded former Jesuit that he is, has a sense of the numinous about his depiction of the sixteenth president's speech, an American Sermon on the Mount by an American Christ. For Wills – and of course in many ways for the idea of "America" itself – the Gettysburg Address heralded nothing less than its own self-declared "new birth of freedom." Lincoln, in such an account, was as Moses on Sinai; the Gettysburg address departs from profane history, and into the sacred. Wills writes that Lincoln's audience "walked off from those curving graves on the hillside, under a changed sky, into a different America." A powerful theophany indeed, for Lincoln's are some pretty well-penned words no doubt, but a changed sky over a different America? But then this is the charged essence of American civil religion.

Civil religion – that amorphous, indeterminate, variable, and yet powerful concept. A collection of symbols, national legends, and mythic narratives which function as a type of subconscious base for the aspirations of a nation – in particular of the United

States. A land whose only true innovation to the liberal political order was neither separation of powers nor federalism, but rather the radical disestablishment of the churches (not to be confused with French *laïcité*). A land where that disestablishment of the churches not only resulted in a tremendous creative ferment for religion itself, but which also lent itself to the development of a type of shadow religion which took "America" itself as its focus, a religion which furthermore could be embraced across denominational lines and by those of no traditional faith at all. Civil religion's holy sites are the Lincoln Memorial and Independence Hall, its scripture the Constitution and the Declaration of Independence, its theologians Lincoln and Martin Luther King, and its theology ostensibly one not about salvation, but rather liberty and equality. What variety of civil religion one embraces, pluralistic and tolerant, or rather a crude strict constructionist letter of the law theology, depends on what the definition of that ever malleable word "America" is. A referent and symbol as open ended and ambiguous as either utopia or Eden. At its best, civil religion can be the inclusive, all-encompassing, universalist rhetoric of King's Dream speech, at its worst the jingoistic defenses for imperialism and exclusion which have perennially marked the American experiment. And civil religion, insomuch as it is "religion" of a type, is an odd one running in parallel next to established houses of worship. Every nation of course has its national symbols; you can trade Uncle Sam for John Bull or the Goddess Liberty, the Stars and Stripes for the Union Jack. But, as the literary critic Leslie Fiedler once noted, "To be an American (unlike being English or French or whatever) is precisely to imagine a destiny rather than to inherit one; since we have always been, insofar as we are Americans at all, inhabitants of myth rather than history."

Myth marks the very idea of America, the very word, from the moment of its invention. Edmundo O'Gorman noted that "America" was always a concept to be invented rather than discovered, and so the construction of myth was always at the center of the American project, in a rather remarkable manner for a country whose arrival in many ways marked the dawn of modernity. A sense of providential meaning accompanied the first migrations of Puritans to New England (and they have certainly been both figured and refigured within the national scripture of our civil religion). Providence seemingly stalks the first stirrings of European colonialism on these shores, for "America" was mythically conceived. As Jonathan Edwards preached in 1742, "When God is about to turn the earth into a paradise, he does not begin his work where there is some growth already, but in the wilderness." That Thomas More wrote *Utopia* a mere twenty-five years after Columbus landed in the Caribbean, and furthermore placed his imagined community in the western hemisphere, is not a historical coincidence. Tragically misunderstood as geographic *tabula rasa,* the American continents were privy to any number of projected dreams of those who arrived. And, contrary to the noxious imaginings of our current crop of nationalists, the project was profoundly multicultural from its beginnings, which only further necessitated the development of a type of invented creed to define what exactly an American is, or as the eighteenth-century Franco-American writer Hector St. John De Crevecoeur answered the question in 1782, "He is an American, who, leaving behind him all his ancient prejudices and manners, receives new ones from the new mode of life he has embraced... Here individuals of all races are melted into a new race of man.... Americans are the western pilgrims." And what would define such a varied people but a type of faith, not necessarily in the Christian god, but in an American God? Even Teddy Roosevelt's "dirty little atheist" Thomas Paine stated with stark millennial fervor that, "We have it in our power to begin the world over again."

As a term "civil religion" can be traced back as far as to Jean-Jacques Rousseau in the eighteenth century, but it gained a new academic import with the publication of the classic sociological text *The Broken Covenant: American Civil Religion in Time of Trial* (1975) by Robert N. Bellah, Gorski's dissertation adviser at Berkeley. Bellah's account of American religious culture traced the ways in which an implicit, in some sense subconscious, and invented faith, which took "America" itself as the central object of its devotion, had evolved "alongside of and rather clearly differentiated from the churches." Bellah argued that this civil religion had its own scripture, in the form of not just the Declaration of Independence and the Constitution, but indeed political speeches such as Lincoln's; that it had its own rituals ranging from patriotic holidays to the duties of civic republicanism itself, its own theology, and its own priesthood (of a sort). After all, a council of learned elders performing exegesis on an ancient document describes both the ancient Jewish Sanhedrin and the Supreme Court equally well. While American civil religion was in some sense indebted to its Christian and in particular Protestant roots, it is not reducible to them either. Central to the American civil religion, as both Bellah and his student Gorski would argue, is the Hebraic concept of the "covenant," the creedal connection between the American people and the highest ideals of the nation. Bellah wrote of this covenant as a "founding myth," and just as the Puritan sees the Old Testament typologically reflected in the New, and both cyclically embodied in present time, so have there been many founding myths of America, from Plymouth Rock to Philadelphia in 1776 and Gettysburg in 1864, the nation ever redefining itself while also recommitting itself in subsequent covenants – just as Noah, Abraham, and Moses had with their covenants. Exodus, in particular, has held a strong resonance in American typology, from the Puritan crossing the Atlantic to the escaped slave crossing the Ohio River, for as Gorski reminds us, the Hebraic analogy "has been a seedbed, not only of most Western forms of nationalism, but also of revolutionary politics as well," and what is the American project but simultaneously both a nationalist and revolutionary one? Myth of course is not history, the former has no concern with the factuality of events so much as with their "truth," and as Bellah emphasized this "religious dimension" was implicit in "the life of every people, through which it interprets its historical experience in the light of transcendent reality." As such, American civil religion is not a "religion" as popularly understood by that word's strictest (and thus also inaccurate) definition, but in marrying providence to an almost numinous sense of ethics (for what could be more abstract than natural rights?) the American civil religion is most definitely a religion in the fullest sense of that word.

One could assume that such a religion must be de facto reactionary, but one of the brilliant aspects of American civil religion is the way in which at its most successful it is supposed to have been able to meld together people of radically different backgrounds through shared ideals rather than appeals to race, ethnicity, language, or religion as conventionally defined – even if obviously the national history has itself been one of exclusion or inclusion at various points based on those very criteria. President Barack Obama, who Gorski correctly identifies as one of the most conversant of contemporary politicians in the rhetoric of civil religion, said that "Being an American is not a matter of blood or birth. It's a matter of faith. It's a matter of fidelity to the shared values we all hold so dear," as apt a definition of the central essence of the idea behind American civil religion as anything more academic, especially because it gestures to a sort of transcendent faith as being the operating power of the ideology – even among ostensibly secular people. G.K. Chesterton, prefiguring Obama's point, once claimed that America was the only nation founded on a creed, and the similarities between the ancient Hebrews bound together by covenant and the American people, whose existence was similarly defined into being by textual fiat at a definite point in history, was not one which was lost on the founding generation, when both Benjamin Franklin and Thomas Jefferson (among the most secular of the revolutionaries) advocated for a national seal depicting the story of the Hebrews' exodus. The Philo-Semitism of the proposal was no mistake, since the Puritan's errand into the wilderness Americans have often typologically conceptualized the nation as a type of New Israel, and as the ancient biblical kingdom was composed of a diversity of tribes so too the *E Pluribus Unum* of the United States – with progressives enlarging the bounds of definition for the American project over the centuries. For those on the left who (only recently) have blanched at the rhetoric of religion in public life, Gorski provides a template for how theology can still be a wellspring for progressive politics, as he reminds us that "Again and again, the covenant between the Israelites and their God was renegotiated, and each iteration was more socially inclusive and more ethically universal than the last. The historical development of America's civil religion had followed a similar pattern." And as Gorski argues, membership in the community only requires adherence to the covenant (a very different matter of fidelity than "assimilation"), in opposition to the noxious idolatries of religious nationalists, as he calls them, who fetishize matters of blood and soil over the transcendent covenant itself.

Remember, as well, that a covenant is different from a contract. A covenant entails the holding of both people and deity (or "Deity") to their higher and shared ideals. Civil religion, in contrast to the religious nationalism of the literalists and fundamentalists, must be steadfastly introspective; its point is not to exult the nation no matter what it does, but to prophetically hold the nation accountable for its sins. Gorski writes that any civil religion which locates "evil outside of itself and claims certain knowledge of divine Providence quickly mutates into self-worship and self-benediction." The best of the American civil religious tradition, from its ur-text John Winthrop's 1620 "A Model of Christian Charity" through King's speeches, avoids the validations of certainty, preferring rather to answer the prophetic injunction by holding Americans responsible for their continual backslidings, to "speak a truth that allows suffering to speak," as Cornel West put it. The most popular genre of sermon in the second and third generation of Puritan New England was that of the jeremiad, based in the rhetoric of that prophetic book of the Old Testament in which Jeremiah holds Israel accountable for the numerous ways that the people and especially their rulers had violated the highest aspirations and ideals which defined the nation. From Puritans like Samuel Danforth and the Mathers in the seventeenth and eighteenth centuries, all the way through Barack Obama's "A More Perfect Union" speech in response to the Jeremiah Wright controversy (another prophetic Jeremiah!), the jeremiad has been the favored mode of American politics. At its crudest it's a variation on the "Golden Age" myth which archetypally reoccurs in seemingly every culture – that there was an Eden and some snake made us lose that paradise. These primitive jeremiads, with their calls to make America great again, merely focus on perceived material plenty or the halcyon joys of cultural uniformity. They are a shell of a jeremiad, a pantomime of the form more than an example of it. Confederates and their Copperhead sympathizers (both in their earlier and current forms) easily conceptualized the golden age of what would become the mythic "Lost Cause." Douglass wrote of the pro-slavery, antebellum churches of the nineteenth century that they practiced "a religion which favors the rich against the poor; which exalts the proud about the humble; which divides mankind into two classes, tyrants and slaves; which says to the man in chains, stay there; and to the oppressor, oppress on," still an accurate description of many evangelicals who've sold their soul to the Mammon of the Invisible Hand. Douglas (who I have heard is doing some tremendous work) says that we must rather commit ourselves to the mighty, ever-living God, who is always a "God of the oppressed," and as such the true jeremiad calls the nation to account not for any loss of power or prestige, but for a violation of its principles. And, what are those principles? Few places better to return than that field in Pennsylvania, where Lincoln simply defined America as a "new nation, conceived in Liberty, and dedicated to the proposition that all men are created equal." If those are the nation's principles, then from *Citizens United* to Stephen Bannon in the White House we've fallen very short of our values, and have more need of genuine jeremiads now than at any point in our recent history. A nation dedicated to the proposition that all men are created equal lets the police martyr her black children while the majority of Americans platitudinously obscure murder by mouthing the jingle "All Lives Matter;" a nation conceived in Liberty splits families up through deportation, or closes the golden door shut to those who are Muslims; a government of the people, by the people, and for the people has increasingly become an oligarchy, replicating the worst iniquities of the Gilded Age. A broken covenant indeed.

So, in the manner of the most scrupulous of Puritans (who after all are our intellectual ancestors), it's worth performing that rigorous self-examination and asking, "Whither the covenant now?" Bellah's subtitle of course alluded to the breaking of that covenant in the era in which his book was written, published the year that Saigon fell. Optimistic, sunny evaluations of American exceptionalism had seemed to die in south-east Asia alongside 60,000 Americans and close to two million Vietnamese. Much as the ancient Israelites continually fell short of their covenant, Bellah emphasized how the participants in the American covenant were also prone to backsliding, and how that covenant was spectacularly challenged at particular points in history, such as during the Revolution, the Civil War, or the period of Bellah's own writing, which he termed America's "third time of trial." Well, it seems that the franchise is a tetralogy, for in this our "Cold Civil War," the American civil religion seems on the verge of collapse (as I've argued elsewhere), with ideological divisions as stark as they have been for the past half century, and with the Oval Office filled with arguably its most demagogic occupant, for whom despite all of his executive and legislative incompetence always seems as if he is only one national tragedy away from transforming himself into a full-on dictatorial tyrant. If there was ever any legitimacy to the model of American exceptionality which understood this country as "the last best hope of earth," where King's contention that the nation is exemplary because "America is the world in miniature and the world is America writ large," than not even Richard Nixon posed as grave a threat to that revolutionary universalism as Donald Trump does, a man who categorically denies both Lincoln and King's vision of the United States. One of Gorski's most potent observations is in correctly identifying American civil religion's moment of fallenness, when Ronald Reagan modified Winthrop's beautiful, humble clarion call to conceive of the American experiment as being a "city on a hill" (itself a quotation from the Book of Matthew) with the gaudy adjective "shining." Suddenly gone was the theological vision which understood our covenant as being one of "charity," replaced with a libertarian, consumerist promise of purely material comforts. Gorski astutely describes Reagan's theology as "Pelagian," that is to say that the Gipper and his California optimism denied original sin, and in the process any sense of national or personal responsibility. Reagan was certainly more responsible for this type of selfish, naval-gazing individualism than the feel-good '60s flower power generation. Gorski writes that Reagan's theology "left out the bitter salt that had given the prophetic stance its sting: the notion of collective sin. And therein lay one of Reagan's greatest, least noted, and most fateful innovations." In the rejection of any kind of understanding of national destiny which has ruthless self-castigation at its center, Reagan adopted the mantra of supply side economics, which advocated no ethic other than that of growth, consumption, wealth, and competition. For those who gnash their teeth over the Republican Party's supposed cooption at the hands of vulgar Trumpians, take heart: the situation has always been terrible, now it's just honest (if seeming to reach some sort of dark culmination). Reagan claimed that the city on a hill was shining, it's only been recently that we've been able to make out that that luminescence was the cheap, tawdry electronic glow of an Atlantic City neon sign. But now that that malevolent geneology has become clear, we face another crisis forcing us to ask what responsibility does American civil religion now have with Caligula in the palace, demanding that all be rendered unto him? When the only God is Mammon, maybe especially the God of the evangelicals who sold whatever slight birthright they had for a mess of meager pottage doled out at the feet of a tyrant as foam-mouthed as any Nebuchadnezzar?

As on cue, arriving right at this fourth time of trial is Gorski's book, perhaps presciently published at our present moment, though conceived of in those comparatively sunnier days of 2008 (economic collapse aside) when Obama's speech on race at the National Constitution Center inspired the sociologist to update his adviser's thesis for a new millennium. The result, as I mentioned earlier, is incomplete – a book both important, welcome, and vital, but that is not quite as radical as it needs to be. Gorski's thesis is that there are three major strands in American public life, his celebrated civil religion which has to contend for dominance alongside a fundamentalist religious nationalism (which interprets America in apocalyptic and specifically Christian terms) and a radical secularism which broaches no role for theological language in public life. As is perhaps the case with any sociological schema, Gorski's tripartite division is a bit too reductionist, even if his overall description is legitimate. American Covenant suffers from a certain whataboutism. The author admirably writes about "the vital center," a third-way charted between the two heretical traditions vying for dominance with civil religion, and he borrows the Anglican term of the via Media to describe this centrist moderation charting a course between the sword-and-flame obsessed eschatological religious nationalists and the radical secularists who apparently spend all their time complaining about "In God We Trust" being emblazoned on our currency. By contrast, Gorski's *via Media* is depicted as a sort of estimably sober, sane, rational alternative to either extreme. The biggest theoretical difficulty in this endeavor lay in defining the admittedly complicated concept of "secularism," and the project is diminished by not fully considering whether such a concept is actually intellectually impossible. Practically, "radical secularism" as a movement poses little threat to the health of the body politic, as rhetorically obnoxious and provincial as the so-called "New Atheists" might be. He defines radical secularism as a "noxious blend of cultural elitism and militant atheism that envisions the United States as part of an Enlightenment project threatened by the ignorant rubes who still cling to traditional religion," continuing later by arguing that the ideology "fails because restricting religious expression violates liberal principles, because the United States was not founded on a 'total separation' of religion and politics." Gorski's account of radical secularism (whose origin he identifies with the Victorian legal thinker Robert Ingersoll) falls short in a few ways: it overstates the actual political threat which the movement poses; it irons out some historical counter-examples which are problematic for his argument, and while beginning to gesture to the proper analysis of secularism, it doesn't fully interrogate the ways in which "radical secularism" (alongside any other political ideology) is simply a type of theology in disguise. No doubt Christopher Hitchens, Sam Harris, and most of all Richard Dawkins (alongside their cultish acolytes), were and are an insufferable lot – poorly educated on the topic of religion, anemic when it comes to theology and history, and nowhere near as clever as they imagine themselves to be. That being said, intellectual boorishness and genuine danger to the Republic are two different things, and the

radical secularist agenda of Margaret Murray-like atheistic zeal-
otry which Gorski writes about holds absolutely no real sway
outside of a few tony zip codes. Maybe this is a bloc with out-
sized power in New Haven, or Cambridge, or Berkeley, or the
Upper West Side, but the vast majority of the country doesn't
suffer from a surplus of too much secularism, far from it. His
contention that the United States was not founded on a "total
separation" of religion and politics is a bit of overly clever jiujut-
su, for nobody credibly claims that the nation was to be founded on a total separation of religion and politics, but rather that
of religion and state; otherwise how could I conceptualize my
own political positions which involve adhering to Amos' desire
to see "justice roll down like waters, and righteousness like an
ever-flowing stream" while using my well-worn ACLU membership card as a bookmark for that passage in my copy of the King
James Bible?

His argument that "Secular liberals who claim that the United States was built on Enlightenment foundation are just as
mistaken as religious nationalists who believe that the American founders were 'orthodox Christians'" is unassailable. When
the left ignores the obvious, if heterodox, religious origins of
American identity Gorski is absolutely correct that they're as in
error as their triumphalist evangelical adversaries. But the legal
"separation of church and state" as implied by the establishment
clause of the First Amendment is also a historical reality; it does
Gorski's argument no good to obscure evidence such as the dip-
lomat Joel Barlow's "Treaty of Tripoli," unanimously ratified by
Congress in 1796, which unequivocally stated that "the United
States of America is not, in any sense, founded on the Christian
religion." Barlow, incidentally, appears nowhere in American
Covenant. I don't wish to impugn or simplify Gorski's argument, he makes clear that "Civil religion recognizes the importance of an institutional separation between church and state,"
yet he overstates both the dangers of radical secularism while

simultaneously minimizing its intellectual genealogy. When he writes that, "it would be a good thing for the more secular minded to reflect on how their values are ultimately grounded in a certain 'transcendent' understanding of reality, that is a reality that transcends their physical self and its narrow interests," I wholeheartedly and uncomplicatedly agree with him in his entirety. My academic criticisms are perhaps reducible to the "narcissism of small differences" as Freud famously put it, which I'll admit is a common affliction, especially among academics, but I'd be remiss not to examine areas of disagreement I have with Gorski.

What I should point out (without having the space to elaborate) is that I don't believe there is anything secular about radical secularism, for the simple reason that I doubt whether secularism, beyond the necessary strict legal fiction of the establishment clause, is even possible. America is not, and never was a Christian nation, but its "secularism" (insomuch as such a thing is even possible), is really a variety of Protestant heresy which evolved into a new religion, taking the nation itself as the god of its supplication, and not incorrectly replacing Christ with an idea of a utopian "America" of charged possibility. Gorski, I think, believes something similar about secularism: that it's not possible to be devoid of all religion, evident when he approvingly quotes the novelist David Foster Wallace's argument that "there is no such thing as not worshipping. Everybody worships. The only choice we get is what to worship." The importance of Gorski's book is that it begins the conversation about the ways in which progressives could reclaim scriptural language and theological thought in the service of a radical agenda. As such I don't want an anodyne via Media, but a radical religious left, of civil religion in the service of what I've called elsewhere "the Augustinian left." Perhaps it's a difference of rhetoric, but the *via Media* of the vital center doesn't move me, nor do the relatively tame prescriptions which Gorski tries to offer at the end of his book. Removing the commercialism from civic holidays, promoting character education in public schools, and advocating for universal national service are all fine and good, but none of those things would have necessarily prevented the moment we find ourselves in now; redemption requires stronger stuff. In Gorski's defense he also clearly understands this, writing about the civil rights movement, the last major left-wing political movement with any theological core, that it "brought together a diverse coalition of social reformers that bridged long-standing divides of race and religion as well as the growing chasm between the religious and secular world-views – the sort of coalition that is needed today to remedy the deepening inequality and cultural malaise of our own era." That the best suggestions for a revitalized version of progressive civil religion rely on proposals for better civics classes and national service isn't to speak ill of the quality of those proposals, but it is to note just how silent our current generation is of prophetic voices that once thundered down from the prodigious hilltops of New Hampshire, and the mighty mountains of New York, and the heightening Alleghenies of Pennsylvania (not to speak of Stone Mountain, Georgia or Lookout Mountain, Tennessee). There is no Martin Luther King in America today, and to our profound detriment. For if we're to be practioners of a prophetic republicanism than we must be willing to listen to prophets! In America today the worst are once again the ones full of passionate intensity, maybe we need a bit of that fire and light as well, to speak in prophetic tongues. Civics class is great and important, but when Canaan is turning into Babylon it requires the fortitude to identify a sin for a sin – and the malignant faux religion of Trumpism is nothing if not sinful.

That finally is the most important observation of Gorski's – that theological thought and scriptural rhetoric can be used for progressive politics, whether Gorski's liberalism or something further to the left (perhaps even more for the later). He's absolutely correct in noting that for the past generation the left has been largely practicing an anemic politics devoid of any sense of sacred justice. It's not that liberal proposals are necessarily wrong – though I'd appreciate less neoliberalism and more New Deal. But it's also that the Democratic Party has confronted the profound injustices of the New Gilded Age with the language of policy papers when what the age requires is the rhetoric of the revival meeting; it's that the Democratic National Committee exhibits all of the cool rationality of the seminar room when the era necessitates the passion of the prophet; it's that campus liberals are conversant in the jargony weak sauce of cultural-studies privilege talk when they'd be better served looking at structural racism, misogyny, homophobia, and classism and calling them exactly what they all are: injustices and sins. As a fundamental truth, religious rhetoric and theological language remains the most potent method of critique against systems of oppression, far more than anemic cultural studies terminology as filtered through social media. W.E.B. DuBois identified a similar problem a century ago, when he wrote that "religion of mere reason and morality will not alone supply the dynamics of spiritual inspiration and sacrifice." The ever-baroque vocabulary of privilege and intersectionality and entitlement and so on has accomplished many necessary and admirable things, but by itself it must ultimately trend towards an emptiness, for such talk cannot on its own supply the inspiration and sacrifice that DuBois spoke of. Gorski says as much when he astutely observes that without scriptural language "Civic poetry would be transformed into political doggerel." There is no Gettysburg Address without the Bible, and we need not literally believe in the latter to know that it is what fuels the former. Contemporary politics remains the continuation of religion by other means, and make no mistake that Trumpism is nothing if not its own dark, occult faith. And what benefit is there then to the left returning to an awareness of its theological origins? The question raises something so much bigger than whatever our own personal faith or doubts may be, or even if questions of theology themselves make any literal sense. But, in our current political moment, I think a beginning might be approached by acknowledging that basic truth as conveyed in the ancient religious formulation which reminds us that "Resistance to tyrants is obedience to God." Any valid emancipatory politics and attendant theology must always flow from that principle, and it is paradoxically true regardless of whether or not there is a literal God. The rest is simply commentary.

The Sacred and the Profane in Pittsburgh

There is an entirely unremarkable looking brown-bricked, dou-
ble-spired chapel in a steep neighborhood on the North Side of
Pittsburgh. Troy Hill is covered in modest houses inching up the
mountainside, overlooking downtown, where two rivers come
together to form a third, that mythic American waterway which
long ago bifurcated this nation as it flowed west between one
land which was free and one which was enslaved. Only eighteen
years after that war, which supposedly erased that boundary, a
visionary Belgian priest named Suitbert Mollinger came to this
hill and founded his church. Troy Hill was then, and is still today, occupied by German stock, and rises high above the flat
neighborhoods to the south, not far from the banks of the Allegheny that still go by the name of "Deutschtown."

Pittsburgh is a confusing place; what national region it belongs to remains ambiguous, though its ethnic history runs parallel to so many other American cities from the Atlantic coast to
the plains. At one time, secessionists wished to call this part of
the country Vandalia; during the Whiskey Rebellion they preferred the less catchy name of Westylvania. Since it was first
settled by the French, then the British, and then the Americans
it was a liminal point between east and west, belonging to neither. Though its reputation and its own understanding of self
eventually saw it as a great industrial forge, making immigrants
into Americans like pig iron into steel, the truth of the matter
is that people often simply recreated their home villages from
Europe in the often strikingly similar topography of Pittsburgh.
First came the Scots-Irish who settled this land after the Quakers of genteel Philadelphia encouraged them to the frontier and
its wars that burnt like a setting sun on the western horizon.
Then came the Irish Catholics, who were so resisted by the nativists that Pittsburgh (which would go on like so many other

north-eastern cities to be ruled by an Irish Democratic political machine) elected a Know Nothing mayor with the disreputable distinction of being the rare elected official to die by being hit by a train. After the Irish came the Germans. And then the Italians. And the Poles and the hunkies, and so on and so on.

Fr. Mollinger's flock were German Catholics, distinctly different from the Pennsylvania Dutch who lived to the east. Unlike their Protestant brethren in the older parts of the state, Pittsburgh's German Catholics huddled together in urban slums such as Troy Hill. The Germans of the nineteenth century had not yet been stripped of their identity by the tragedies of the twentieth, and like the Irish before and the Italians after they were viewed with native suspicion by those chance had made American by birth and not through choice. It was here that Fr. Mollinger – a physician by both training and inclination – gathered his congregation. The priest was a wealthy and well-educated man with a profound personal devotion to Anthony of Padua, to whom he dedicated this new church. Anthony is the patron saint of that which is lost, and cheekily enough his skull in Padua has one lost tooth that is now in Troy Hill, the first relic of many.

Mollinger paid for the construction of a small chapel, on a site that from the Victorian era towards the period of post-industrialization would have smelled of vinegar from the Heinz Factory below, of yeast from the breweries not far away, and of sulfur from the gargantuan steel mills that would come to punctuate these river valleys. Indeed as a visitor in that late-nineteenth century recorded:

In the rear a hill slopes gently downward into a beautiful valley, and from the porches of the residences an interesting panorama of the surrounding hills and valleys is afforded. In decided contrast is the view from the riverfront. Instead of a clear atmosphere and the bright hills covered with foliage, can be seen nothing but a huge cloud of black smoke that seems to settle continually over the city, with here and there a church spire, a smoke stack or tower projecting through the cloud.

If you visit St. Anthony's Chapel today, the front of the church, though handsome, is as regular as any other Catholic immigrant church you might see in the cities and towns of the north-east and the industrial Midwest. But inside is a sacristy sanctuary as lush and baroque as any a tourist or pilgrim would visit in Europe. Rich violet reds and deep lush greens and celestial blues adorn fourteen carved life-size depictions of Christ's Stations of the Cross lining the walls of the church, and in-between, in every single conceivable corner, there are relics – 5,000 of them. This is a place that seems not so much pre-Vatican II as pre-Tridentine: if you ever wished to travel to the twelfth century you only need take the 6A bus. Bits of bone, cloth, skulls, skeletons, chips of wood are all housed in ornate gem-encrusted reliquaries as if in some crusader knight's personal temple, fresh from Jerusalem. Indeed this church contains more Roman Catholic relics than the entire Holy City; the only location with more relics is the Vatican. Jerusalem may be where David and Solomon built their Temple, where the Ark of the Covenant once resided in the Holy of Holies, where Jesus Christ was crucified, resurrected, and ascended to heaven. But Pittsburgh has more relics.

The notion of the relic triggers derision among rational-minded materialists as surely as it did Protestant reformers. Indeed, it was John Calvin who wondered if the several examples of Christ's foreskin, the holy prepuce which multiple medieval churches claimed ownership of, indicated a miraculous size in the divine member. Nowadays, "relic" may make the modern secular reader think of nothing so much as Chaucer's Pardoner with his collection of pig bones. But this misses the point. Relics are evidence of faith, not of prosaic reality. They are not laboratory specimens to be scientifically analyzed; they are objects that in their sacramental urgency force observers to consider the existence of divinity within the pain of everyday life. Consider the people who once sat through Mass at St. Anthony's (and still do), men and women who had perhaps lost limbs to accident or in the many wars in which the working classes of this country have fought (and still do). Here, under the altar, stacked to the rafters, in small boxes, are slivers of physicality. An arm like your arm, a skull like your own, a body with a connection to God. People believe that relics can heal their infirmities, and whether we believe with them or not the relics remain a symbol of divinity dwelling in mere matter.

Consider Annie Moore of Oil City who, though nearly blind, claimed she could see again after visiting Fr Mollinger, or Michael O'Regon of Youngstown, whose spine was injured at work and believed that the relics of St. Anthony's restored to him the ability to walk. This may not be the religion of the scholastics, but it is religion, and it instills in men and women the ability to hope. In a long and conflicted history, that may be one of religion's most important gifts. Is it right to mock the faith of the father who lost his son in a mill accident? Of the mother who lost hers in war? Of people who pray for the little bit of grace that life too often withholds? Not everyone may need to believe in the miracle. But we mock at our own peril; if we deprive others of their belief, we may wind up starving our own souls.

St. Anthony's is part of the gentle surrealism that permeates Pittsburgh. Why shouldn't this city have the second-largest collection of relics on Earth? Fr. Mollinger saved these thousands of objects with his personal finances as the iconoclasm of Bismarck's protestantizing Kulturkamp as well as the anticlericalism of Italy's unification scattered thousands of relics. The priest himself died from heat exhaustion after celebrating Mass on, appropriately enough, St. Anthony's feast day. A Pittsburgh Press article from 1892 records his fame, stating that "the venerable priest-physician, has spread to all parts of the continent, and he now numbers among his patients invalids from nearly every state and territory in the union."

It is endlessly said that Pittsburgh is a "city of neighborhoods" (ninety at last count) but it's more correct to say that it is a city of villages. With its rivers, mountains, and valleys it resembles no place as much as some central European province, with dozens of villages scattered across the green wooded floor (for all its Rust Belt associations Pittsburgh is if still a stunningly forested city in some parts). If one stands atop Mount Washington – from which the most clichéd (and yet beautiful) photos of the city are taken – you see a rolling carpet with these little villages hidden in hamlets behind the sparkling façade of the modern downtown. Some villages have onion-domed churches, some steeples. It is a holy city, and if not a city of dreaming spires than a city of working ones.

If the essence of religion is finding the holy in the normal, the sacred in the profane, then what city could be more holy than Pittsburgh? It is a city "of brick and tired wood" where it seemed that "Christ and the Father were still fashioning the Earth" as the poet Jack Gilbert had it. It may seem like a joke to say that Pittsburgh is a holy city – but it is, in its strangeness and its savage beauty. And its holiness is multifaceted; while someone might sarcastically quip that the only real objects of faith in this city are the Steelers, it takes a special type of spiritual perception to describe a football play as the "Immaculate Reception." The earthy nature of religion in Pittsburgh is such that there is nothing blasphemous about such a coinage – the physical and the spiritual exist in tandem here, how could it be any other way in a place so committed to production but so inhabited by the pious? Industrial Pittsburgh was the inverse of Giordano Bruno's Naples – if the latter was a paradise inhabited by demons then turn-of-the-century Pittsburgh was a hell with the lid taken off inhabited by angels.

In Polish Hill there is a cathedral that is a perfect miniature of St. Peter's in Rome. An inaccurately white-faced St. Benedict the Moor looms over Pittsburgh's Hill District. In the northern mill town named, appropriately enough, Millville, St. Nicholas Croatian Church sits in view of the modern skyscrapers of Downtown Pittsburgh while inside are the leftish murals of the Maxo Vanko, who painted Herod as a Gilded Age capitalist and the centurions who executed Christ as Great War doughboys. Squirrel Hill is dotted with Hasidic synagogues, men davening over the Torah as if it was seventeenth century Lithuania or Galicia. In the suburb of Penn Hills sits a massive ivory-colored Hindu temple, Sri Venkateswara, one of the earliest of its kind in North America, where the faithful believe an incarnation of Vishnu resides. A massive Gothic Presbyterian cathedral marks the skyline of inner-city East Liberty, looking more St. Giles than New Kirk and colloquially coined "Mellon's fire escape" after the banker who funded it – seemingly with little knowledge of Calvinist theology.

Religion is often thought of as rarefied and abstract, the metaphysical speculation of how many angels can dance on the head of a pin. But in Pittsburgh – where life was often very physical – religion had to be as well. And so we have the tired stone eyes of the Moorish saint looking out over subsidized housing, the communist paintings of Vanko, the swaying of the black-hatted Hasid, and the sheer physicality of the incarnated Hindu god who resides above the Parkway East. And we have the bones and cloth of St. Anthony's Chapel.

There is an old and admittedly not-terribly-funny joke that has it God gave John Knox Scotland and threw in Pittsburgh for free. Indeed the prevalence of Presbyterian churches demonstrates the fact that Pittsburgh really is the great metropolis of the trans-Appalachian frontier, reminding us that before Tennessee was the south and Pennsylvania the north, both were simply the west. And in what had once been the burnt-over country of the second Great Awakening the physicality of that frontier religion remains, and though John Knox would be revolted to hear it, that type of physical faith still exists in the Catholics, Jews, Hindus and so on who adopted this place as their new home. In many ways they all had more in common than they would have ever expected. It's an earthy city, and regardless of theology the religion that is practiced there is going to be the same. During the last 500 years, besieged both by Cartesian rationalism and Luther's Reformation, civilization attempted to distance us from the sacred, or even to abolish it in some sense. A disenchantment of the world, as the sociologists would put it. The sacred and the profane and the holy and the physical were to be separated. Yet in Catholicism – especially medieval Catholicism – mankind may be fallen but the world is still God's creation. And the brilliance of medieval Catholicism is that sparks of the divine could exist within corporeal reality. If it is the incarnational logic that has it that God could become man, then simple objects can also be holy.

Nothing is sacred without the profane, that's the fundamental rule of faith, which cannot be forgotten if faith is to remain faith.

The saints serve to remind us that holiness exists within creation. If modernity's primary instincts were to separate the two cities of God, our present one and the one to come, then St. Anthony's is itself a blessed relic of the past. The cynic may decry this as pre-modern superstition, but faith is not faith because it is respectable, it is such because the lived experience of it is real. The beauty of this understanding is that one can believe in the sacred even if you don't believe in God, you can acknowledge these things of the saints even if you are not one yourself. Sacredness is an experience, not a worldview, and it is accessible to the pious and apostate alike. St. Anthony's does what it has always done, providing a continuity of belief from the Gilded Age till today. When it was built the working class were sacrificed on Frick and Carnegie's altar of capital. Today the gap between those of the Kingdom of God and the others who find it harder to enter that Kingdom than to fit through a needle's eye again find the gulf separating each other almost insurmountable. They no longer make ketchup and vinegar in the Heinz factory; the building is now condos, and the mills have been silent for a generation. The *New York Times* seemingly discovers this city every month with some article declaring it the new Williamsburg or the new Portland, this place of aching beauty, with its ancient hills and rivers that will remain long after the last person is gone. And despite it all St. Anthony's goes on, the pilgrims come day after day looking for a cure to whatever causes them suffering, a respite from whatever haunts them. It's the humanity that is beautiful.

So what does St. Anthony's teach us? What does it teach us especially if we are not really the faithful, or sometimes the faithful, or wish we could be the faithful, or even never could be the faithful? It teaches us that no matter the pain – illness, poverty, death – there is nobility in our bodies. That the soul may be holy but that the body can be as well. That the saints may have been otherworldly but that they also had hands that were held, lips that were kissed, tongues which spoke, feet that walked, eyes that saw, ears that heard. That the back, which aches from labor, or the feet calloused from travel are not so dissimilar to those which belonged to God's favorites. The saints were all born, all lived, they ate, drank, defecated, slept, loved, and died, just like you do and you will. Nothing is sacred without the profane, that's the fundamental rule of faith, which cannot be forgotten if faith is to remain faith. It is after all our bodies that connect us.

A half millennium of modernity has tried to make religion respectable, but if it is respectable it's not really faith. That is to say that faith must always be Other, it must be visceral, lived, experienced, sensory, seen, felt, tasted, smelled, touched, and listened to before it is ever merely believed. Religion isn't just in the head or the heart, it's in the body, and the relics remind us of that. A religion exorcized of its strangeness is scarcely religion. St. Anthony's welcomes the pilgrim searching for real religion.

Zero Books

CULTURE, SOCIETY & POLITICS

Contemporary culture has eliminated the concept and public figure of the intellectual. A cretinous anti-intellectualism presides, cheer-led by hacks in the pay of multinational corporations who reassure their bored readers that there is no need to rouse themselves from their stupor. Zer0 Books knows that another kind of discourse – intellectual without being academic, popular without being populist – is not only possible: it is already flourishing. Zer0 is convinced that in the unthinking, blandly consensual culture in which we live, critical and engaged theoretical reflection is more important than ever before.

If you have enjoyed this book, why not tell other readers by posting a review on your preferred book site.

Recent bestsellers from Zero Books are:

In the Dust of This Planet
Horror of Philosophy vol. 1
Eugene Thacker
In the first of a series of three books on the Horror of
Philosophy, *In the Dust of This Planet* offers the genre of horror
as a way of thinking about the unthinkable.
Paperback: 978-1-84694-676-9 ebook: 978-1-78099-010-1

Capitalist Realism
Is there no alternative?
Mark Fisher
An analysis of the ways in which capitalism has presented itself
as the only realistic political-economic system.
Paperback: 978-1-84694-317-1 ebook: 978-1-78099-734-6

Rebel Rebel
Chris O'Leary
David Bowie: every single song. Everything you want to know,
everything you didn't know.
Paperback: 978-1-78099-244-0 ebook: 978-1-78099-713-1

Cartographies of the Absolute
Alberto Toscano, Jeff Kinkle
An aesthetics of the economy for the twenty-first century.
Paperback: 978-1-78099-275-4 ebook: 978-1-78279-973-3

Malign Velocities
Accelerationism and Capitalism
Benjamin Noys
Long listed for the Bread and Roses Prize 2015, *Malign Velocities* argues against the need for speed, tracking acceleration as the symptom of the ongoing crises of capitalism.
Paperback: 978-1-78279-300-7 ebook: 978-1-78279-299-4

Meat Market
Female Flesh under Capitalism
Laurie Penny
A feminist dissection of women's bodies as the fleshy fulcrum of capitalist cannibalism, whereby women are both consumers and consumed.
Paperback: 978-1-84694-521-2 ebook: 978-1-84694-782-7

Poor but Sexy
Culture Clashes in Europe East and West
Agata Pyzik
How the East stayed East and the West stayed West.
Paperback: 978-1-78099-394-2 ebook: 978-1-78099-395-9

Romeo and Juliet in Palestine
Teaching Under Occupation
Tom Sperlinger
Life in the West Bank, the nature of pedagogy and the role of a university under occupation.
Paperback: 978-1-78279-637-4 ebook: 978-1-78279-636-7

Sweetening the Pill
or How we Got Hooked on Hormonal Birth Control
Holly Grigg-Spall
Has contraception liberated or oppressed women? *Sweetening the Pill* breaks the silence on the dark side of hormonal contraception.
Paperback: 978-1-78099-607-3 ebook: 978-1-78099-608-0

Why Are We The Good Guys?
Reclaiming your Mind from the Delusions of Propaganda
David Cromwell
A provocative challenge to the standard ideology that Western power is a benevolent force in the world.
Paperback: 978-1-78099-365-2 ebook: 978-1-78099-366-9

Readers of ebooks can buy or view any of these bestsellers by clicking on the live link in the title. Most titles are published in paperback and as an ebook. Paperbacks are available in traditional bookshops. Both print and ebook formats are available online.

Find more titles and sign up to our readers' newsletter at http://www.johnhuntpublishing.com/culture-and-politics

Follow us on Facebook
at https://www.facebook.com/ZeroBooks

and Twitter at https://twitter.com/Zer0Books